QUENTIN TARANTINO

First published in Great Britain in 2024 by

Greenfinch
An imprint of Quercus Editions Ltd
Carmelite House
50 Victoria Embankment
London EC4Y 0DZ

An Hachette UK company

A CIP catalogue record for this book is available from the British Library

ISBN 978-1-52943-877-2
Ebook ISBN 978-1-52943-878-9

10 9 8 7 6 5 4 3 2 1

Cover design by Luke Bird
Interior design by Ginny Zeal

Printed and bound in Slovakia by TBB, a.s.

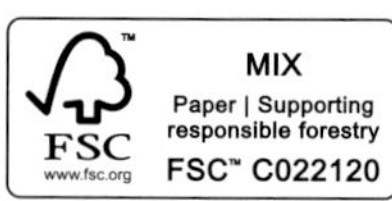

Papers used by Greenfinch are from well-managed forests and other responsible sources.

ICONIC DIRECTORS SERIES

QUENTIN TARANTINO

THE COMPLETE UNOFFICIAL GUIDE

DAN JOLIN

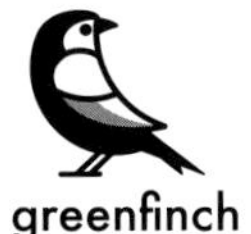

greenfinch

CONTENTS

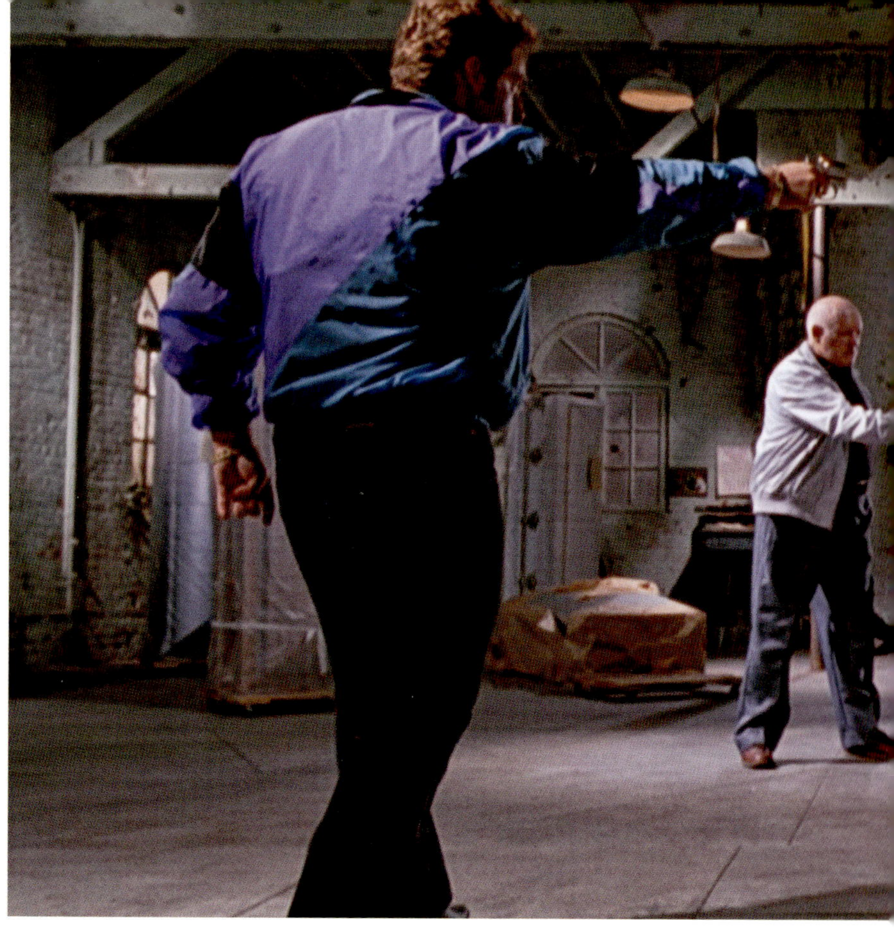

ABOVE: Nice Guy Eddie (Chris Penn), Joe Cabot (Lawrence Tierney),
Mr White (Harvey Keitel) and Mr Orange (Tim Roth) during *Reservoir
Dogs'* much analyzed climactic stand-off.

*'If we've grown up at the movies we know that
good work is continuous not with the academic,
respectable tradition, but with the glimpses of
something good in trash. . .Trash has given us
an appetite for art.'*

PAULINE KAEL

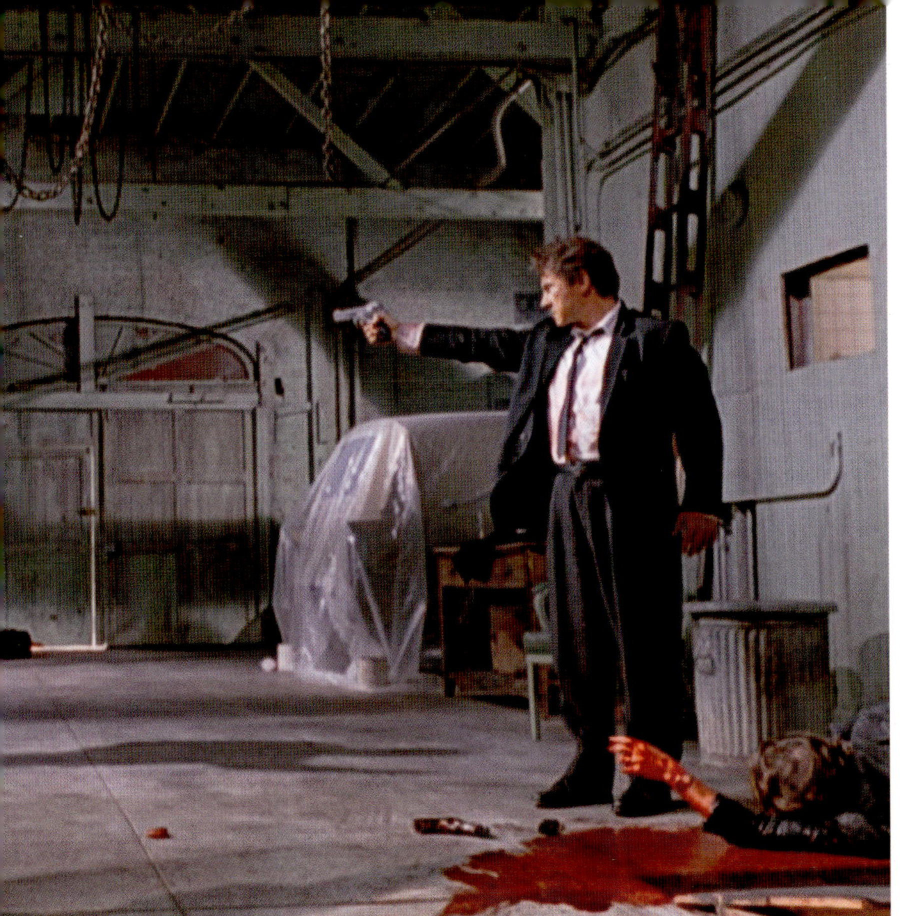

INTRODUCTION

Who shot Nice Guy Eddie? If my memory is to be trusted, this was the question on everybody's lips when Quentin Tarantino's debut feature *Reservoir Dogs* was unleashed in late 1992. The movie ends with its diamond-heisting hoods yelling at each other in a warehouse-based Mexican stand-off. Gang boss Joe Cabot (Lawrence Tierney) has his gun pointed at the prone, bleeding Mr Orange (Tim Roth), whom he suspects, correctly, of being a cop. Veteran thief Mr White (Harvey Keitel), who is sure Orange is to be trusted, has his gun on Joe. And Joe's son Nice Guy Eddie (Chris Penn) has his gun trained on White. Suddenly, triggers are squeezed and the three standing men fall to the ground with gunshot wounds that instantly kill Joe and Eddie. Joe shot Orange. White shot Joe. Eddie shot White. But who shot Eddie?

Reservoir Dogs was a cinematic phenomenon: cool, funny, disturbing, inventive and familiar, with a great cast and a killer soundtrack to boot. It got us all talking, debating, quoting and rewatching like no other movie that year. It was notorious, too, becoming swept up in a fresh moral panic about movie violence. I don't recall another time in my life when a first-time filmmaker without even a background in commercials, music videos, TV or theatre became an overnight household name.

It hasn't hurt that Tarantino himself is such a compelling presence: an articulate, bona fide cineaste with towering self-assurance and a combative edge that has seen him come through a cycle of controversies relatively unscarred, despite some undeniable missteps and misjudgements. He was, as writer Peter Biskind put it, 'our first rock-star director'. Although for a time, he was more than that, even. He was a one-filmmaker genre.

For years, sharp-suited, pop-culture-plundering criminals strutted all over the cinematic landscape, especially in the wake of Tarantino's masterful second film *Pulp Fiction*. But there was nothing more exciting than the genuine article, even after he left the crime movie behind in the 20th century and started kicking around in other sandboxes: martial-arts flicks, slasher films, men-on-a-mission adventures and, of course, spaghetti Westerns. Whether lifting directly or nailing a vibe, Tarantino's films are deeply referential, often to some very trashy and obscure material. But that's rarely been an obstacle to appreciating them. You don't need to know of all the ingredients to enjoy the cocktail.

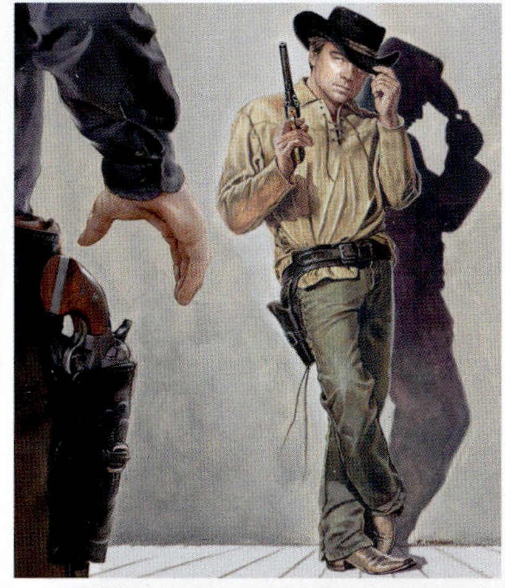

Almost every new Tarantino film feels like an event (the unfortunate exception being 2007's *Grindhouse*), and those events are heightened by the wait, usually at least three years between movies. This is the result of Tarantino's refusal to churn, work for hire or direct someone else's material (the fortunate exception being 1997's Elmore Leonard-adapting *Jackie Brown*). He typically spends years on each of his scripts, scrawling them in longhand and stacking up hundreds of pages, as if he's working on a novel rather than a screenplay, before cutting it all down into something manageably filmic, but still epic.

This is how, over the past three decades, Tarantino has painstakingly and passionately sculpted his own cinematic universe, with its own in-jokes, fake products, character connections and history, as well as all the stylistic touches and tropes you'd expect of any independently minded filmmaker's body of work. His cinematic universe even contains its own cinematic universe. After taking off on Zed's chopper and making it to Knoxville, *Pulp Fiction*'s Butch and Fabienne might have settled down with some Big Kahuna burgers to watch *Kill Bill*, before falling asleep to re-runs of *Bounty Law* starring *Once Upon a Time. . . In Hollywood*'s Rick Dalton.

However, it is not a universe so complete that every last detail is explained. Tarantino knows that leaving his audience wondering is a great way to engage them. What is in the suitcase that Marsellus Wallace wants back so badly in *Pulp Fiction*? How did Lieutenant Aldo Raine from *Inglourious Basterds* get his rope-burn neck scar? Did *Once Upon A Time. . . In Hollywood*'s Cliff Booth intend to kill his wife on that boat?

It is not the remit of this book to answer all those questions, but rather to explore the universe that raises them, and how it intersects with our own. But before getting stuck in, I will answer the question that started it all. Chris Penn's blood-spurting squib went off a moment too early, and he instinctively fell to the ground before Keitel had a chance to bring his gun around on Penn, as the script indicated he should. Nice Guy Eddie's mysterious death was a glitch, then, that Tarantino decided would make a great feature. He liked the mystery of it. He knew it would get people talking.

And he was right.

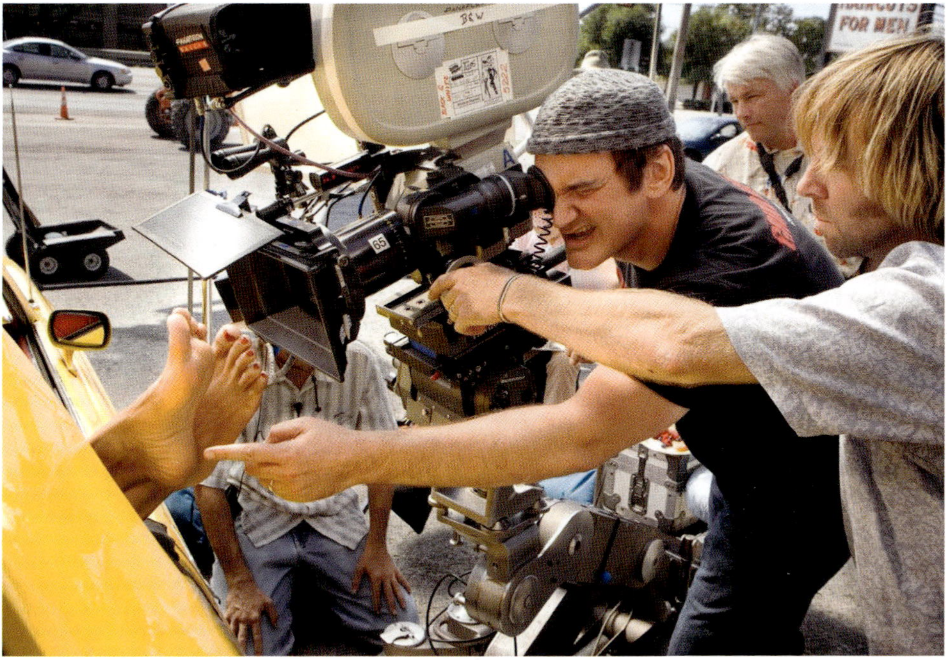

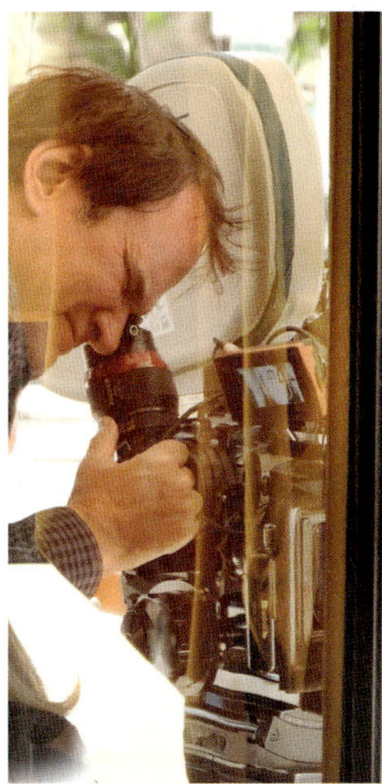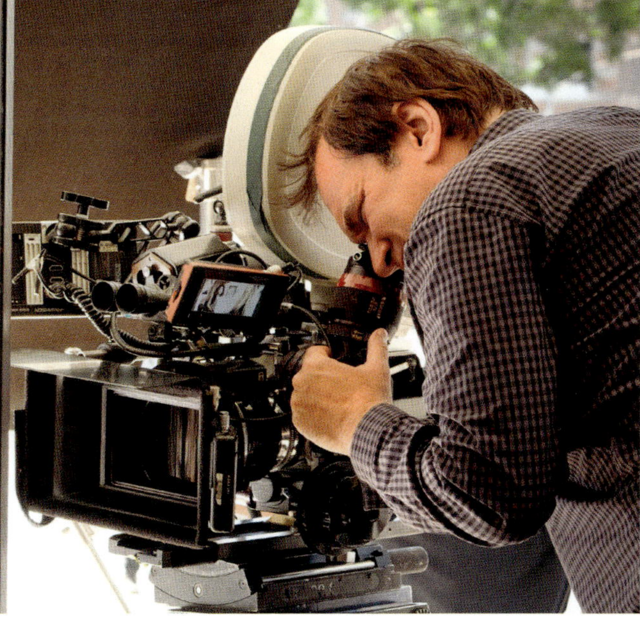

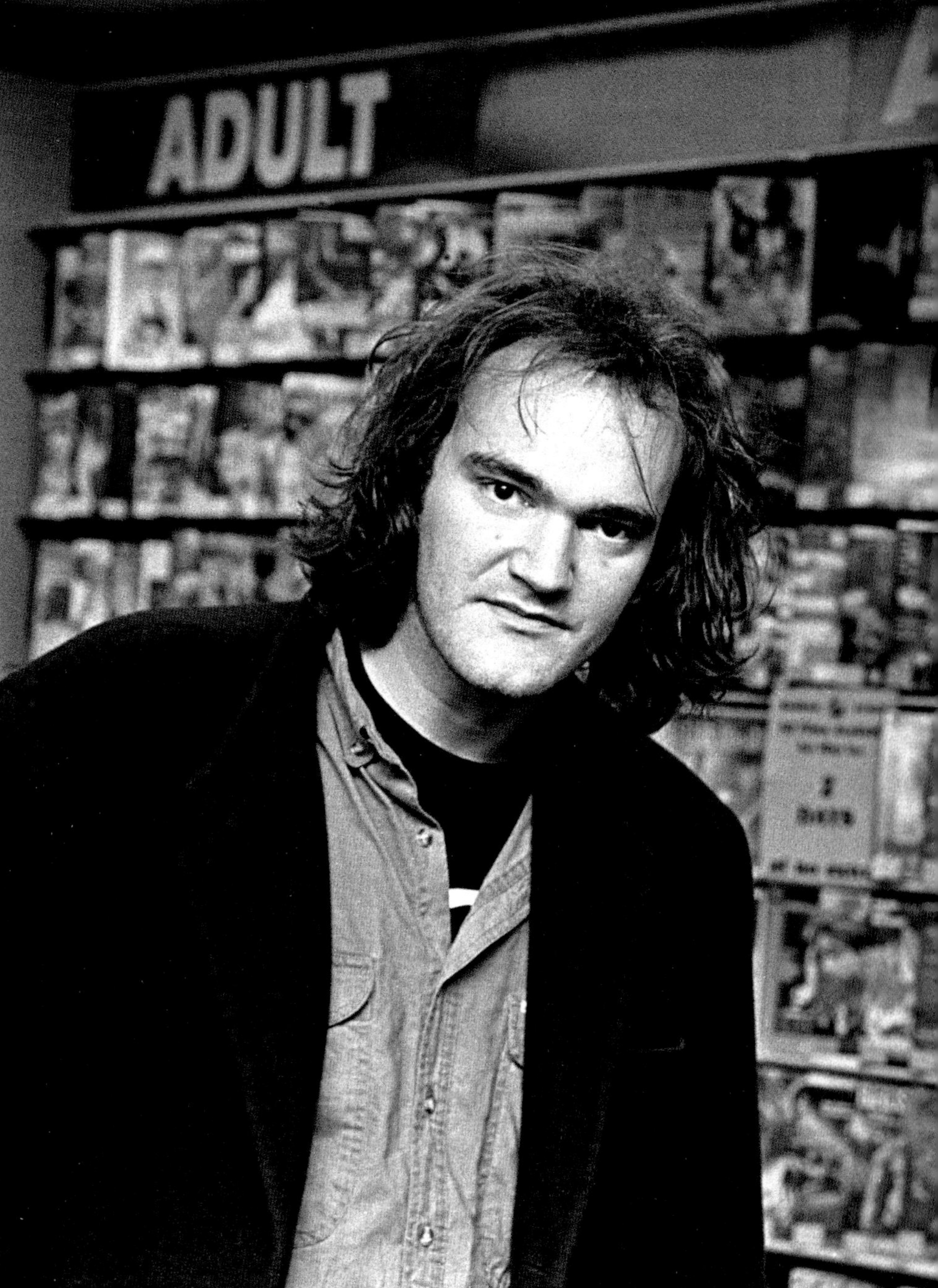

ADULT

FROM CHILDHOOD TO MY BEST FRIEND'S BIRTHDAY

1963–1990

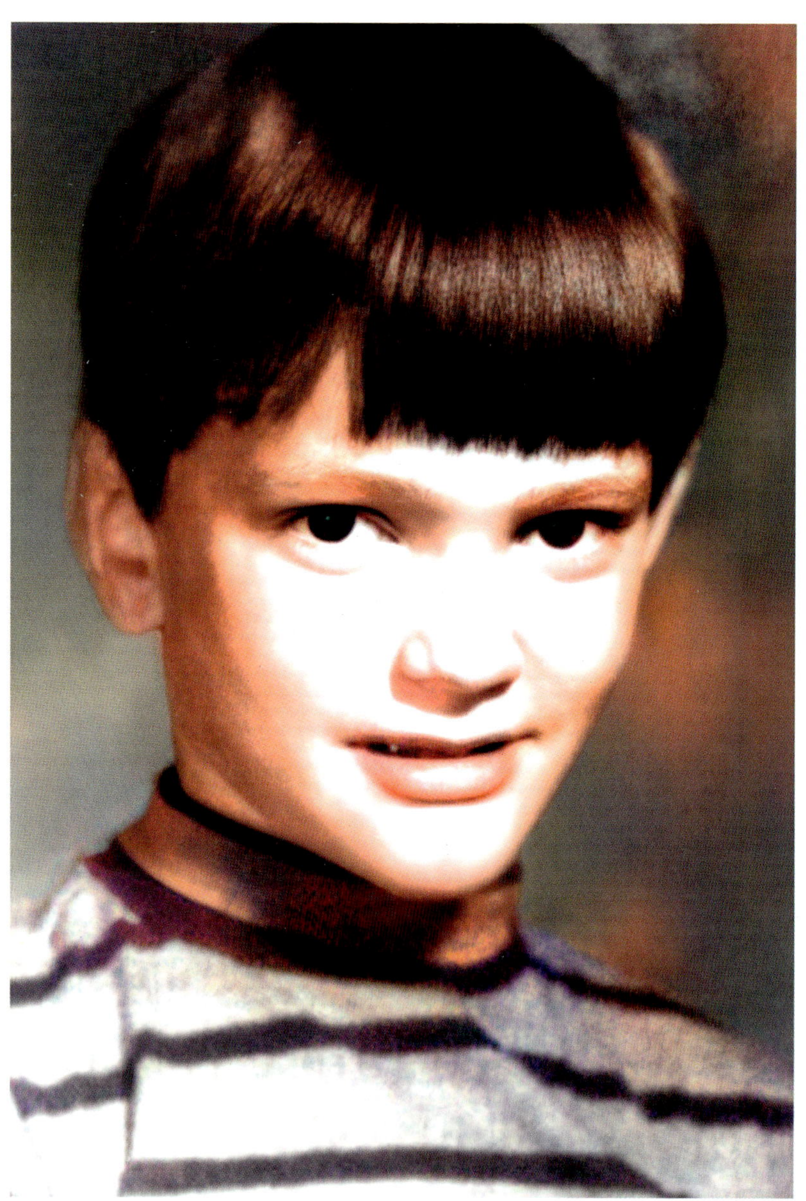

Quentin Tarantino can't remember a time when watching movies wasn't the 'number one thing' in his life. As a child, growing up in the South Bay area of Los Angeles County during the mid-to-late Sixties, young Quentin Jerome Zastoupil (named after his then-stepfather Curt Zastoupil, a musician) would sit for hours close to the TV set, just like the young Butch Coolidge in *Pulp Fiction*. His favourite film at this time was 1948's *Abbott and Costello Meet Frankenstein*. He remembers appreciating the way it blended horror and comedy, so that 'the scary parts are scary and the funny parts are really funny – two great tastes that taste great together.' One scene that really impressed the young Quentin was the moment the Monster (Glenn Strange) threw a nurse through a window. Someone just died horribly? In a movie that also makes you laugh!?

But Tarantino's true cinematic awakening occurred in the silver glow of the big screen. His mother Connie, a healthcare worker originally from Knoxville, Tennessee, figured that rather than hiring a babysitter she and Curt might as well just bring little 'Quint' along to the cinema with them. 'We took him to every movie, regardless of whether it was appropriate, from the time he was three,' said Connie, who figured there was nothing he would see in a film that could ever truly harm him. But she never anticipated how deeply inspired her boy would be by such exposure to the bold and challenging New Cinema of the late Sixties and early Seventies.

Tarantino's strongest memory of this time was seeing a double bill of Sam Peckinpah's 1969 Western bloodbath *The Wild Bunch* and John Boorman's 1972 survival thriller *Deliverance*, when he was 11. 'It's one of the greatest nights of movies of my life,' he said.

OPPOSITE: Eight-year-old Quentin Zastoupil, not looking
a million miles different to the young Butch Coolidge in
Pulp Fiction.

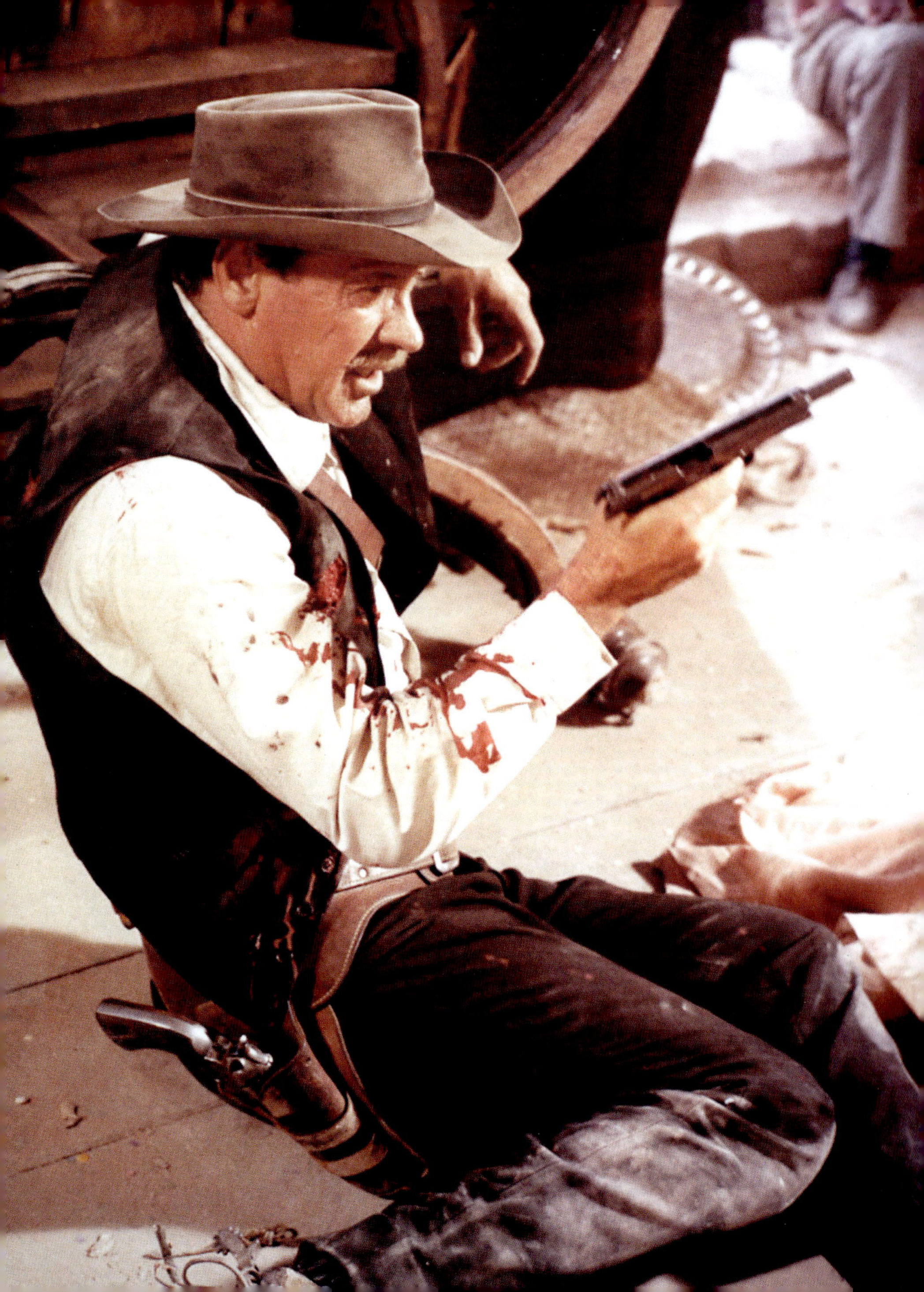

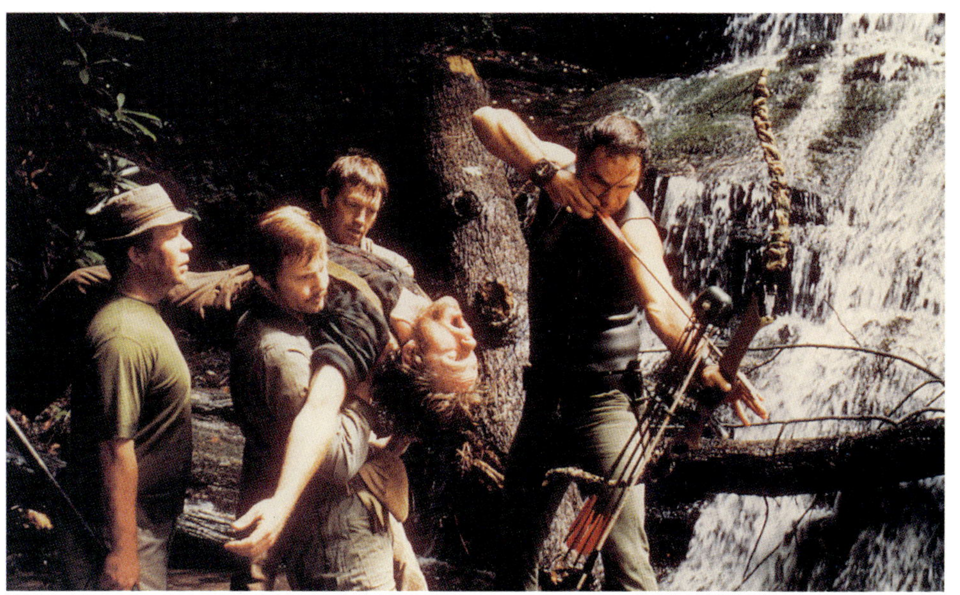

Though he admitted that *Deliverance* terrified him. 'For a while, I didn't want to go camping. The way people were scared of the beach after *Jaws* was how I was scared of camping.'

If Connie and Quentin's shared love for movies formed a bond between mother and son during Tarantino's early childhood, his obsession became a source of friction during his teenage years. He fixated on becoming an actor, and also wrote screenplays, scribbled on whatever scraps of paper came to hand. One of his earliest was *Captain Peachfuzz and the Anchovy Bandit*, a pastiche of the *Smokey and the Bandit* car capers starring Burt Reynolds. Meanwhile, his academic attention deteriorated. Matters came to a head when Connie confronted her son about risible grades and singled out his problematic focus on scriptwriting, telling him his 'little writing career' was over. It was

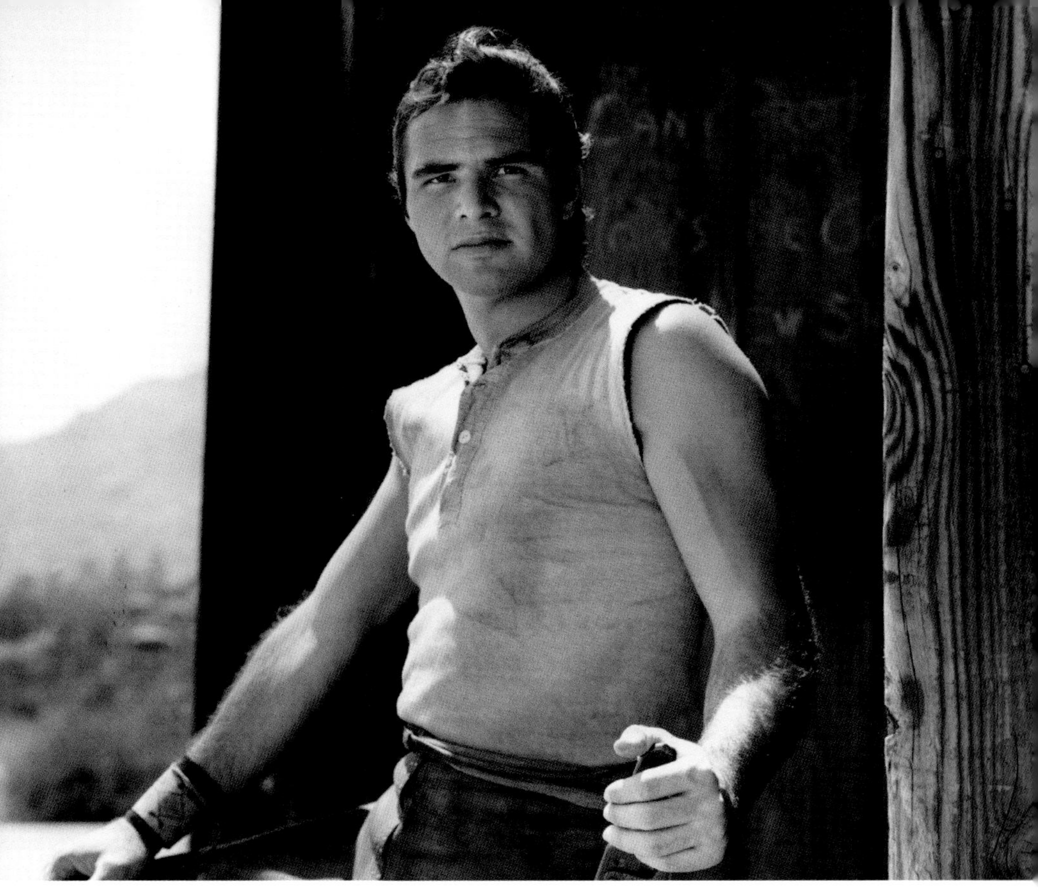

ABOVE: Quint Asper (Burt Reynolds), a half white, half Comanche blacksmith from TV Western *Gunsmoke*, inspired Connie Zastoupil to name her son Quentin.

something he never forgot or, apparently, forgave. He vowed then to deny her any financial benefit from his success, a promise he claims to have kept.

Connie can hardly be blamed. From her perspective, he was lazing around all day, watching TV all night and neglecting his studies. Perhaps she didn't like the idea of Quentin following in his biological father's footsteps. Tony Tarantino, whom she'd met while attending high school in California and got pregnant by when she was only 14 (marrying then leaving him four months later), was a wannabe actor. Not that he was an inspiration to his son; Quentin never expressed any interest in meeting his father, and claims to have spurned Tony's attempts to connect. He only took his surname, he said, because it sounded 'cool'.

Still, Connie did support her son's efforts to achieve his dreams. After grounding him all summer for a shoplifting incident, where 15-year-old Quentin had attempted to pocket a copy of Elmore Leonard's *The Switch* (the first of the pulp writer's novels to feature characters who would later appear in *Jackie Brown*), she allowed him to attend a local theatre group. Here, he immediately landed the lead role, playing a twentysomething man in a production of *Two and Two Make Sex*. When Quentin turned 17, Connie also reluctantly allowed him to drop out of high school to focus on his acting, on the condition that he find work. He did: as an usher in a Torrance porn cinema called The Pussycat Theatre. It was not a job he enjoyed, but it was at least Hollywood-adjacent.

Tarantino's path from the outskirts of the US film industry to its thumping heart took in two major milestones: joining an acting class at the James Best Theatre Center in 1981, and then – more famously – the film-geek staff of VHS rental outlet Video Archives in 1985.

Two or three evenings a week, he would make the 30-mile bus journey from Manhattan Beach to Toluca Lake, where the theatre centre was based in a studio above a deli. The school had been established by Best (most famous for playing the sheriff in TV hit *The Dukes of Hazzard*) two years earlier, and focused on preparing actors specifically for TV and film work. 'He taught you how to act for the camera,' said Tarantino. 'His whole idea was, "You're in Los Angeles. The way you're gonna make your living is two or three lines on Quincy".' It was while attending the school that Tarantino

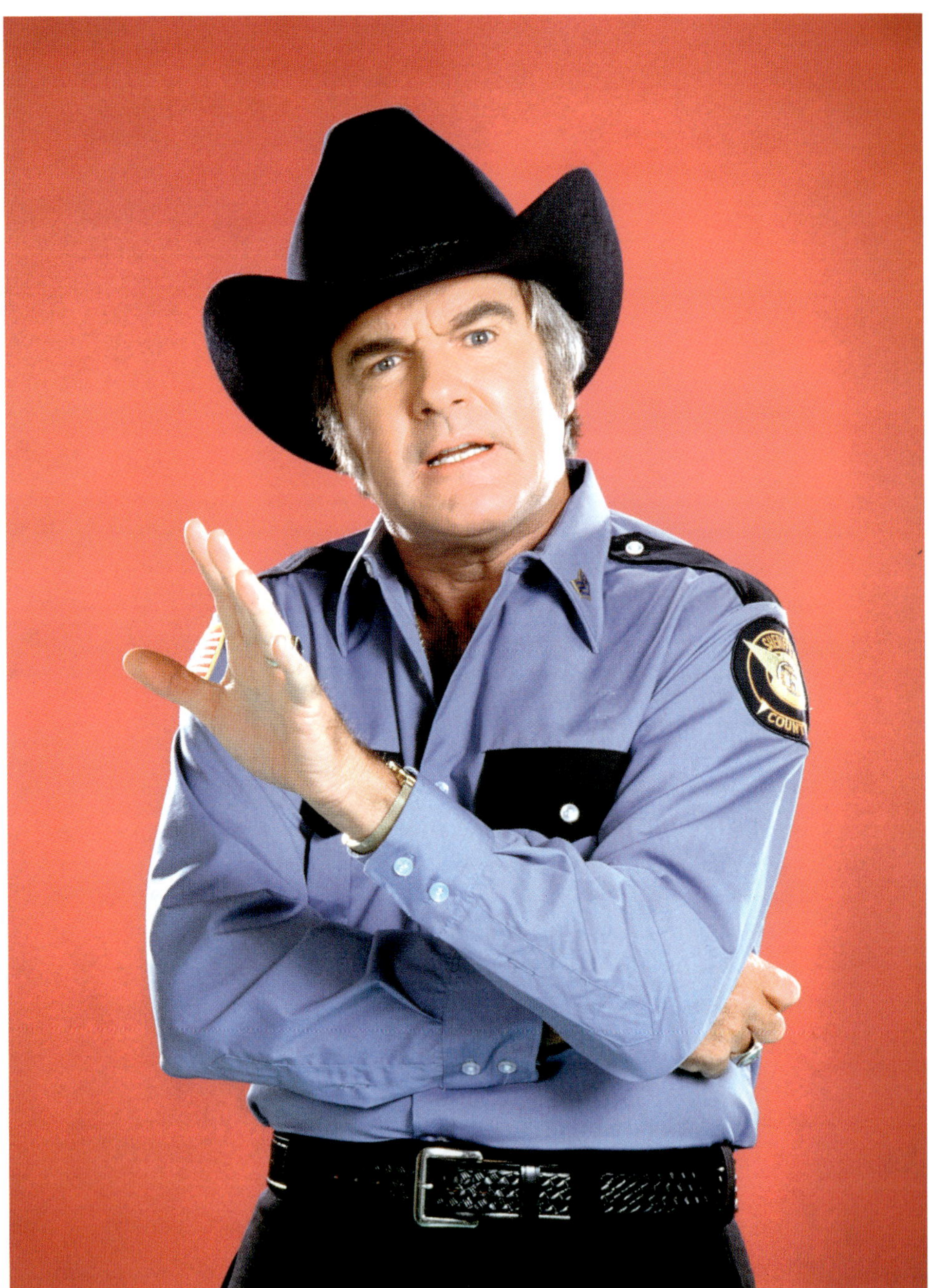

decided he wanted to direct, too. 'I loved movies too much to simply appear in them. I wanted the movies to be *my* movies.'

He penned his own scenes for workshops, usually adaptations of scenes from recent movies he'd enjoyed. The most memorable was a spin on John Carpenter's *Assault on Precinct 13*, for which Tarantino and his acting-school buddies Craig Hamann and Rick Squery brought some problematic props: a real assault rifle, revolver and pump-action shotgun. 'That really bothered people,' recalled Hamann. 'They got kinda freaked out.' Hamann was Tarantino's closest friend at the time, the pair bonding over kung fu movies. As well as partnering up during acting class, they also wrote screenplays together, including one which, in 1984, they started shooting, intending it as their big Hollywood calling card. It was titled *My Best Friend's Birthday*.

Around this time, Tarantino formed some other significant friendships. At school, he'd always been the 'hip' (his word) outsider. But in his early 20s he finally found his tribe: a group of 'crazy movie guys' with whom he could endlessly debate and compare notes.

His love for hanging out in mom-and-pop video stores, searching the racks for new discoveries, had pulled him into the orbit of Video Archives on North Sepulveda Boulevard in Hermosa Beach. Its owner was Lance Lawson, who 'knew more about movies than any living person I had ever met,' Tarantino said. Lawson became his movie-geek mentor, generously taking him to rockabilly gigs and theatre performances. He also gave Tarantino a job at the store, which became a defining moment in the future

OPPOSITE: Before setting up Tarantino's acting school,
James Best was best known as lawman Roscoe P. Coltrane
in *The Dukes of Hazzard*.

Elvis has entered the building

While Tarantino was working on the scripts that would one day make his name, he also scored his first-ever acting gig. In 1988, when he was 25, his then-manager Catherine Jaymes recommended him to a casting agent friend who was looking for Elvis impersonators for an episode of popular sitcom *The Golden Girls*. Jaymes pitched Tarantino as 'Elvis meets Charles Manson', and he made the cut. In the Season 4 episode 'Sophia's Wedding: Part 1', a mix-up sees Sophia's nuptials attended by a gang of Elvises in lieu of real guests. At the show's climax, they perform 'Hawaiian Wedding Song', and Tarantino can be spotted emphatically twitching his arms in the back row. He's the only one who isn't decked out in Vegas-era duds; instead, he turned up in his own clothes, representing The King's Sun Records days.

director's career. It would be much mythologized, positioning his time there as an equivalent of film school, where he would absorb all the influences that resulted in his early features. It was never quite that – Tarantino brought more knowledge than he gained during his time at Video Archives – but it was, for a while, his ideal job. And it was here that he became close friends with fellow employee Roger Avary. A film studies drop-out who shared Tarantino's and Hamann's movie-making ambitions, Avary later collaborated with Tarantino on his early film scripts, and in 1987 the pair earned their first crew credit together as production assistants on *Maximum Potential*, a workout video by Swedish action star Dolph Lundgren. Although that year is more notable for marking the completion of Tarantino's first movie – or rather, half-movie.

My Best Friend's Birthday was a shoestring passion project that Tarantino and Hamann toiled over during evenings and weekends between 1984 and 1987, with the help of Avary (who produced) and other friends, including Scott McGill (another Video Archives staffer) and Rand Vossler. Shot on black-and-white 16mm, it had a budget of around $5,000. 'It was almost like a Martin/Lewis kind of thing,' said Tarantino, referring to the screwball comedies of Dean Martin and Jerry Lee Lewis. 'I thought we were making something really special.'

It was certainly something really personal, drawing heavily from both Hamann and Tarantino's lives and tastes. As well as writing, directing, producing and editing, Tarantino stars as Clarence Pool, an overbearing, Elvis-obsessed DJ who tries to give his best buddy Mickey Burnett (Hamann) a birthday to remember by hiring him a call girl (Crystal Shaw Martell) named Misty Knight, after the Marvel Comics character. But Mickey's day is memorable for all the wrong reasons. First he discovers his ex-girlfriend (Linda Kaye) has an obnoxious new boyfriend (Rich Turner). Then he is attacked by Misty's pimp (Al Harrell), who shouts 'Your ass is grass – and I'm the lawnmower!' before a slapstick kung fu sequence kicks off. Finally, Clarence falls for Misty during a scene where she reveals she was inspired to become a call girl after seeing Nancy Allen in Brian De Palma's *Dressed to Kill*.

The film allowed Hamann to show off his martial arts skills and Tarantino to showcase his love for rockabilly, movies and the sound of his own voice. Meanwhile, several of the film's elements foreshadow Tarantino's later works. The call-girl birthday gift device was used to spark the plot of *True Romance*, while Clarence's statement that if he 'had to fuck a guy...I'd fuck Elvis,' is also delivered by *True Romance*'s main character (Christian Slater) – named Clarence, too. Other names will ring bells for Tarantino fans: Yolanda (*Pulp Fiction*), Mickey (*Natural Born Killers*), and a reference to actor Aldo Ray, who inspired the name of Brad Pitt's *Inglourious Basterds* character, Lieutenant Aldo Raine.

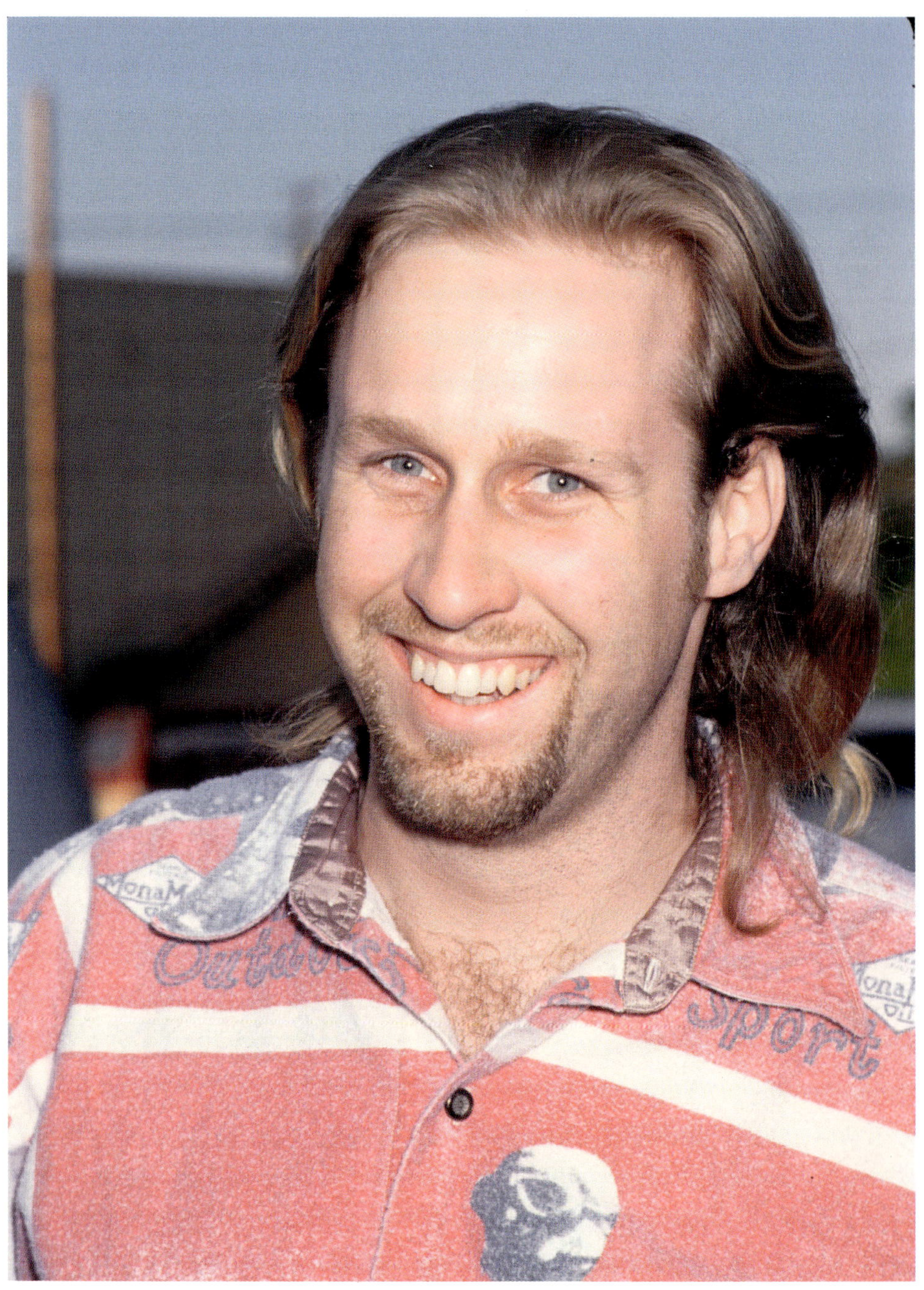

There may have been further similarities, but thanks to a lab mishap in 1987, around half of the 70-minute film was destroyed. A story circulated that the lost reels went up in smoke during a fire, but this wasn't true. Tarantino chose never to deny it, figuring it was a better-sounding reason for the loss of the movie. Also, by the time he'd completed it, he saw that there was in fact nothing 'special' about *My Best Friend's Birthday*. It was, he later admitted, 'amateurish' and 'kind of embarrassing'.

For a couple of weeks, he was despondent. All that time, effort and passion had been for nothing. But while the film was by no means the calling card he'd hoped it would be, it still had value. 'Well, of course the stuff I did in the first year sucks,' he later admitted. 'I really truly didn't know what I was doing. I was learning

The return of Video Archives

Tarantino's appreciation of the Manhattan Beach video store he once worked and virtually lived in has never dimmed. In a great show of nostalgic affection, when the store closed in 1995 he bought all of its stock and effectively recreated it in a room in his home. Yet even this wasn't enough for Tarantino. He also wanted to revive the spirit of the place. To that end, in July 2022, he started the Video Archives podcast, in which he and his old pal Roger Avary plucked those original video tapes from those original shelves, and based each episode on a great double or triple bill, from *Dark Star/Cocaine Cowboys* to *The Hospital/ Ulzana's Raid/Steel*. The result is probably the closest most of us will ever get to being a store regular, hanging out with Avary and Tarantino during the late Eighties, and listening to them bang on entertainingly about the movies they love.

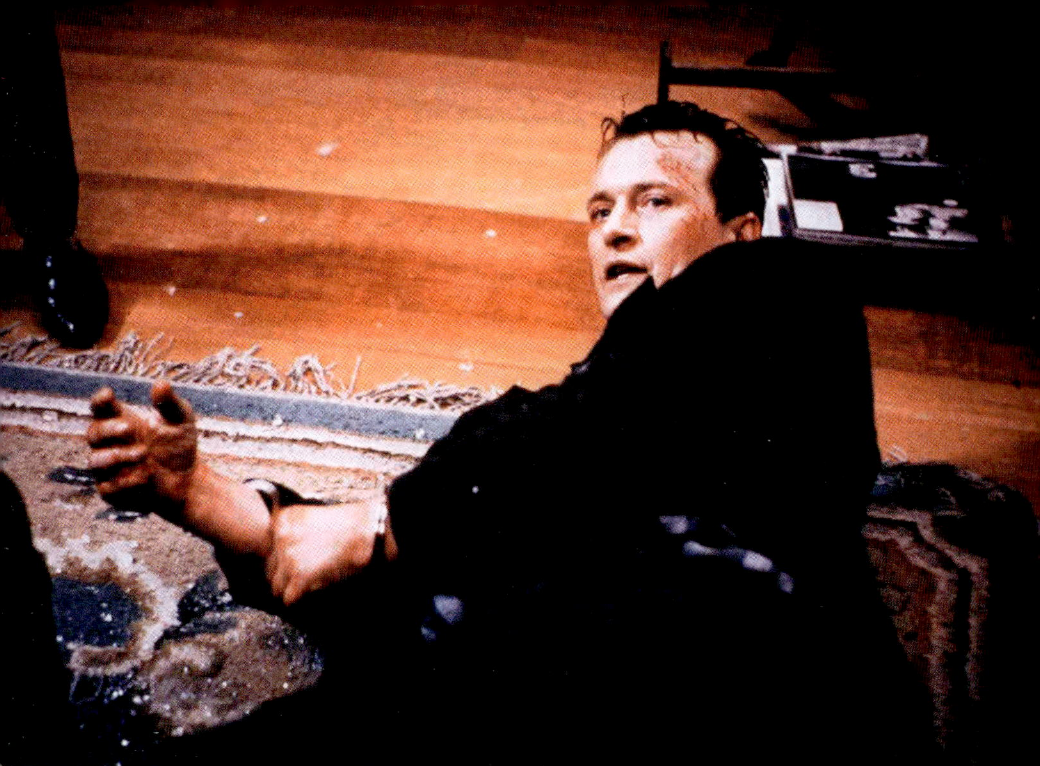

ABOVE: Rutger Hauer in *Past Midnight*. Tarantino received an associate producer credit for the film.

on camera. But the stuff I did in the last year was drastically better. I'd learned now to juggle the coverage, how to pace the scene.' All the money (both his own and other people's) he'd spent had not resulted in a film. But he'd taught himself how to make a movie. As he once said in a masterclass at the Cannes Film Festival, 'trying to make a feature film yourself with no money is the best film school you can do.' He'd also learned that he never again wanted to scrape together his own budget and make a film on a shoestring. He wanted to write a *real* script, and get *real* money to make a *real* movie.

The failure of *My Best Friend's Birthday* spurred Tarantino to write *True Romance*, which he based in part on an 80-page script he and Avary had written titled *The Open Road*. Tarantino intended to direct it himself, so he then wrote *Natural Born Killers* to hopefully fund it. But he eventually decided to leave *Natural Born Killers* in the hands of Vossler, who quit his job in development at MGM to produce and potentially direct the film. Tarantino also received his first paid writing assignment: $1,500 from special effects make-up artist Robert Kurtzman to flesh out a vampire movie concept he wanted to direct, titled *From Dusk Till Dawn*. This was soon followed by a more lucrative gig, doing a script rewrite for the romantic thriller *Past Midnight*, which would eventually be released in 1992, starring Rutger Hauer and Natasha Richardson.

By now, Tarantino had the confidence to quit his job at Video Archives and become a full-time filmmaker, despite still struggling financially. However, he hadn't yet succeeded in getting *True Romance* off the ground. He knew he had a distinct voice, but recognized that voice was just too commercially risky for a studio or production company to commit. 'As far as they were concerned, I didn't know what I was doing because I wasn't following the format,' he said. So, in 1990 he gave up on the idea of making *True Romance* himself, selling it for $30,000, the Writer's Guild minimum.

But, just as *My Best Friend's Birthday* had pushed him forward rather than convincing him to quit, relinquishing *True Romance* hardly quelled Tarantino's ambition. 'Out of frustration,' he said, 'I wrote *Reservoir Dogs*.'

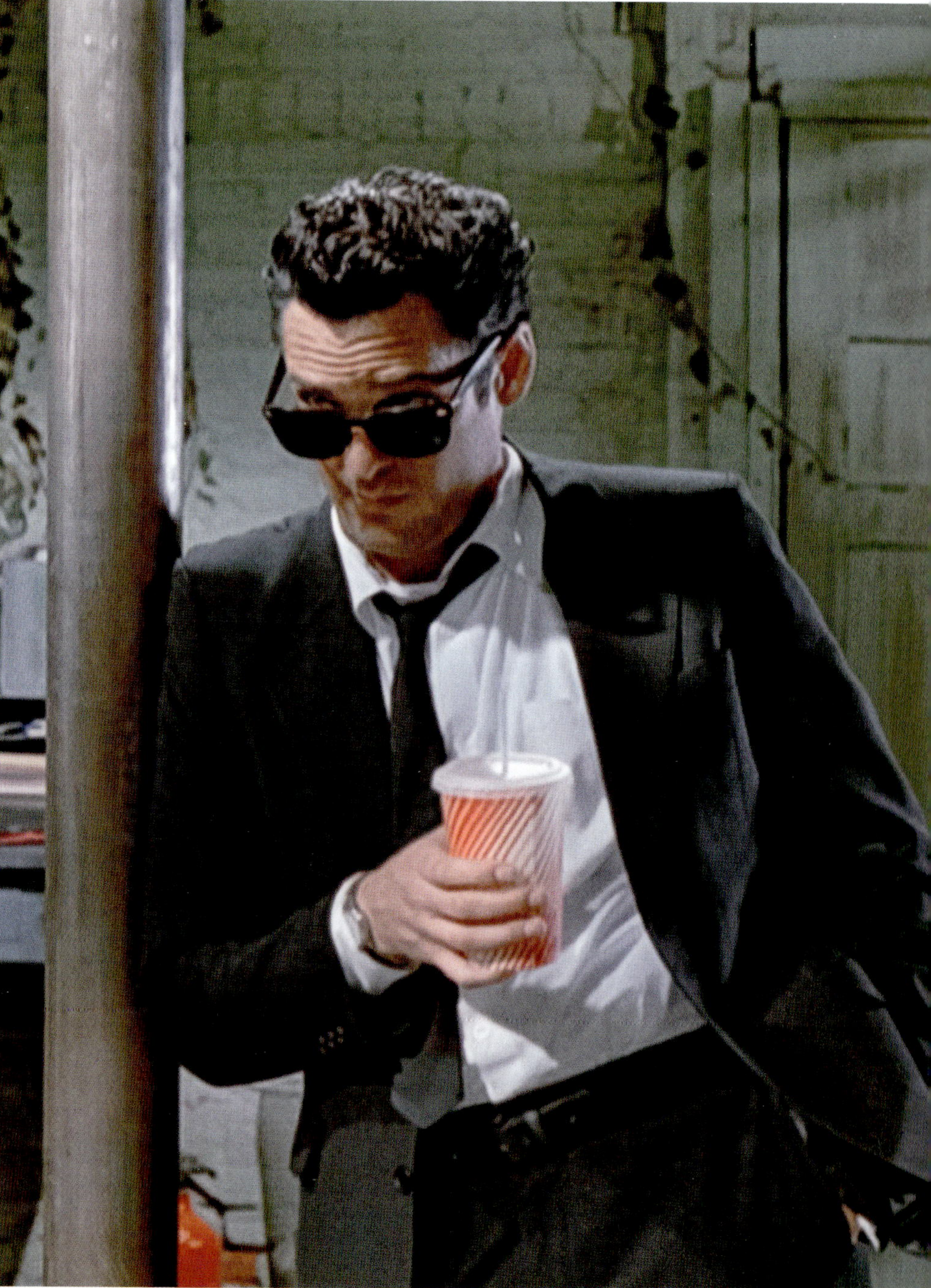

'Let's go to work'

RESERVOIR DOGS
1992

In late July 1991, Quentin Tarantino sat in a Malibu beach house enjoying a pre-shoot dinner with the producers and cast of his proper directorial debut. Their host was Harvey Keitel, who'd made his name during the Seventies with groundbreaking movies such as Martin Scorsese's *Mean Streets* and *Taxi Driver*, the latter being one of Tarantino's favourite films. The other guests included Steve Buscemi, Michael Madsen, Chris Penn and British actor Tim Roth. As the guys bantered, Tarantino looked around the table and, in a moment of quiet reflection, realized he could stop worrying about how the following weeks would go. 'If I don't have a single solitary idea of how to shoot a given scene, it'll be dynamic,' he thought. 'These guys are so great I could put them in a white shirt up against a white wall and I got a movie!'

Driving home to Glendale, he took a long diversion to fully take in the moment. He'd never felt happier. His life had never been better. He was finally making that real movie, for real money, with a real cast. He was living his dream.

Little did he know, it was a dream that would also inspire the biggest shake-up in Hollywood since the films he'd grooved on as a kid.

That dinner may never have happened if it wasn't for the least experienced of three producers present at the gathering: 33-year-old Lawrence Bender, who had been introduced to Tarantino by director Scott Spiegel at a party the previous year. He'd only produced two small movies, one of which was Spiegel's straight-to-video horror *Intruder*. Tarantino was, of course, a fan. He described *Intruder* as 'like the Coen brothers had made a slasher film'.

Impressed by Bender, Tarantino pitched him his latest idea: a script he'd hammered out in three weeks, about a daylight diamond heist that goes horribly wrong, pulled off by a gang of professional thieves with colour-themed codenames, most of

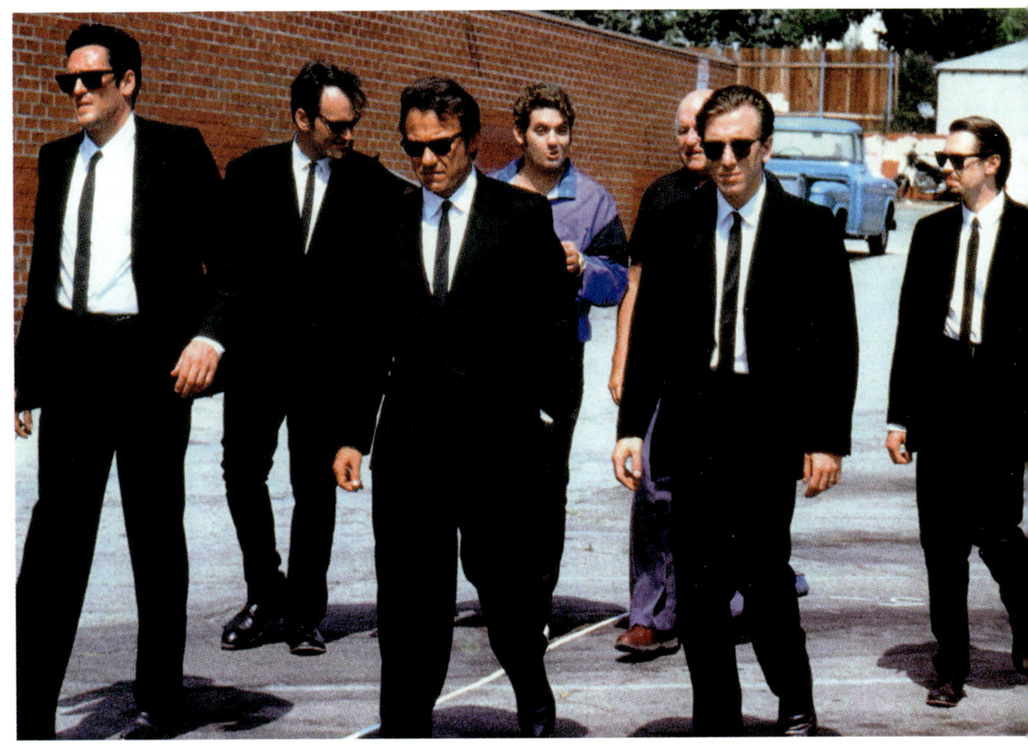

ABOVE: The gang members head towards their heist as the film's opening credits roll.

whom have never previously met. To keep costs down, the robbery itself goes unseen, with the majority of the action taking place after the event, as the surviving criminals convene in a garage and realize there's an undercover cop among them. Tarantino's plan was to shoot the film on 16mm using his *True Romance* fee, casting himself in the role of Mr Pink. He wondered if Bender would like to produce and help raise a little more money.

Over at Tarantino's apartment, Bender read through the script. It was badly formatted and riven with spelling errors but, said Bender, 'I just knew we were off and running into something really great.' He talked Tarantino into giving him two months to find

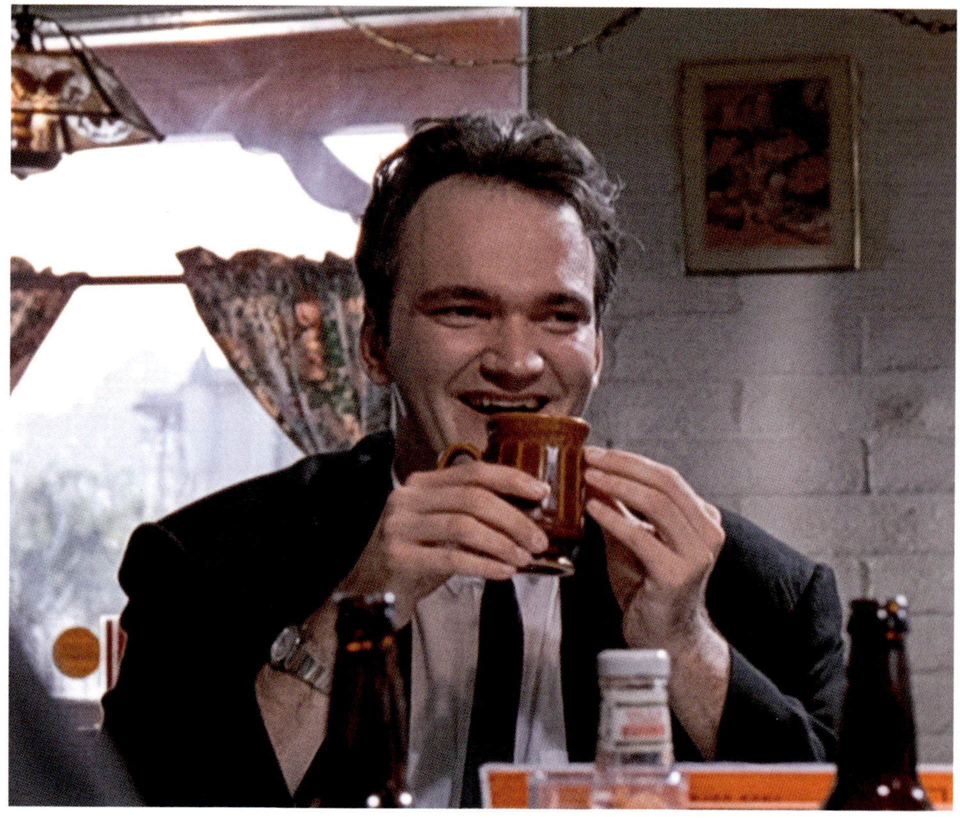

ABOVE: Tarantino gave himself the first of many minor roles
in his own films: Mr Brown, whose 'Like A Virgin' monologue
memorably opens the movie.

some serious financing; if that didn't work out, he could always
revert to Plan A. Bender began frantically shopping it around
Hollywood, and eventually the script found its way into the hands
of Keitel. He loved the screenplay, finding in it a 'Hemingway-esque
code, which guided the characters in a world without meaning.'
The dialogue was so rich and realistic, he was astonished when he
learned that Tarantino had no close friends or relatives from the
criminal world. Keitel promptly called Bender and said that not

The big influences

Tarantino has been open and unapologetic about the many cinematic inspirations for *Reservoir Dogs*. It wasn't hard to spot the influence of 1974 hijack thriller *The Taking of Pelham 123* on the colour-coded character names, or of *The Good, The Bad and The Ugly* on the climactic Mexican stand-off. *Reservoir Dogs* also snatched elements from Stanley Kubrick's *The Killing*, Brian De Palma's Vietnam movie *Casualties of War*, John Carpenter's paranoid sci-fi *The Thing* and Jean-Pierre Melville's heist drama *Le Doulos*.

Even more boldly, the movie closely resembled the final act of Ringo Lam's *City on Fire*, about an undercover cop (Chow Yun-Fat) who becomes involved in a jewellery-store robbery and is shot in the stomach. In 1995, a Michigan film student named Mike White called this out by making a 10-minute short provocatively titled *Who Do You Think You're Fooling? (The Story of a Robbery)*, which highlighted the similarities by combining footage of both films.

Not that this bothered Tarantino. 'I steal from every single movie made, all right?' he said when challenged about his debt to Lam's film. 'If my work has anything it's because I'm taking this from this and that from that, piecing them together. If people don't like it, tough titty. Don't go see it.'

only would he like to be in the movie, he would be happy to support them any way they needed, in return for a producer credit.

Tarantino was overjoyed to hear that one of his favourite actors was willing to come on board. But, more importantly, Keitel gave the project legitimacy. No longer were Tarantino and Bender just two random guys in Hollywood trying to get their first movie made. They were now two random guys with a *Harvey Keitel* movie.

The Keitel factor certainly hooked the attention of veteran exploitation filmmaker Monte Hellman, who, after expressing interest in directing it himself, shepherded the script toward Richard Gladstein of Live Entertainment, Carolco Pictures' home

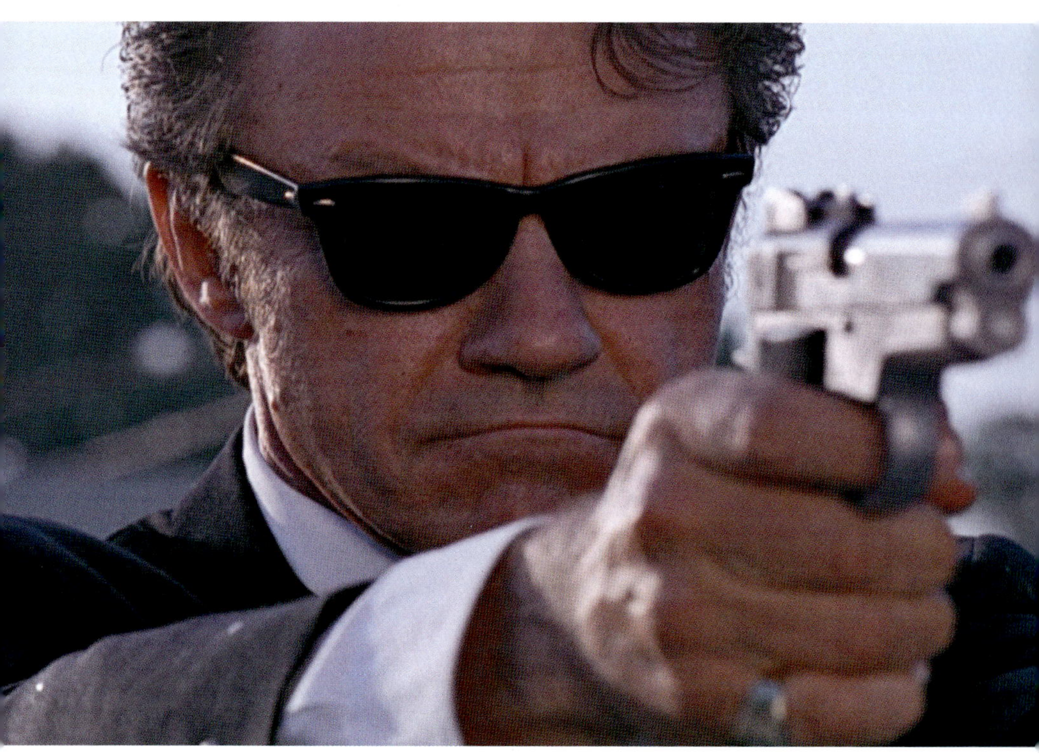

entertainment division. Gladstein was so impressed that he decided to accept the script's cocky cover-page assertion that it was 'written and directed by Quentin Tarantino', and committed to the tune of $1.3 million. With a far bigger budget than he'd ever hoped for, Tarantino could finally get to work.

While Live Entertainment's budget still placed the film very much in the indie realm, it did raise *Reservoir Dogs* to a whole new level. Now Tarantino had to gather an appropriately adept cast around Keitel, who took the role of Mr White, aka Larry, the heist veteran who unwittingly takes undercover cop Mr Orange under his wing, at the cost of his long-term friendship with crew boss Joe Cabot (Lawrence Tierney) and ultimately his life. No longer would the

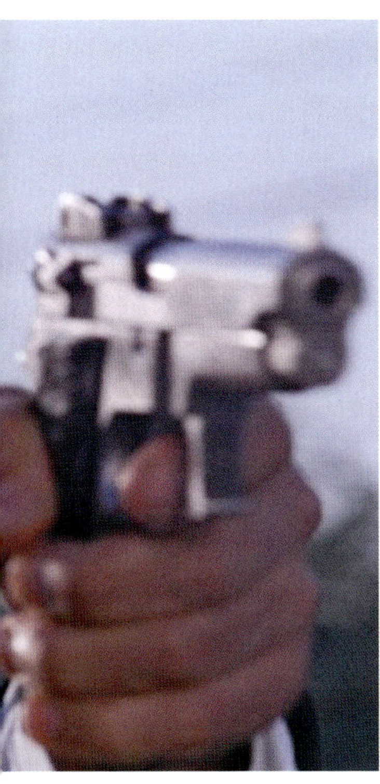

ABOVE: Harvey Keitel engages in a little twin-gun action as Mr White has to shoot his way out of the botched heist.

ensemble be drawn from Tarantino's social circle (though a few friends do appear in minor roles, including Bender as one of the cops pursuing Mr Pink in a flashback). Tarantino even downscaled his own front-of-camera involvement, relinquishing his favoured role to Steve Buscemi and taking instead the smaller part of Mr Brown.

Casting primarily took place in New York at Keitel's suggestion, with the actor even covering the cost of their flights from LA. Bender recalls spending most of the auditions sitting in a chair as tortured cop Marvin Nash (eventually played by Kirk Baltz), being knocked about by hopeful diamond robbers.

Tarantino, meanwhile, wasn't so sure of his directing savvy that he didn't seek some guidance. In early July 1991, he attended Robert Redford's Sundance Institute Filmmakers' Lab in Park City, Utah, where upcoming directors could workshop scenes with established filmmakers. After presenting some scenes he'd shot with Buscemi, Tarantino's first feedback session didn't go so well. The group (whose members have remained unnamed) castigated him for his long takes. The second session was a different story. Comprising Ulu Grosbard, Volker Schlöndorff, Jon Amiel and Terry Gilliam, the mentors applauded

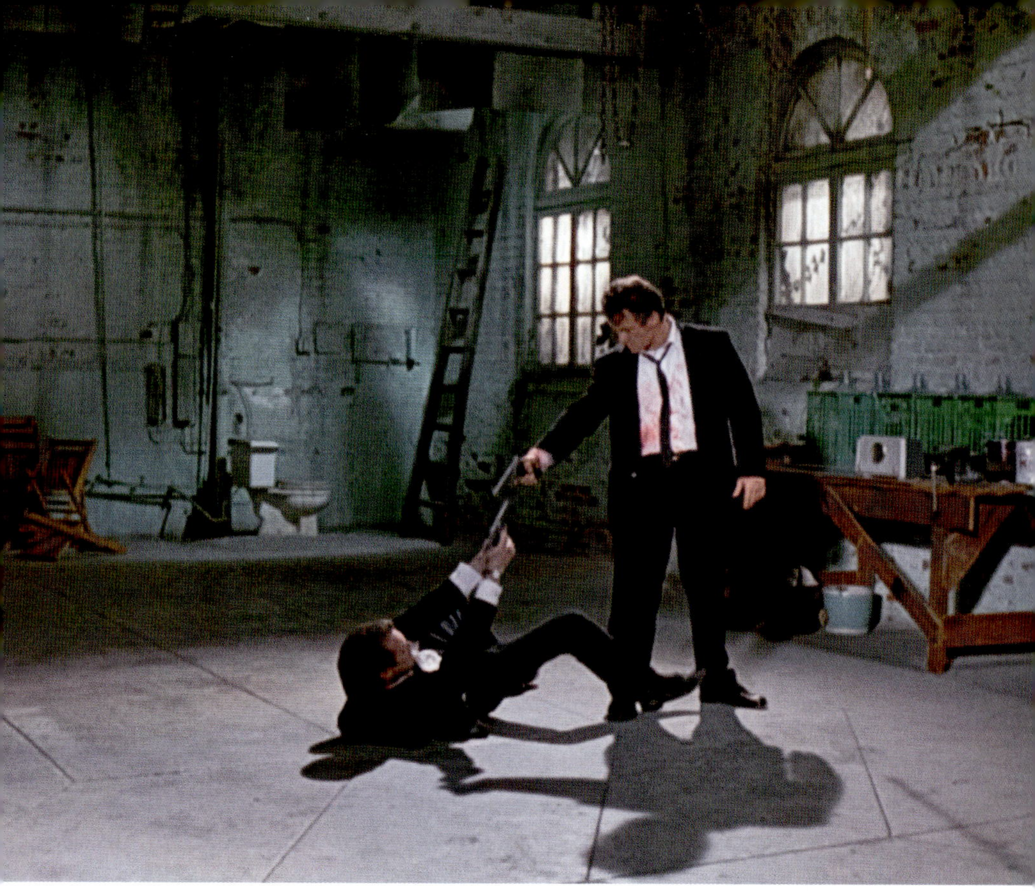

Tarantino's bold vision. 'Here was a man with such incredible enthusiasm and this outrageous script,' recalled Gilliam. 'Amazing energy, great dialogue.' Their advice was constructive, focusing on his need to just calm down a little. 'The camera wouldn't stay still,' said Gilliam. 'It was up people's noses, down their throats. You couldn't see anything. I think that was a really useful thing for him to get out of his system.'

Following a two-week rehearsal period, *Reservoir Dogs* was filmed on location in Los Angeles over five weeks, from late July to early September. It was mostly based in a mortuary on Figueroa and

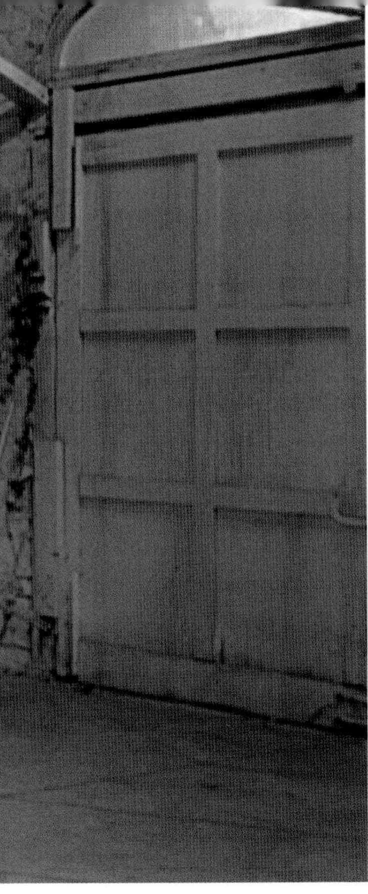

ABOVE: 'I'm acting like a professional!' Steve Buscemi (as Mr Pink) and Harvey Keitel perform one of the film's most iconic scenes.

59th Street, which provided the warehouse set and, in an embalming room they found upstairs, Mr Orange's apartment.

As Tarantino suspected, the sheer quality of his actors took him a long way, but Keitel gave the neophyte director his due. 'He had these different styles of acting and different personalities to contend with,' he said. 'All very dynamic men. And Quentin won their confidence and their trust from day one.'

To Buscemi, shooting *Reservoir Dogs* didn't feel like working with a newbie. During one dialogue scene between Mr Pink and Mr White, Tarantino kept the camera on Keitel, slowly pushing in on his face while Buscemi said his lines out of shot. When the scene was done, Bender – along with the script supervisor and first assistant director – suggested he film Mr Pink's side of the conversation, so he'd have it as an option during the edit. 'No, I'll never use it. I don't want to waste time shooting it,' said Tarantino. 'Wow,' thought Buscemi. 'This guy is a first-time director and he is so sure of what he's doing.'

The only cast member Tarantino didn't vibe with was Tierney, the grizzled, Brooklyn-born 72-year-old who'd broken through in the mid-Forties playing bank robber John Dillinger. 'He was personally challenging to every aspect of filmmaking,' said Tarantino, who described Tierney as 'a complete lunatic by that time'. The director became so tired of Tierney's objectionable behaviour that the pair came to blows at the end of the first week of shooting, which had been scheduled to focus on the Joe scenes, and Tarantino fired him. When that happened, he claimed, 'the whole crew burst into applause'.

Aside from that incident, it was a largely amicable shoot, though for some of the cast, it occasionally proved uncomfortable and physically demanding. Baltz, for example, suffered a real ride in the trunk of a car after Madsen, playing the insouciantly psychotic Mr Blonde, went for a half-hour drive in his Cadillac with Baltz in the back. Madsen has insisted it was Baltz's idea, to give him an idea of how it felt, but admitted the drive was longer than Baltz had expected, because Madsen felt it would be a good way for him to get into character, too. 'He was very brave,' said Madsen years later, 'and that scene bound us together in cinema history.'

The film's most notorious sequence finds Mr Blonde left alone with Officer Marvin Nash (and the seemingly unconscious Mr Orange). Blonde decides to torture the chair-bound cop, just for fun. He turns on the radio, pulls a razor blade from his boot and, while shuffling around to Seventies ditty 'Stuck in the Middle With You' by Stealers Wheel, slices off Nash's right ear.

Tarantino would later joke that *Reservoir Dogs* became known as 'the movie where the guy gets his ear cut off'. When it first screened, at the Sundance Film Festival in January 1992, there were reports of viewers walking out during that very moment. And when the movie was first picked up by independent American distributor Miramax, run by brothers Bob and Harvey Weinstein, Tarantino had to fight to keep the torture scene. Without it, Harvey told him, it would reach a mainstream

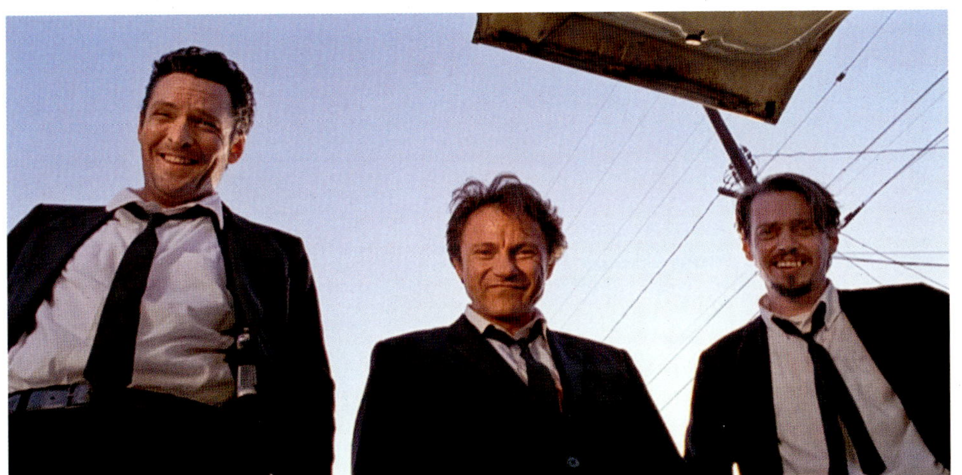

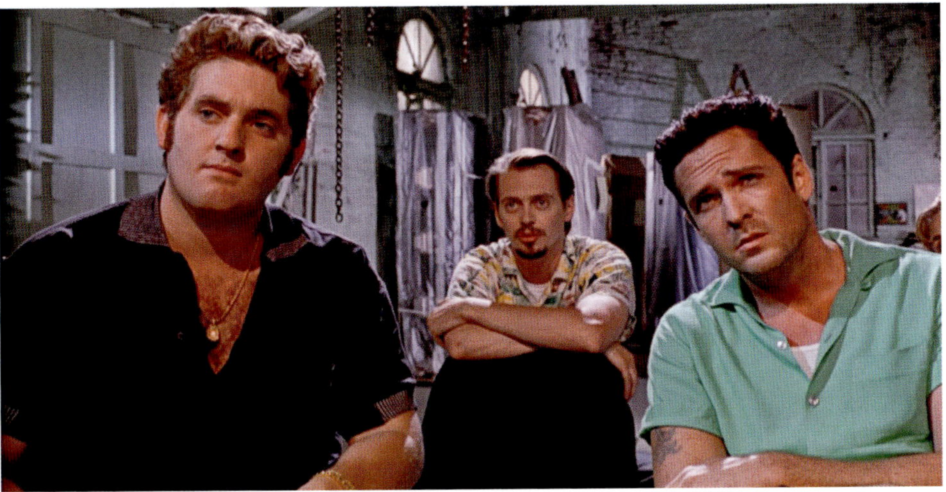

TOP: *Reservoir Dogs* saw the first example of Tarantino's trademark trunk shot – a point-of-view shot looking up at the characters looking in.

ABOVE: Nice Guy Eddie (Chris Penn), Mr Pink and Mr Blonde (Michael Madsen), during a heist-planning flashback.

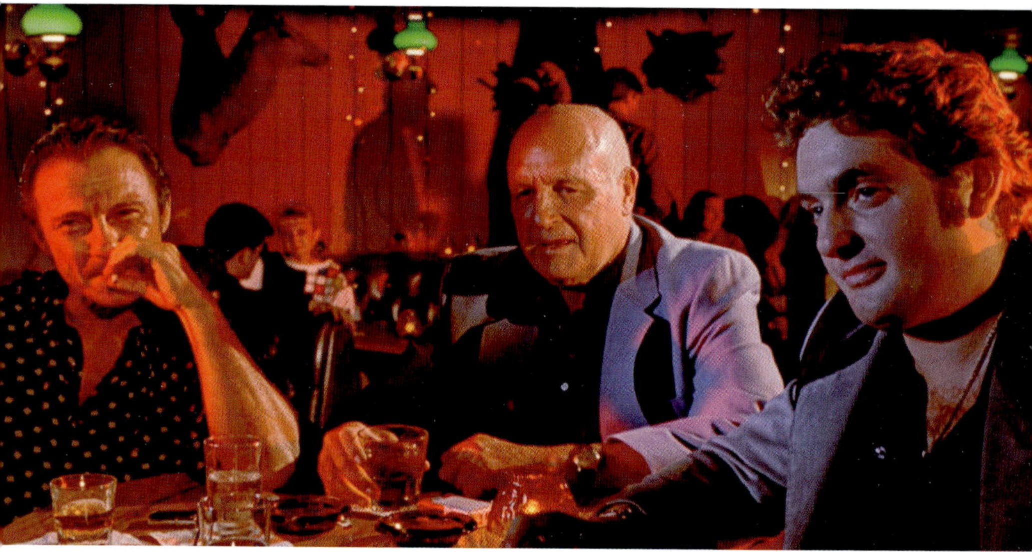

ABOVE: Mr Blonde, Joe (Lawrence Tierney) and Nice Guy Eddie, taking in Mr Orange's (off-screen) fictional story.

audience. 'This movie was never meant to be everything for everybody,' Tarantino responded. 'I made this movie for myself, and everybody else is invited. It's staying in.' It is, he's repeated, his favourite moment in the film.

It is a truly queasy scene, accentuated by the fact that up until now Tarantino has so effectively humanized these crooks, with their naturalistic diner-table small talk. To describe them as likeable is a stretch, given all the racism, sexism and homophobia that litters their banter, but with the help of their black-suit-and-tie cool, they're a compelling bunch to hang out with. Besides, we've been led to believe they're professionals, specialists, a more meritocratic breed of criminal than the Mafia gangsters we'd become accustomed to in the movies of Francis Ford Coppola and Martin Scorsese. And until now, Mr Blonde's 'unprofessional' psychoticism has only been reported and so excellently hinted at by Madsen, beneath the twinkling of his eyes.

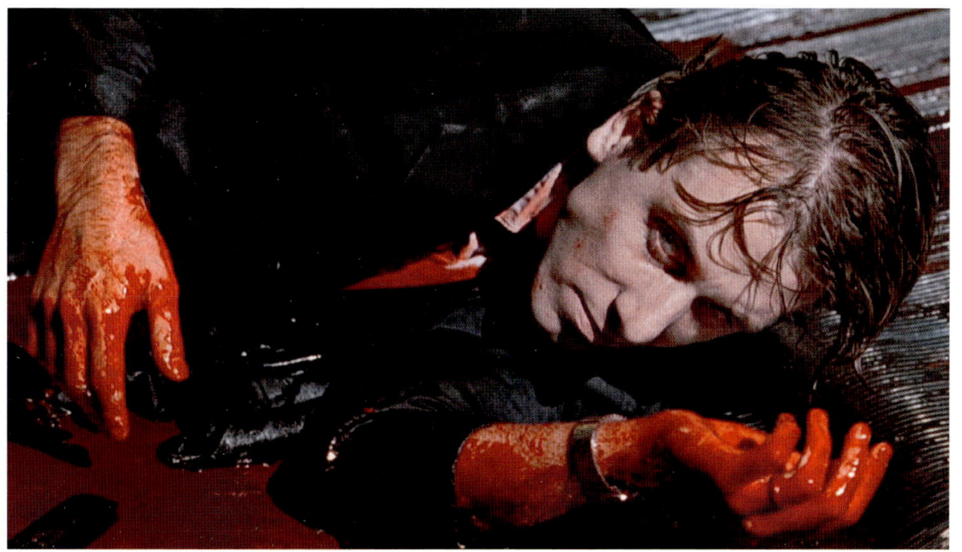

ABOVE: As the gut-shot Mr Orange, Tim Roth spent much of the shoot slathered in bright red Karo syrup.

But it is not a graphic scene. As Blonde closes in with his razor, Tarantino's camera pans away, settling on a wall which, ironically, has the words 'Watch your head' daubed on it. We hear the screaming, but we never see the cut. What irked Tarantino most about the reaction to the scene, and the criticism of the film's portrayal of violence, was that it was misdirected. 'They talked about *Reservoir Dogs* as if it was the most violent movie ever made,' he said. 'Now, someday I may make the most violent movie ever made, and I wouldn't mind people saying it. But I didn't.'

The excitement and cult of *Reservoir Dogs* went beyond its use of violence, and even its refreshing portrayal of criminal characters. Its pop-cultured dialogue and astute use of music drew approval, establishing a trend for retro-tastic soundtracks which, in Tarantino's case, became almost as popular as the movies themselves, their track lists tellingly punctuated by dialogue excerpts.

There was also Tarantino's audacious disregard for linearity, chopping the narrative up into different intertitled chapters ('Mr White', 'Mr Blonde', 'Mr Orange'), presented out of chronological order – and also, interestingly, giving up on the 'who's the undercover cop?' mystery about halfway through so we can follow Mr Orange's story. Tarantino put this down to his novelistic approach. 'There's a complexity to a novel that you don't get in original screenplays,' he said. 'A novel thinks nothing of starting in the middle of a story. And if a novel goes back in time, it's not a flashback, it's so you learn something. I've always thought that the closer we hitch movies to books, the better off movies will be.'

Remarkably, there is an entire sequence in the film that depicts an event that didn't even happen. Drawing on his own acting-school experience, Tarantino has Mr Orange rehearse then deliver 'a scene' to make his cover persona more convincing. As Orange tells 'the commode story', Tarantino presents it as authentically as any 'real' scene, and even nests within it a whole second anecdote told by one of its characters. It was the first example of the narrative diversions he'd make in future films (such as the animated 'Origin of O-Ren' sequence in *Kill Bill Volume 1*), to give his characters more depth.

When *Reservoir Dogs* debuted at Sundance, it was identified as part of an exciting new wave of American independent film, alongside the likes of Allison Anders' *Gas Food Lodging*, Gregg Araki's *The Living End*, Tom Kalin's *Swoon* and Alexandre Rockwell's *In The Soup*, which also starred Steve Buscemi and beat *Dogs* to the Grand Jury Prize at the festival. But, as good as they were, none of those films had the same cultural impact.

Nor did their creators create such a stir in the media as Tarantino, who left the United States for the first time to screen the film at the Cannes Film Festival, where the world's press lapped up his confidently geeky patter. While he'd gathered a strong cast for *Reservoir Dogs*, which repaid Keitel for his initial support by rejuvenating his career, it was clear that the film's true star was its director. The big question was: how was he going to follow it up?

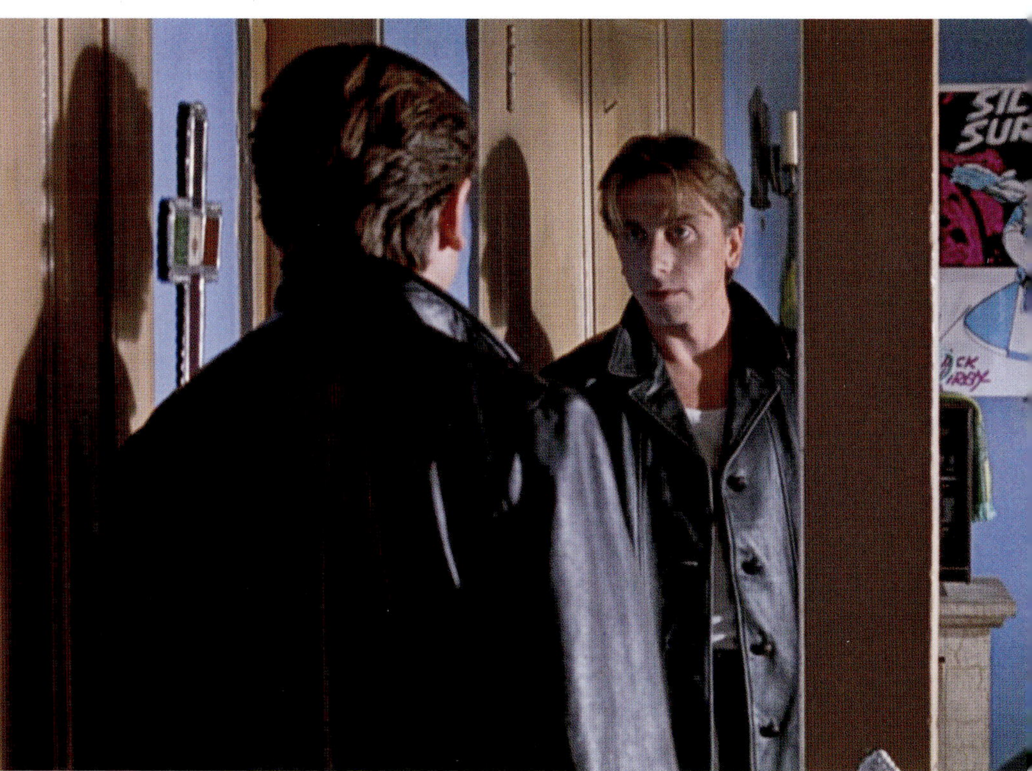

BELOW: 'You're super-cool': Mr Orange (Tim Roth) gives himself a final pep talk before it all goes south.

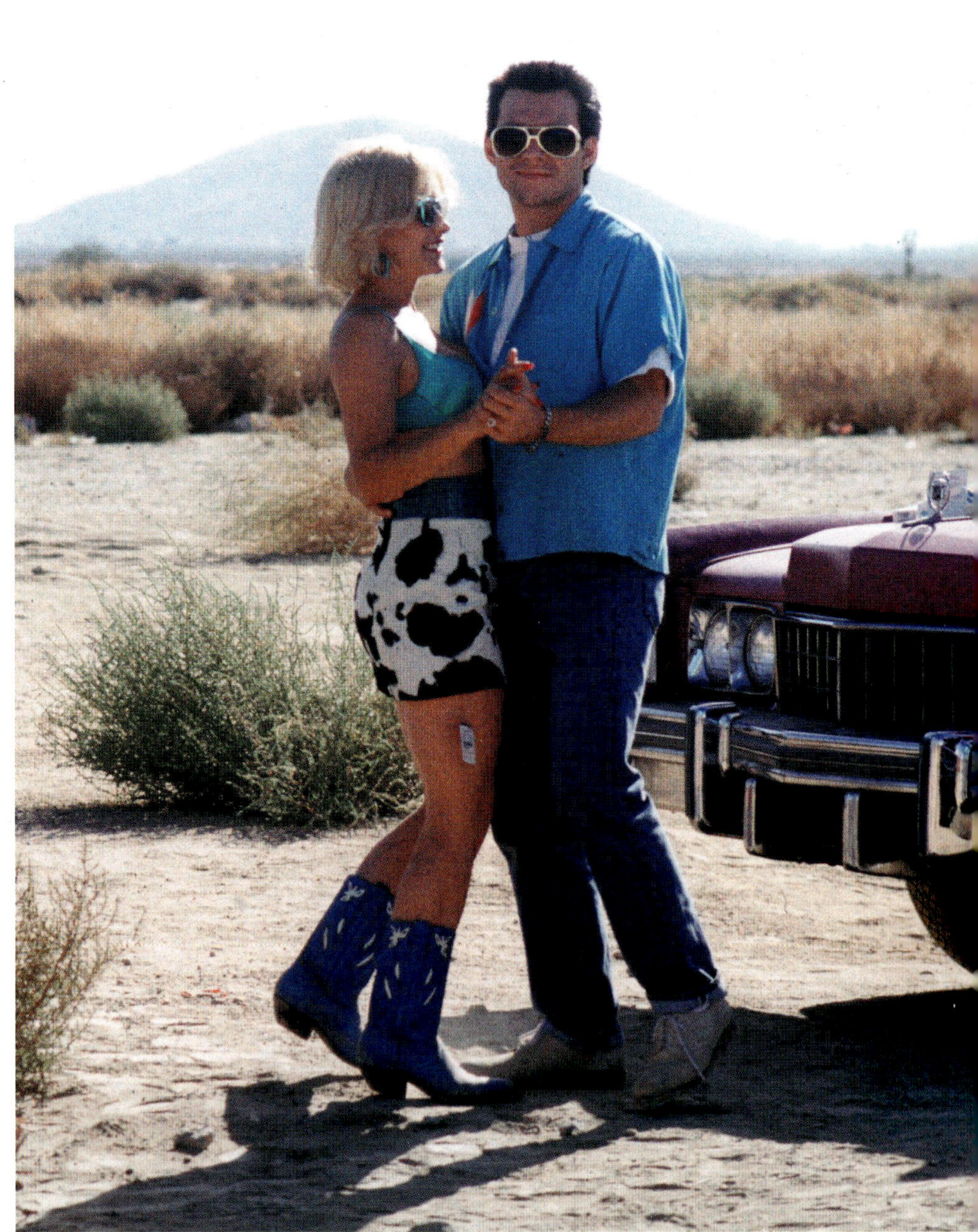

TRUE ROMANCE
ROMANCE
&
NATURAL
BORN KILLERS
1993/1994

While the world waited to see what Tarantino would do next, two of his earlier scripts manifested as movies by other directors. Both involved young married couples on the run – from the Mob in one case, from the law in the other – yet their treatment of Tarantino's material, and his regard for the results, couldn't have been more different.

First came 1993's *True Romance*, a project already running before *Reservoir Dogs* was made. This was the script Tarantino had originally hoped to make himself, a hybrid of reclaimed components from *My Best Friend's Birthday* and his and Roger Avary's *The Open Road*. Detroit comic-store clerk Clarence Worley and Tallahassee call girl Alabama Whitman fall in love after Alabama is hired as a birthday present for Clarence. Going full Travis Bickle, Clarence murders Alabama's pimp, Drexl, and the couple accidentally acquire a suitcase full of Mafia cocaine. They abscond to Los Angeles to sell it via the Hollywood contacts of a wannabe actor friend, but the gangsters are hot on their heels, leading to a massive shoot-out, during which Clarence is killed.

Alongside *My Best Friend's Birthday*, it is Tarantino's most solipsistic work, in the sense that he obviously cast himself as the main character. 'Clarence was me,' he confirmed years later – a fact not hard to spot given Clarence's amplified obsession with Elvis (who mentors him from beyond the grave), his geeky workplace (run by someone called Lance), and the fact that he meets with Alabama during a triple bill starring Japanese martial-arts star Sonny Chiba (who would, years later, appear as legendary katana forger Hattori Hanzo in *Kill Bill*). Alabama, meanwhile, is Tarantino's dream girl incarnate: she's hot, she's tough and she goes weak at the knees when her beau waxes lyrical about the artwork in *Spider-Man* comics. Rather more problematically, she also treats Clarence's outbursts of violence less as red flags than as acts of affection, and spends much of the story pliantly affirming his self-perceived coolness. Fortunately, the young Tarantino's ego was diluted somewhat by another director's vision. And it hardly hurt that they were a director who Tarantino loved.

At the time he made *True Romance*, British filmmaker Tony Scott had established himself in Hollywood as a prime purveyor of high-concept action cinema, delivering hits for überproducers Don Simpson and Jerry Bruckheimer in the form of *Top Gun* and *Beverly Hills Cop II*. But Tom Cruise vehicle *Days of Thunder* had been badly reviewed, while its wisecrackingly violent follow-up *The Last Boy Scout* (starring Bruce Willis) underperformed at the box

BELOW: Young lovers Alabama (Patricia Arquette) and Clarence (Christian Slater) don't exactly take the easy road.

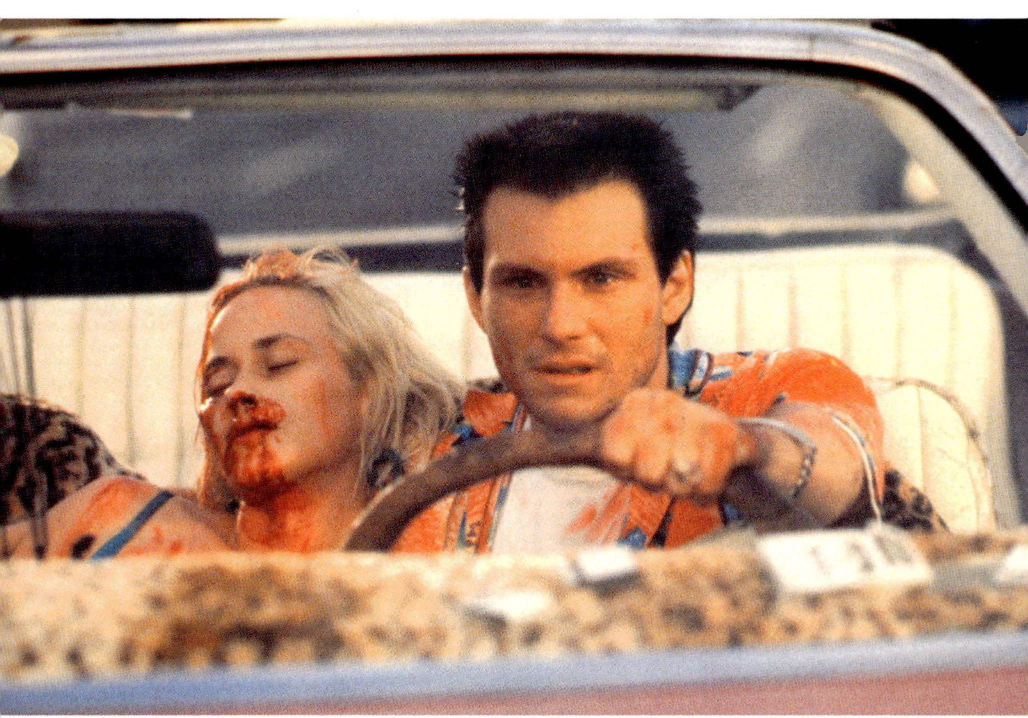

office. Scott was looking for something less dependent on big stars and bigger explosions. Something more interesting and challenging. He found it in *True Romance*, which Tarantino managed to put into Scott's hands via a friend on *The Last Boy Scout* crew. 'What I fell in love with were Quentin's characters,' Scott said of the script. 'It's an actor-based movie, the first time I've had one of those.'

Scott certainly cast some great actors. Christian Slater, then in his mid-20s, imbued the role of Clarence with the same edgy charm he'd exhibited in *Heathers* a few years earlier. Patricia Arquette, whose biggest film previously was *A Nightmare on Elm Street 3: Dream Warriors*, proved the perfect Alabama, adding some much-needed texture through her own doubts about the character. Her struggle to understand Alabama's reaction to Clarence killing Drexl, for example, adds valuable tension to the scene. 'My acting coach and I came up with the idea that here's a man I barely know, who killed someone and is eating a burger. He could kill *me* next,' she said. 'As a female, the way to stay safe is to be in a love bubble.' Although, for the relationship to work, she recognized that part of Alabama did genuinely find the act romantic. 'Like, kill all the mistakes I ever made.' It also helped that their on-screen chemistry was, both she and Slater admitted, fed by a mutual off-screen attraction.

According to Scott, both Brad Pitt and Val Kilmer loved the script so much they begged to be in the film, and were happy to take the minor roles of the scene-stealing stoner room-mate Floyd and 'The Mentor' (aka Elvis), respectively. Gary Oldman delivered a typically transformative performance as the scarred, dreadlocked Drexl, the pimp who, we're told, 'thinks he's Black'; while James Gandolfini makes an early-career impression as Mob thug Virgil, who brutally beats Alabama in a distressing sequence that required several cuts for the film to avoid an NC-17 rating in

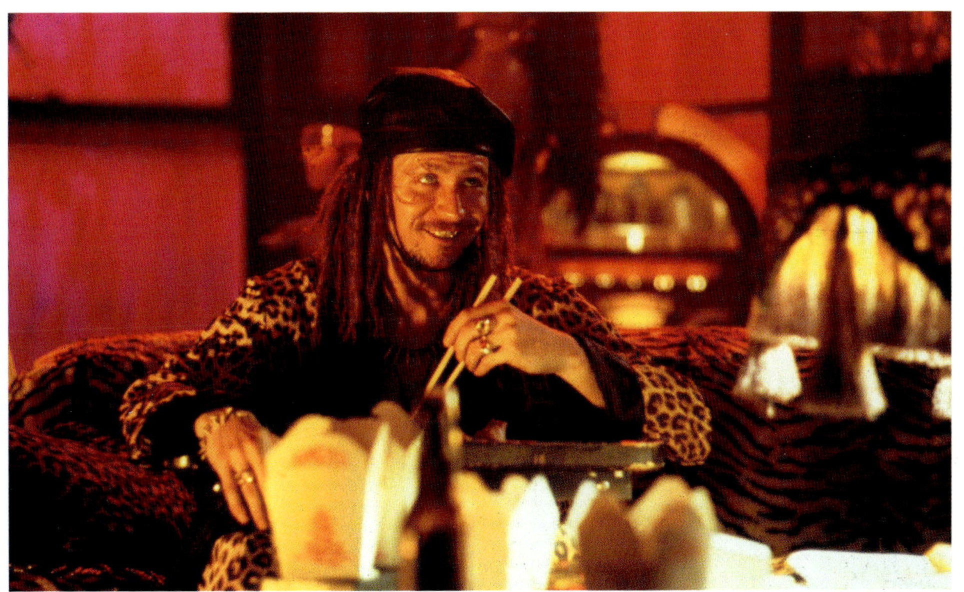

ABOVE: Gary Oldman in his brief but hugely memorable appearance as the short-lived pimp Drexl.

the United States. Most memorably, two Hollywood heavyweights went toe-to-toe in the scene where Dennis Hopper, as Clarence's doomed father, delivers a slur-filled monologue about the racial provenance of Sicilians to his senior Mafioso interrogator Christopher Walken. It is an electrifying scene, seemingly refereed by Scott rather than directed.

For all the mutual respect between Scott and Tarantino, the director wasn't above restructuring the script to make it more traditional and linear; originally it started with the Clarence/Drexl showdown, followed by the Walken/Hopper scene, before going back to Clarence and Alabama's meeting, and then continuing with the coke-selling plot. Scott's narrative rearrangement irked Tarantino, but not so much that he wanted to fall out with the director over it.

He was more bothered by Scott's decision to allow Clarence to survive the climactic shoot-out and escape to Cancún, in Mexico, with Alabama, where they raise a family. Tarantino tried to convince Scott to leave the ending as it was. 'You're losing your balls,' he told him. 'You're trying to make it Hollywood shit. Why are you doing this?' Scott heard him out, and mollified Tarantino by saying he'd shoot the ending both ways. 'Then I'm going to look at them, and then decide which one I want to go with.' However, Tarantino point-blank refused to write the new ending, and Avary stepped in to do it for him, uncredited, for a $1,000 fee. Scott stuck with the happy denouement, and in the end, Tarantino had to admit that he was right. 'He added a fairy-tale element to it,' said Tarantino.

Despite its more conventional structure and Hollywood ending, *True Romance* flopped at the box office, barely making its $12.5 million budget back in the United States. Interestingly, it hasn't aged so gracefully as the films Tarantino directed himself, perhaps because it is shot very much in early Nineties style, with slo-mo action and a cheesy neon-washed sex scene, while Tarantino instead emulated the filmmakers of the Seventies. But Scott considered it one of his best movies, and his good relationship with Tarantino persisted.

It was all a very different story to the fate of Tarantino's other early script, even though that one ended up in the hands of no less impressive a director.

OPPOSITE: Playing Clarence's ill-fated father, Dennis Hopper shared a scene with Christopher Walken that was as celebrated for its dramatic tension as it was criticized for its use of racial slurs.

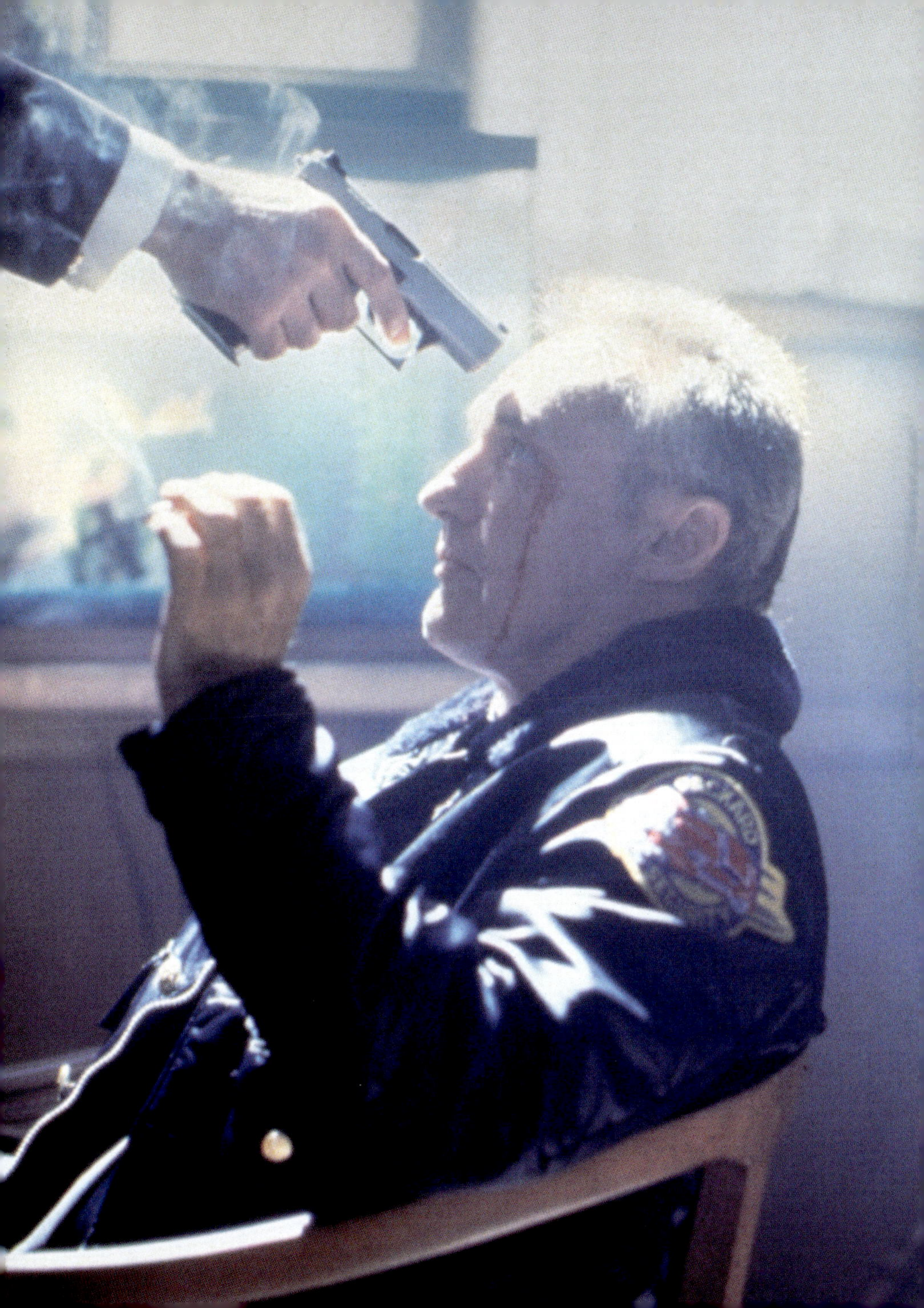

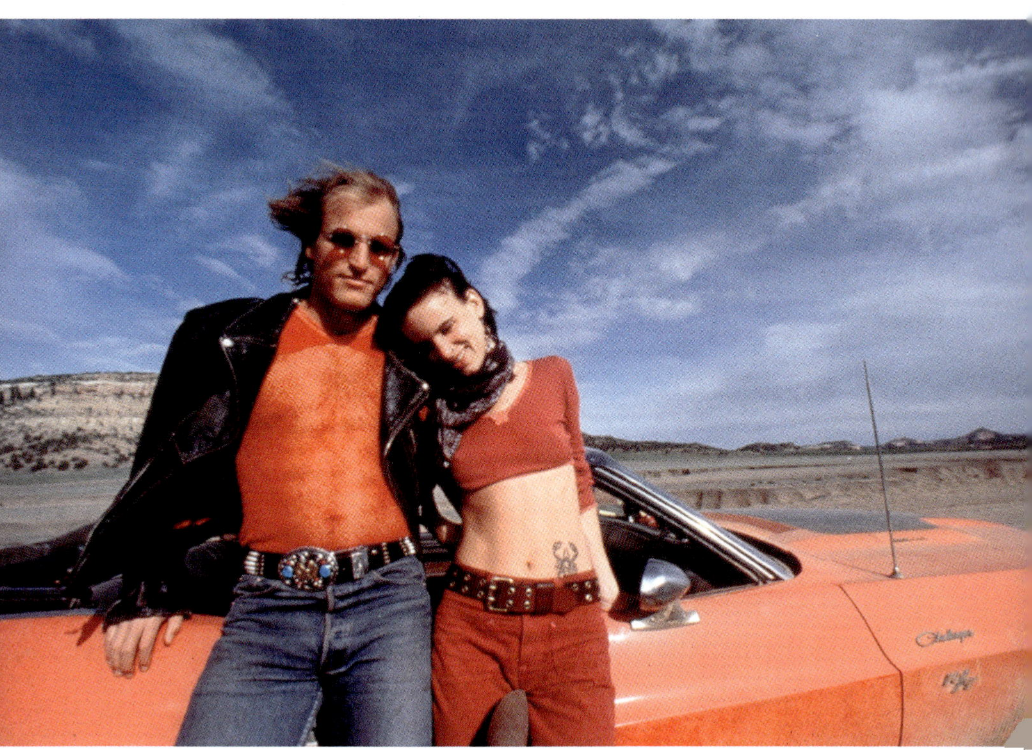

By the time Oliver Stone first read the script for *Natural Born Killers*, Tarantino's old friend and *My Best Friend's Birthday* co-producer Rand Vossler was out of the frame to make it. Tarantino had sold the option for $10,000 to up-and-coming producers Jane Hamsher and Don Murphy, who succeeded in setting the project up at Warner Bros. Stone, who enjoyed *Reservoir Dogs*, appreciated *Natural Born Killers'* sense of humour, and its 'insanity'. He felt he could say something interesting and provocative with Tarantino's material: the misadventures of Mickey and Mallory Knox, a young couple who are incarcerated after embarking on a 55-victim killing spree (starting with Mallory's parents), and become celebrated by the media, embodied by tabloid TV hack Wayne Gayle (Robert Downey Jr), who secures a big-scoop interview with Mickey.

But Stone felt the script was a little one-note and needed some added layers. Together with writers Richard Rutowski and David Veloz, he embarked on a 'tearing-down plan' that would add 'character, violence and humour,' and downgrade Tarantino's contribution to a 'story by' credit. Stone also thickened the satire. He was concerned by the commercialization of the American media and the way news was becoming violence-obsessed entertainment. 'The salvation of moronic violence grew enormously in the early Nineties,' he later reflected. 'The film is about an entire culture going down the toilet.'

Tarantino was not enamoured of Stone's heavy-handed style, and expressed as much to Hamsher and Murphy. He asked them not to make the film with Stone, but they refused to shop it elsewhere. The resultant hostility Tarantino felt towards the pair only intensified when he realized just how much Stone had reworked his script, and later had to engage in a legal battle to publish his original version.

To this day, Tarantino claims not to have seen the entire movie, having walked out of the only screening he attended, but, based on reports from friends, he objected to Stone's explanation of the protagonists' sociopathy by giving them a background of childhood abuse. Tarantino particularly disapproved of a scene in which Mickey (Woody Harrelson) fantasizes about a female captive he's bound and gagged in his and Mallory's (Juliette Lewis) motel room while making love to his wife. 'Mickey would never do that,' Tarantino insisted. 'The point is, they unnaturally live for each other at the expense of everybody else on planet Earth.'

On the film's release in 1994, Tarantino did not hold back from expressing his dissent in interviews, much to Stone's annoyance.

OPPOSITE: *Cheers* star Woody Harrelson with *Cape Fear*'s Juliette Lewis as killer couple Mickey and Mallory Knox.

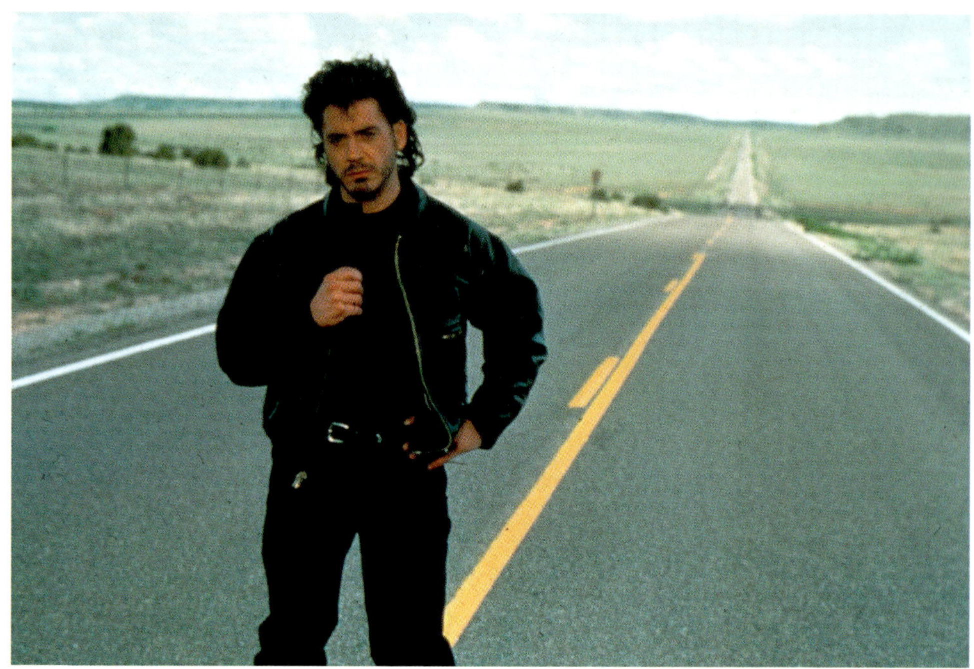

'It's embarrassing because I'm trying to sell a film and not only is he bad-mouthing me, he's damaging the possibility at the same time for us to make money,' Stone said. 'Tarantino was a holy god at that point. He could do no wrong. He had the biggest fan club in the world, every fucking critic! I tried to let it go by, but it did hurt the film, no question.'

As it turned out, *Natural Born Killers* performed robustly at the box office, taking over $100 million worldwide. But in disassociating himself from it, Tarantino dodged a bullet. Stone's film was stylistically bold, taking its cue from MTV with its disorientating collage of film stocks, lurid flash-frames and back-projected images. But while it had its fans, the critical response was largely

Tarantino's universe

Quentin Tarantino considered many of his films as taking place in the same 'realer than real universe', and the same names tend to crop up in his movies. There are references in *Reservoir Dogs* to a Marsellus Spivey, combining *Pulp Fiction*'s Marsellus Wallace and *True Romance*'s Drexl Spivey, while Mr Blonde/Vic Vega's parole officer Seymour Scagnetti shares a surname with *Natural Born Killers*' cop Jack Scagnetti, and Vega himself shares a surname with *Pulp Fiction*'s Vincent. Tarantino confirmed the latter pair were indeed siblings, and even considered writing a Vega brothers script. Other family connections appear between *True Romance*'s sleazy producer Lee Donowitz and *Inglourious Basterds*' Donnie Donowitz – son and father – and *Pulp Fiction*'s Captain Koons and *Django Unchained*'s Crazy Craig Koons – descendent and ancestor.

vitriolic. '*Natural Born Killers* is dense and unmodulated enough to be exhausting,' wrote Janet Maslin in *The New York Times*. 'It is finally less an epiphany than an ordeal.' As a satirist, she jabbed, Stone is 'an elephant ballerina'.

The film's depiction of violence, meanwhile, was found by many commentators to be disturbingly glorified to the point of depravity, even after Stone had to make 155 cuts to secure the picture a commercially acceptable R-rating in the United States. The movie and its violence were *supposed* to be disturbing, Stone pointed out. That was the whole point of it.

Tarantino had taken flak for the violence in *Reservoir Dogs*, and would continue to do so throughout his career, but none of his works would attract the furore that whipped up around *Natural Born Killers*. Its reputation as the most controversial film of the 1990s was sealed by its association with a spate of supposed

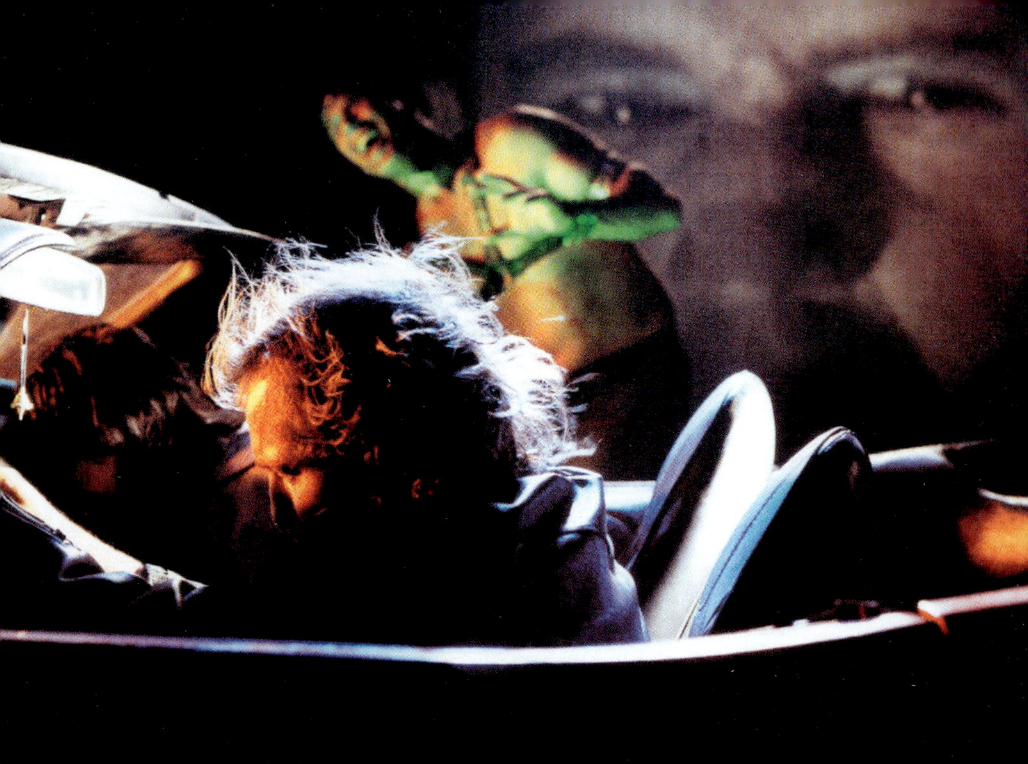

copycat killings in the United States. Incitement lawsuits were filed against Warner Bros and Stone by the families of the victims in three such incidents, although ultimately they were dismissed. When a Louisiana judge ruled in Stone and Warner Bros' favour in the case of an 18-year-old couple who committed armed robbery and killed shop assistant Patsy Byers after watching the film in 1995, Stone stated that he didn't see the result as a victory. 'We've created a new legal hell where everyone is entitled and no one is responsible,' he said.

Compared with that experience, to have Tarantino disapprove of his handling of the script was a minor event, as much as it

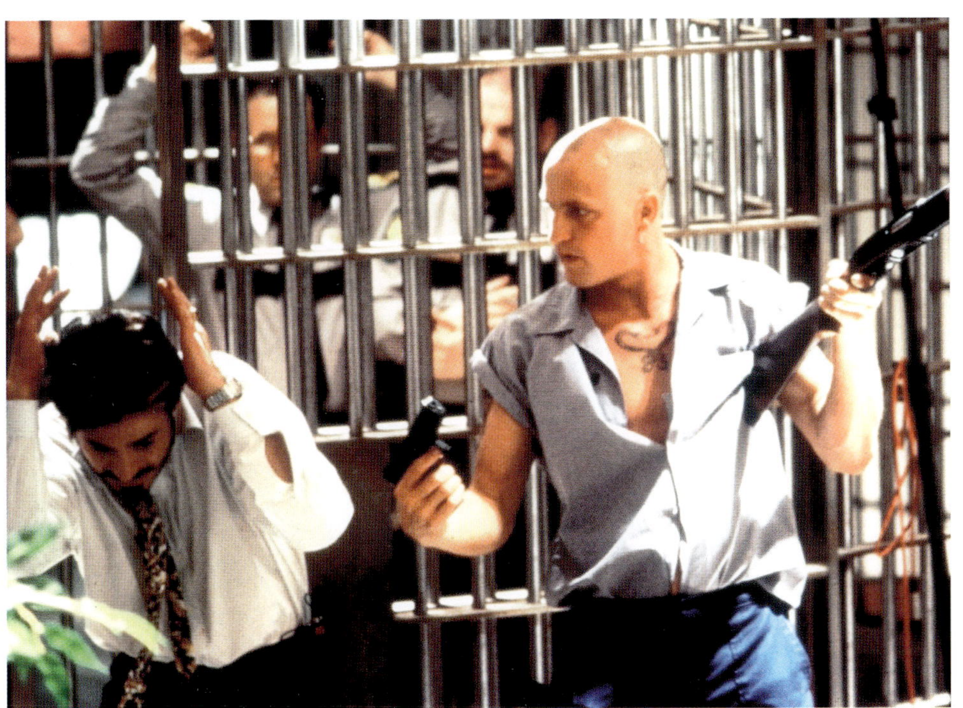

ABOVE: Mickey is about to prove to Wayne that no prison can contain his murderous wrath.

pained Stone. Eventually, the pair reached a truce. 'We get along,' said Stone in 2009. 'We talk here and there. He likes some of my movies and I like some of his.'

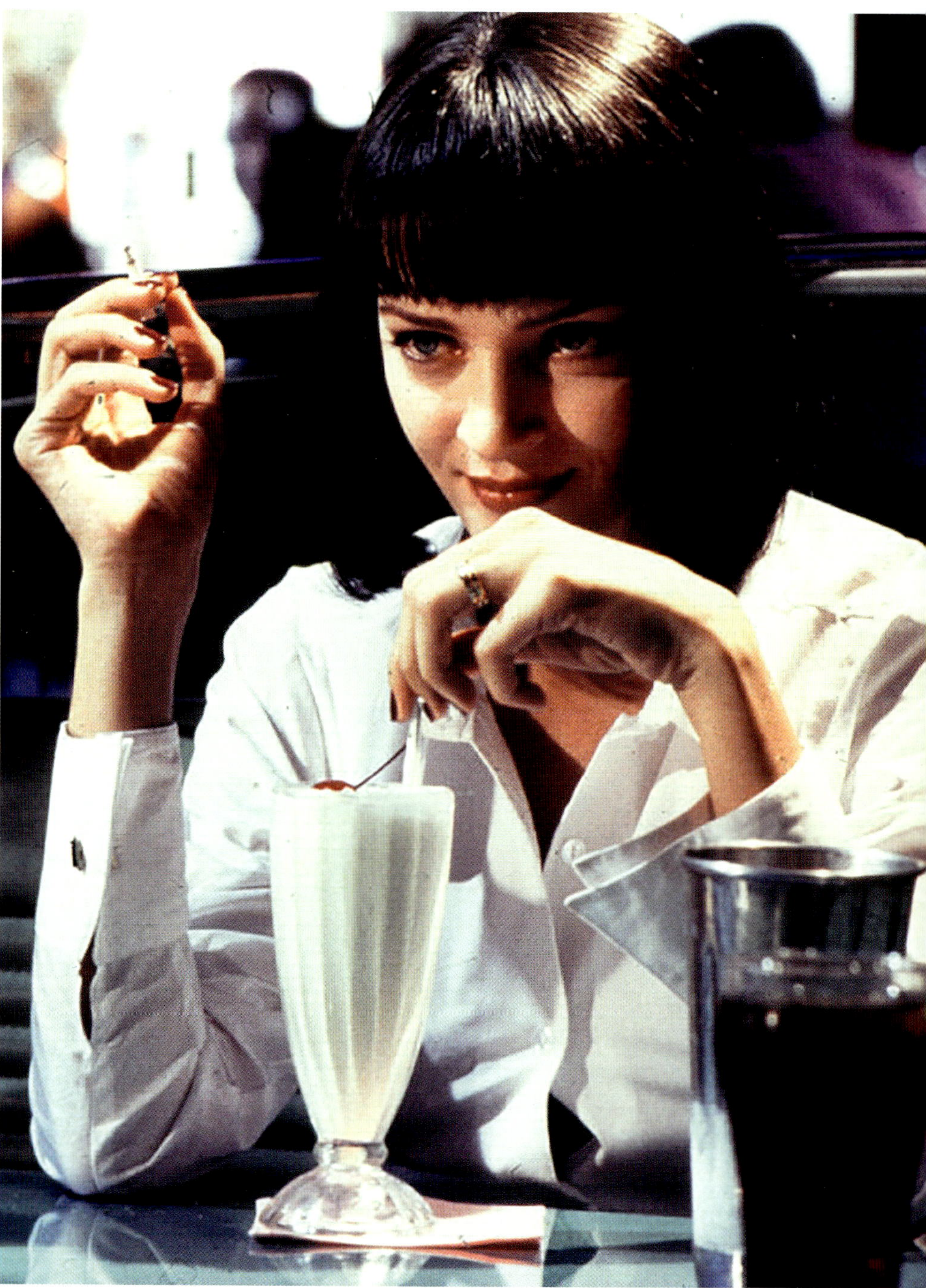

*'Now, if you'll excuse me,
I'm going to go home and
have a heart attack'*

PULP FICTION
1994

On 23 September 1994, *Pulp Fiction* opened the New York Film Festival. Tarantino was in the audience at the Lincoln Center, along with many of his cast and crew. About an hour in, the movie's signature scene played out. Tarantino's favourite in the film, it would become as notorious as *Reservoir Dogs'* ear slice.

After a date night with Vincent Vega (John Travolta), one of her gangster husband's sharp-suited employees, Mia Wallace (Uma Thurman) discovers a bag of white powder in Vincent's overcoat pocket. Assuming it to be cocaine, she snorts a line. But, as it is in fact high-grade heroin, she overdoses and collapses. Vincent, who has been tasked by his boss to treat Mia to a fun night out, returns from the bathroom to find her twitching on the floor, and rushes her to the home of Lance (Eric Stoltz), his dealer. Lance has the only means of saving Mia: a huge syringe loaded with adrenalin that must be slammed directly into her ailing heart.

The sequence is chaotic, darkly comical and shot in long takes that only intensify the tension as the moment of penetrating truth arrives. When, on the count of three, Vincent brings down the needle, Tarantino cuts away, just as he did when the other Vega applied razor to ear. The dull thud we hear is still excruciating.

At this very moment, a woman's voice rang out in the stalls, screaming for the film to be stopped. The man next to her had collapsed, apparently in the throes of a heart attack. The casualty was, it turned out, a diabetic suffering a sugar crash, which abated when he was given a cup of soda. Still, as the story spread the legend stuck: *Pulp Fiction* had given someone a heart attack. And what was Tarantino's first thought when those cries rang out? 'This movie fucking works!'

Two years earlier, while Tarantino was touring the world with *Reservoir Dogs*, absorbing the adulation and spitting out soundbites, Danny DeVito's production company Jersey Films secured a $900,000 development deal with the writer-director for his next script, on which major studio TriStar Pictures had first refusal. The deal allowed Tarantino to have final cut and final say over casting choices, while also giving him a percentage of the box-office gross receipts. For a filmmaker in their early 30s with only one movie under their belt, this was virtually unheard of.

You can imagine Jersey Films' anxiety, then, when as soon as the ink was dry, Tarantino seemingly absconded to Amsterdam, only checking in over the phone from time to time. However, while

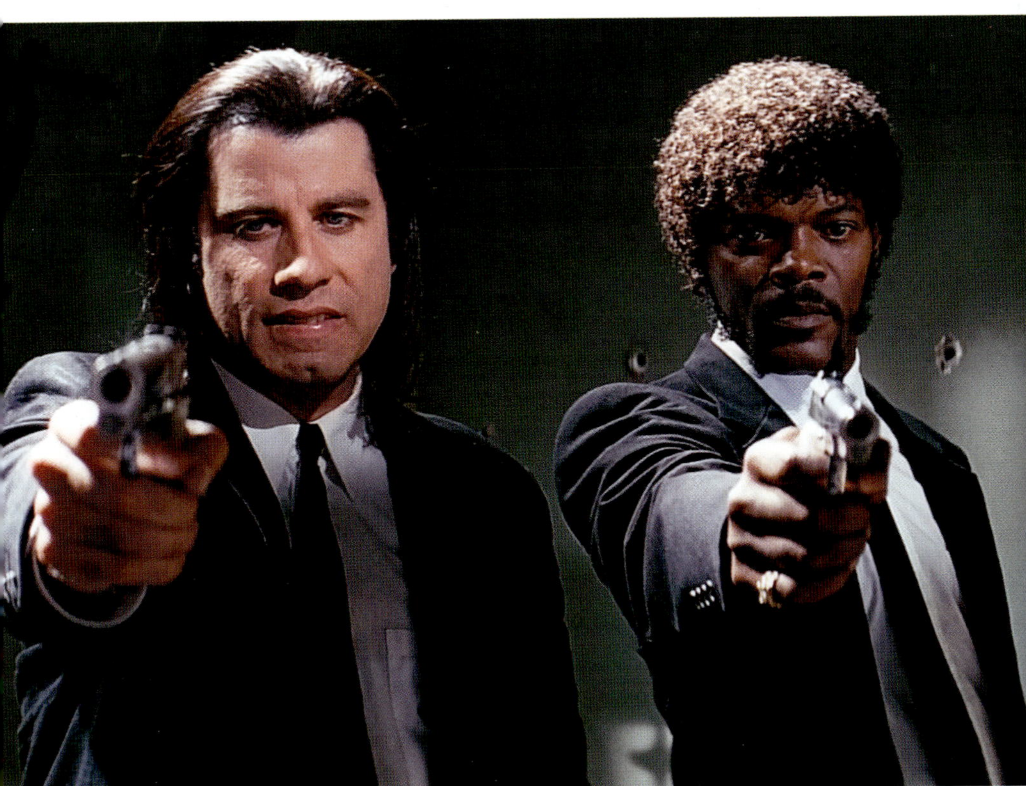

BELOW: John Travolta and Samuel L Jackson as chatty hitmen Vincent and Jules, having just narrowly cheated death.

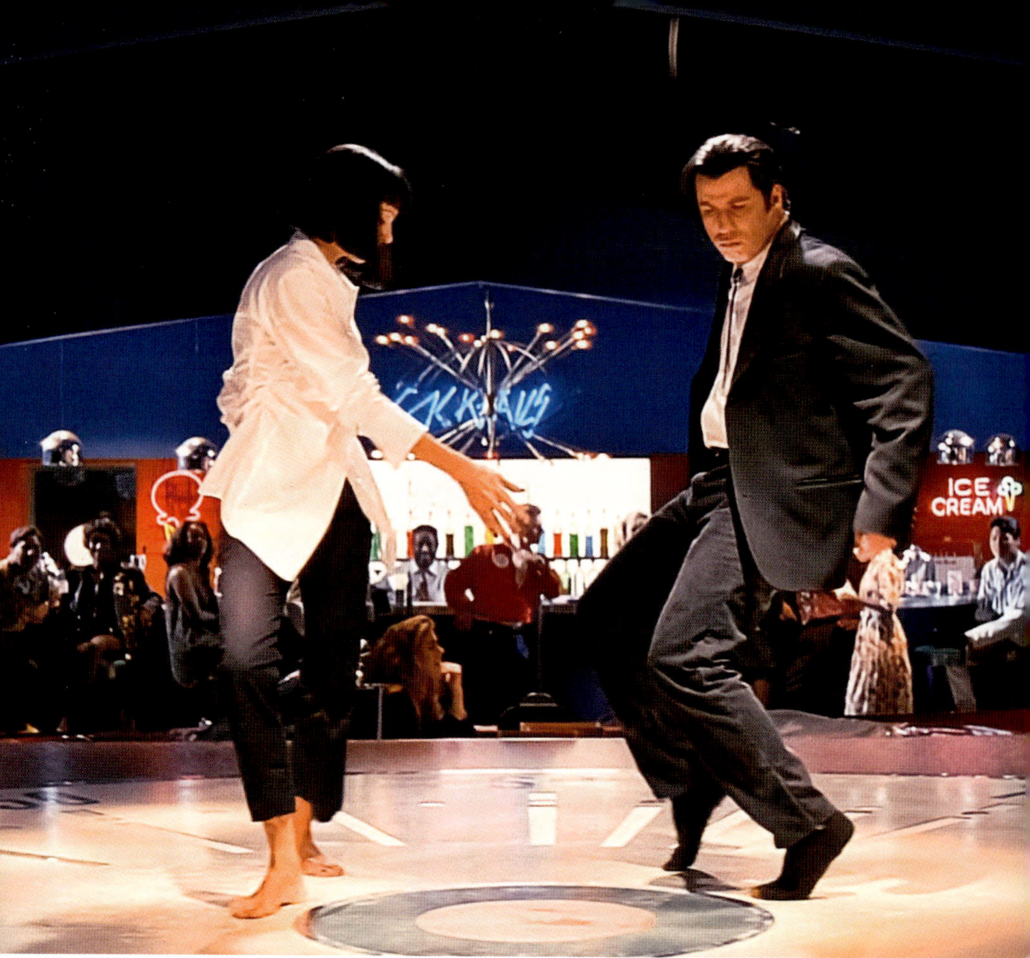

he was certainly enjoying himself in the city's coffee shops and cinemas, he was in fact hard at work on his new script, *Pulp Fiction*.

It was an anthology film, weaving together the kinds of hard-boiled, antagonist-driven crime stories he used to consume in *Black Mask* magazine, which since its launch in 1920 had introduced the world to the likes of Raymond Chandler and Dashiell Hammett. Similar to *Reservoir Dogs*, the film would be non-linear, peppered with pop culture references, and written with great music in mind, from the frenetic surf rock of Dick Dale

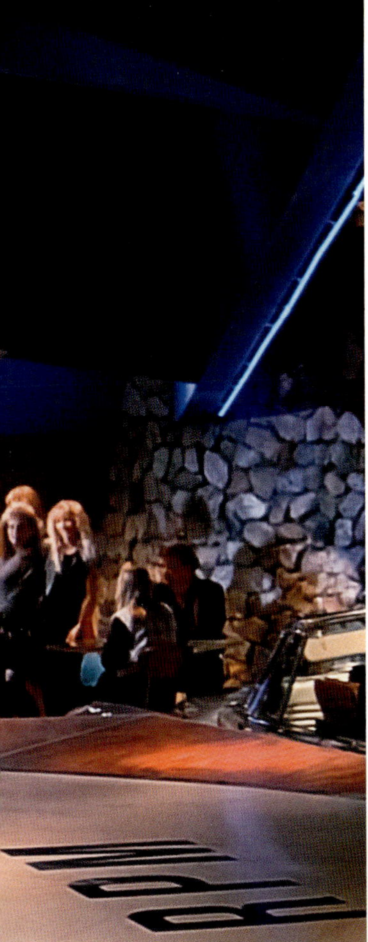

to the Urge Overkill cover version of Neil Diamond's 'Girl, You'll Be a Woman Soon'. More importantly, it would, like *Reservoir Dogs*, display Tarantino's Elmore Leonard-inspired attitude to dialogue and genre: taking something familiar and giving it a real-life twist.

'You've seen these stories a zillion times before,' said Tarantino, referring to the crime-genre staples of the guy who has to take out his crime-boss' wife, the boxer who throws a fight, and the hit men who carry out a job. 'But you've never seen them quite play out like this. Part of the trick is to take these genre characters and these genre situations and apply them to some of real life's rules. And see how they unravel.'

It is in this conceit that we find the film's novelty, charm, impact and comedy. So, we meet hired killers Vincent and Jules (Samuel L Jackson) who chat about European McDonald's and foot massages before getting into 'character', executing their marks, and narrowly avoiding death thanks to what Jules can only interpret as 'divine intervention'. We have the aforementioned date, complete with uncomfortable silences, a dancing competition and that spectacular overdose. And we get the fight-throwing boxer (Bruce Willis) randomly bumping into the boss he's just double crossed

(Ving Rhames) while retrieving his precious heirloom watch, with the rivals then falling afoul of some hillbilly rapists. For some added flavour, Tarantino cross-hatched his LA-based plot lines so that characters from one story would turn up in the others, and squeezed them all into the same, short time frame (around two days).

The screenplay was an evolution of everything that made *Reservoir Dogs* so impressive, with much wider scope, a bigger cast of characters and far greater ambition. Jersey Films had a winner. Except TriStar declined to make it. The studio's main problem was the depiction of drug use, specifically the scene in which Vincent shoots up. Once Tarantino returned from Amsterdam, he took a meeting to try and reassure them, but failed. Instead, the script was snapped up by Miramax, which had distributed *Reservoir Dogs* in the States. Harvey Weinstein was so smitten by *Pulp Fiction*, he committed to backing the entire production to the tune of $9 million, where previously his company had only over acquired (and often brutally repackaged) completed films. He even agreed to Tarantino's terms, though was reluctant to allow him final cut, and would fight the director over his casting choices. But, as

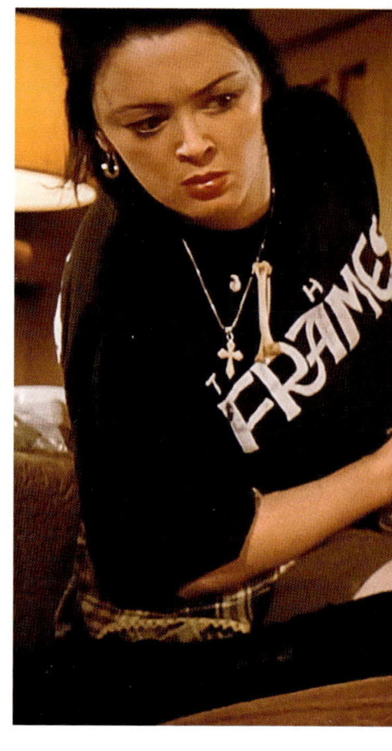

ABOVE: 'That was fuckin' trippy.' Mia (Uma Thurman) comes back from the brink thanks to a direct-to-the-heart adrenalin shot.

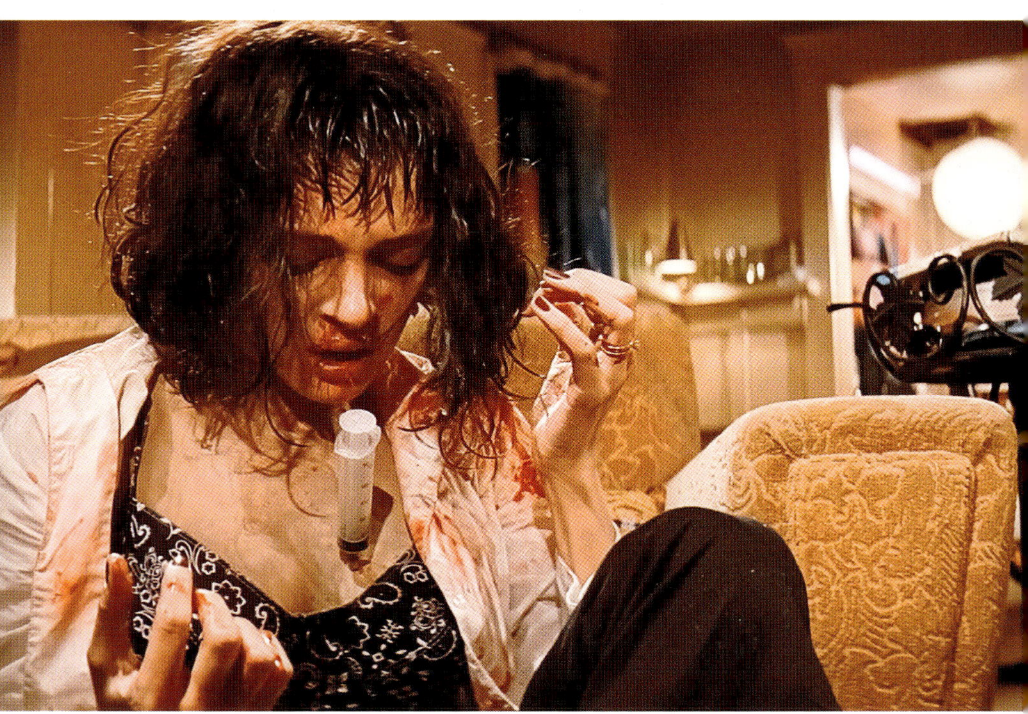

Harvey's brother and co-chairman Bob later put it, Miramax was now very much 'in the Quentin Tarantino business.'

Pulp Fiction involved one of the most celebrated casting decisions of Quentin Tarantino's career. He'd always loved the idea of putting John Travolta in one of his movies. The star of *Grease*, *Saturday Night Fever* and *Blow Out* had, but for his appearance in 1989 baby comedy *Look Who's Talking*, been largely forgotten by the early Nineties. Yet Tarantino still saw him as 'one of the greatest stars Hollywood has ever produced,' and felt he could reignite Travolta's spark. When they first met, he told Travolta he'd love him to play the lead role in *From Dusk Till Dawn*, which at the time he was trying to revive. But Travolta admitted that vampires weren't really his thing. He was more interested in the other upcoming film Tarantino mentioned, *Pulp Fiction*. Until that point, Tarantino had pictured Michael Madsen in the role of long-haired hitman Vincent Vega. But after a night of talking and reminiscing with Travolta, he recalibrated his plans. Six months later, the actor got a phone call. 'Quentin Tarantino has rewritten *Pulp Fiction* with you in mind,' he was told.

He'd already given Harvey Keitel's career a boost with *Reservoir Dogs*, but it was the casting of Travolta in *Pulp Fiction* that would establish Tarantino's reputation as the saviour of forgotten stars. A reputation he never fully embraced. It was not his intention, he insisted, to bring people back from Hollywood limbo. 'I'm just trying to cast the best actors or the coolest actors in whatever role. I'm just not using, you know, the "hot star list" in order to do it.'

However, Miramax was very much using the 'hot star list', and favoured Oscar magnet Daniel Day-Lewis for the role of Vincent. Tarantino stood his ground and was ultimately proven right: Travolta was superb in the role, his loose, laidback delivery perfectly complementing the preacher-like precision of Samuel L Jackson as his on-screen partner-in-murder, Jules.

Jackson's casting was a different story. He'd been Tarantino's first choice for Jules, and considered *Pulp Fiction* the best script he'd ever read. He was no doubt encouraged by the fact that he'd have arguably the best part in it: a 'bad motherfucker' who has a life-changing experience and seeks redemption, all ingeniously reflected in his two very different deliveries of Biblical passage Ezekiel 25:17. But Jackson nearly blew his chances when he assumed he'd already bagged the part and underperformed in an audition that he didn't realize was an audition. The role of Jules almost went to Paul Calderón (eventually cast as Marsellus' barman), but Jackson was allowed a second chance and was reportedly so mesmerizing at his next reading that the casting assistant feeding him his lines kept freezing up.

CHAPTER THREE

The Tarantino cameos

The same year *Pulp Fiction* was released, Tarantino made a memorable *Top Gun*-analysing cameo in Rory Kelly's romantic comedy *Sleep With Me*, produced by and starring Eric Stoltz. This was just one of a rash of appearances he made in films (other than his own). The first was in 1992's *Eddie Presley*, a comedy about an Elvis impersonator, in which the former Elvis-impersonating Tarantino appeared as a hospital orderly alongside *Evil Dead*'s Bruce Campbell. Then he appeared as a bartender in his friend Alexandre Rockwell's *Somebody To Love*, reuniting with Harvey Keitel and Steve Buscemi.

Post-*Pulp*, Tarantino would make a number of appearances for another filmmaking buddy, Robert Rodriguez – in *Desperado* (1995), *From Dusk Till Dawn* (1996) and *Planet Terror* (2007) – while also showing up in the likes of Spike Lee's *Girl 6* (as a creepy director), misfiring crime comedy *Destiny Turns on the Radio* (as the mysterious Johnny Destiny), Adam Sandler comedy *Little Nicky* (as a blind preacher), Takashi Miike's *Sukiyaki Western Django* (as a weird gunslinger) and *The Muppets' Wizard of Oz* (as himself).

However, Tarantino's acting stints were rarely reviewed as well as his movies, something that never failed to vex him. 'They almost resent the fact that I want to act,' he said.

It was not hard to convince the Weinsteins to go with A-lister Bruce Willis for Butch, after Tarantino met him at a barbecue at Harvey Keitel's Malibu beach house. Encouraged by Keitel's glowing reports from the set of *Reservoir Dogs*, the *Die Hard* actor happily took a major pay cut to be part of its follow-up.

The field was far more open for Tarantino's first major female character, slinky moll Mia Wallace, whose barefoot padding would mark the start of his on-screen fascination with women's feet. He took meeting after meeting with different actresses, including Holly Hunter, Alfre Woodard and Rosanna Arquette (who got the smaller part of Lance's wife, Jody), waiting for the magical moment

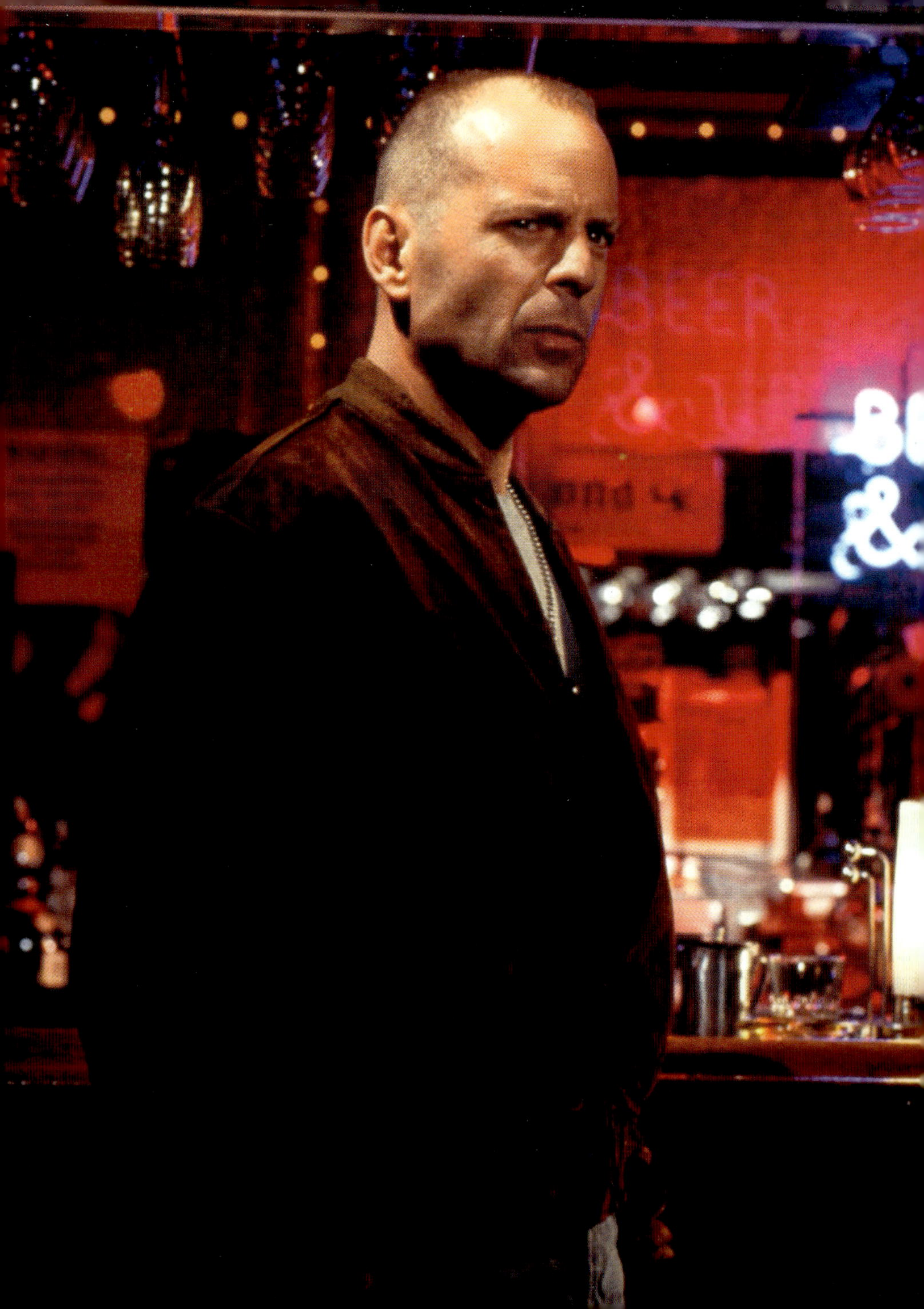

he'd just instinctively know he'd found Mia. That came only minutes into his lunch with Uma Thurman, who'd made her breakthrough four years earlier as love goddess Venus in Terry Gilliam's *The Adventures of Baron Munchausen*. The pair got on so well during the shoot, they hatched a plan for a Thurman-led reunion, inspired in part by the references to Mia's failed TV show *Fox Force Five*, in which she'd played one of an all-girl gang of kick-ass secret agents. Almost a decade later, this would be executed as *Kill Bill*.

With twice as much time to shoot and a much larger budget, production on *Pulp Fiction* was far less pressured than on *Reservoir Dogs*, and Tarantino always kept the mood light. While the movie was much bigger and more complicated than his debut, he took it all in his loping stride, fuelled throughout by an infectious boyish enthusiasm. 'Quentin has an energy about him that's very wild and open,' said Jackson. 'He's so excited about seeing his words come to life, it's contagious. It turns out to be a real productive energy.'

Tarantino never once lost control, thanks to a very fixed, focused idea, as the film's writer, of how every scene should work. And also how the movie should look: bright, crisp, almost hyper-real, in keeping with his conception of his stories as taking place in an alternate, heightened reality. *Pulp Fiction* was shot by his *Dogs* cinematographer Andrzej Sekula on 50 ASA film stock, the slowest available. 'It creates an almost no-grain image, it's lustrous,' said Tarantino. 'It's the closest thing we have to Fifties Technicolor.'

In no sequence is the film's vibrancy more pronounced than Vincent and Mia's arrival at Jack Rabbit Slim's, a larger-than-life, kitscher-than-kitsch restaurant staffed by Golden Age Hollywood cosplayers, whose clientele eat beneath posters for *Attack of the*

OPPOSITE: Playing Butch Coolidge, Bruce Willis was Tarantino's biggest star yet. Willis' salary for Tony Scott's *The Last Boy Scout* had been almost twice *Pulp Fiction*'s entire budget.

50 Foot Woman and *Shock Confessions of a Sorority Girl*, and watch live entertainment on a stage with a speedometer dance floor. Constructed in a Culver City warehouse under the supervision of production designer David Wasco, the set cost around $150,000, and blended an archetypal Fifties diner with the bar from Howard Hawks's *Red Line 7000* and the nightclub from Elvis Presley picture *Speedway*. It was never an option to rent out a real restaurant, Tarantino insisted. It had to be built from the ground up. But once it was, he confessed to being almost intimidated by the space. 'How do I make it live?' he worried. The answer was to introduce it through Vincent as he blearily wanders in, gliding between its tables. 'But the scene ain't about the restaurant,' Tarantino pointed out.

The scene is, firstly, about Vincent and Mia's dinner-table conversation, which is as enthralling for the stretches in which they don't talk as it is for the moments they do. It is also, of course, about the now-iconic twist competition scene, performed by Travolta and Thurman to Chuck Berry's 'You Never Can Tell'. The *Saturday Night Fever* star was, of course, no stranger to grooving on camera, and suggested to Tarantino that he and Thurman mix things up by throwing in other dance moves, such as the Batman and the hitchhiker. Thurman, however, confessed she didn't feel capable of pulling it off. Tarantino assured her that the point wasn't to be proficient, it was simply to enjoy it. He took her and Travolta to a trailer and played them the 'Madison' dance scene in Jean-Luc Godard's nouvelle vague classic *Bande à Part*, where Anna Karina, Sami Frey and Claude Brasseur almost carelessly pull off a little rough-and-ready routine in a café. 'They're not dancers,' he told her. 'They're not executing a dance perfectly. But they're having

OPPOSITE: Harvey Keitel was treated to a juicy guest spot in the film, as impeccable fixer Winston Wolf.

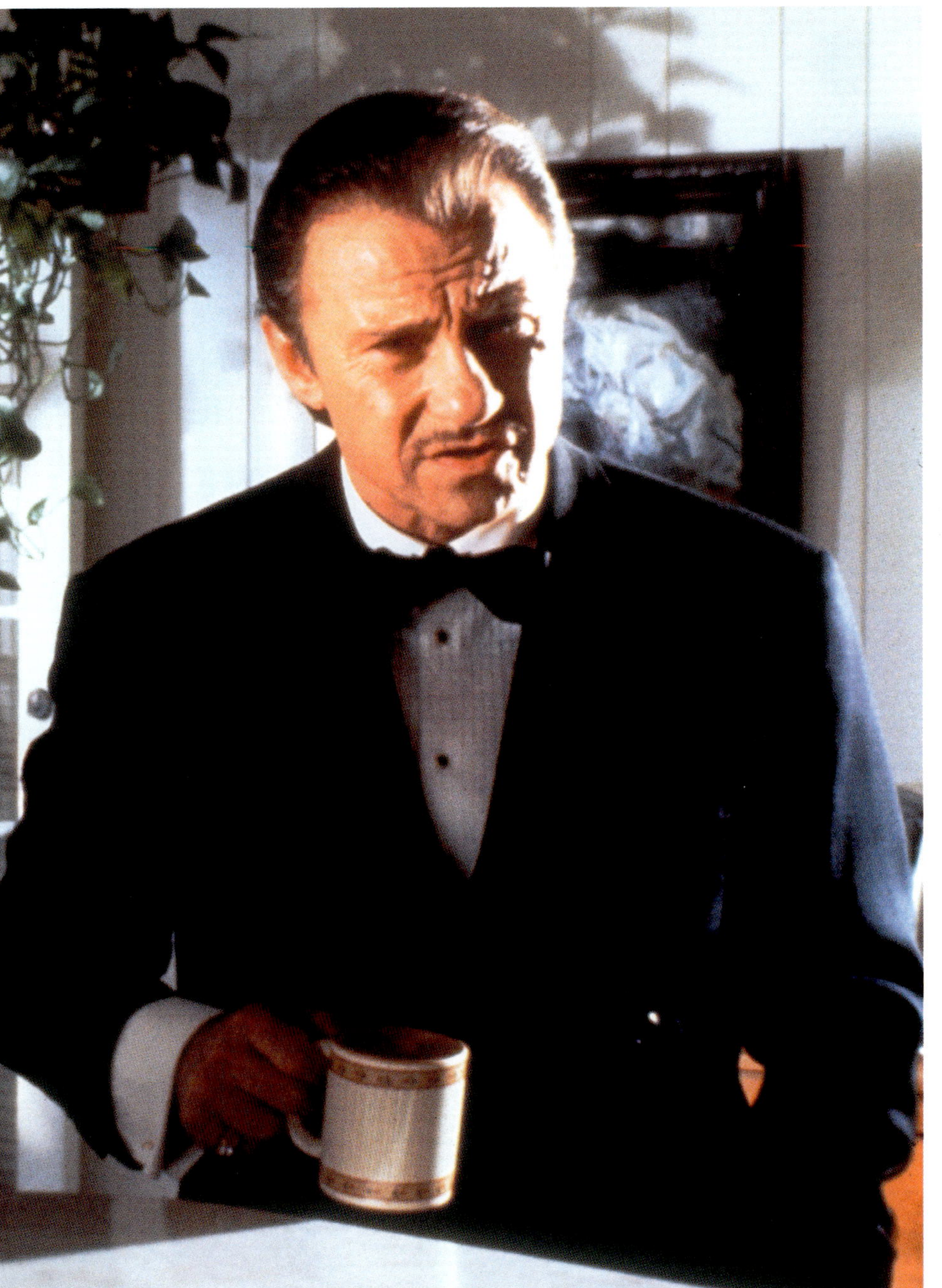

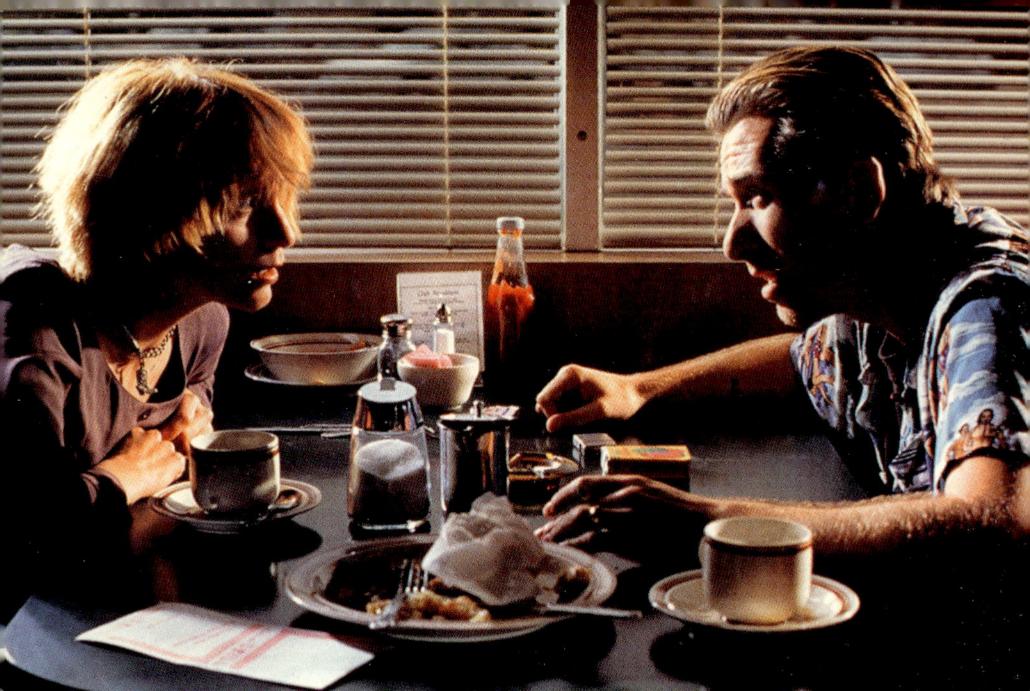

ABOVE: Tim Roth, as 'Pumpkin', alongside his real-life friend Amanda Plummer as 'Honey Bunny'.

fun. They're actually dancing great because they're having fun.' Thurman totally got it. Her worries evaporated. Tarantino was evidently pleased with the results. In behind-the-scenes footage he can be seen, shoes off, a big silly grin plastered across his face, twisting along with Thurman and Travolta from the side lines. Dancing joyously, like nobody's watching.

When it came to the film itself, everybody was watching. Or at least, far more people than might reasonably have ever been expected for a two-and-a-half-hour-long independent movie by a second-time director that features a heroin overdose, a guy accidentally getting his head blown off in the back of a car, anal rape, and conversations about pot bellies, eating pork and European junk-food nomenclature.

Boosted by a savvy marketing campaign fronted by Thurman-as-Mia on a poster destined to decorate student walls across the world for years to come, the film grossed almost $214 million worldwide, making it the most successful indie yet made. (Although, ironically, by this time Miramax had been absorbed by Disney, meaning *Pulp Fiction* was distributed by the same company that released *The Lion King* and *The Santa Clause*.) The critical reception was rapturous and the movie received seven Oscar nominations (including Best Picture, Best Director and Best Actor for Travolta), winning for Best Original Screenplay. Even before *Pulp Fiction* was released, it was a winner. Earlier in the year it had been shown in competition at the Cannes Film Festival and bagged its top award, the Palme D'Or.

What was, and remains, so astonishing about Tarantino's second picture is just how pristinely accomplished it is. It's hard to think of a greater leap in filmmaking quality than from *My Best Friend's Birthday* to *Pulp Fiction* in just two movies – and from a director with no formal training (other than as an actor). *Pulp Fiction* not only confirmed Tarantino as a masterful synthesizer, able to absorb and blend his influences into compelling new packages, it also – even after *Reservoir Dogs* – felt completely, invigoratingly fresh. 'I like the idea that I'm taking a genre that already exists and reinventing it, like Leone reinvented the whole Western genre,' he said.

He's not wrong. Just as Leone's late Sixties *Dollars* trilogy sparked a trend for less moral, more stylish Westerns, in the wake of *Pulp Fiction* the crime genre took a turn towards dark humour and cool soundtracks. Among its most obvious imitators were 1995's *Things To Do in Denver When You're Dead* (which featured Steve Buscemi as a suit-wearing hitman named Mr Shhh), 1996's *2 Days in the Valley* (which starred Eric Stoltz and exactly shared *Pulp Fiction*'s time frame), and 1999's *Go* (in which director Doug

Liman played with chronology and perspective across three different crime-driven plot threads). The word 'Tarantino-esque' was used to describe all three, and dozens more movies, for the rest of the Nineties and well into the early 21st century. In just two moves, Tarantino had gone from a filmmaker to an adjective.

Though the movies *Pulp Fiction* inspired were occasionally excellent (*Amores Perros* and *Get Shorty* were among the best), none matched its ballsy playfulness. While convincing Vincent to eat at Jack Rabbit Slim's, Mia tells him not to be a square. She doesn't say the word, but draws it out in the air – and it literally appears in animated dotted lines, which then puff away with a tinkling sound. It is unexpected, delightful and revels in the unreality of cinema while taking nothing away from the truth of the moment. For Tarantino, cinema is its own reality, a beautifully malleable one in which he, as its creator, can have his cake and eat it.

This is best exemplified by his predilection for messing with chronology. In presenting *Pulp Fiction*'s chapters out of order, he

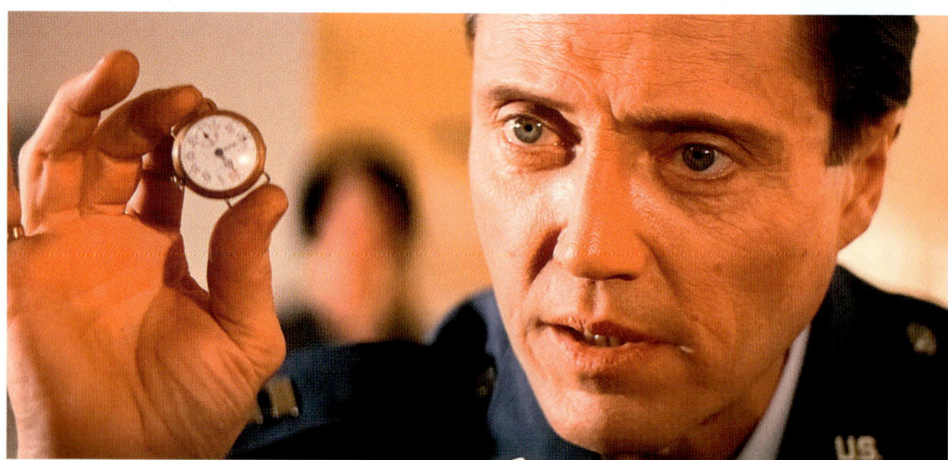

can shock his audience by having Butch unceremoniously kill Vincent only two-thirds of the way through the movie. Then, a few scenes later, Vincent is back, alive and well in the apartment where he and Jules have just whacked the guys who stole Marsellus Wallace's mysterious briefcase. Tarantino has effectively resurrected Vincent – an act of directorial intervention that is immediately (and ironically) followed by the act of 'divine intervention', whereby Jules and Vincent are missed by every bullet from the surprise gunman in the bathroom, leading to Jules' climactic moment of life-changing revelation. Though Vincent doesn't survive this story, and goes out in the manner of a disposable goon, he will get to star in the film's final hero shot, coolly strolling out of the diner alongside the also-reborn Jules.

Not everyone was a fan. As Tarantino took to the stage of Cannes' Palais on 23 May to collect his Palme D'Or, a woman yelled from the audience, '*Pulp Fiction* is shit!' Tarantino responded with a

'The Gold Watch'

The boxer strand in *Pulp Fiction* originated with Roger Avary, as a short film he had written titled *Pandemonium Reigns*. Tarantino loved the concept and bought the script for $25,000, to adapt and incorporate into his new anthology, with Christopher Walken appearing to deliver a fantastic monologue as Captain Koons, an old war buddy of Butch's dad (opposite). But Avary claimed his involvement went far further than this, and that the whole feature was co-written. So when Tarantino insisted Avary take only a 'story by' credit, enabling Tarantino to say the film was 'written and directed by' him alone, the two fell out. Though Avary did go up on stage with Tarantino to collect a shared Best Screenplay Oscar for *Pulp Fiction* in 1995, and the pair have since reconciled.

giddy giggle and, ever the enfant terrible, a one-finger salute. During his speech, he told the audience he hadn't expected to win, as the award was decided by a jury. 'I don't make the kind of movies that bring people together,' he said. 'I make movies that kind of split people apart.' But while the film certainly had its detractors, whether they took issue with its casual violence, its unjudgmental depiction of drug use or the prevalence of the n-word, he was proven wrong. His film was a unifier more than it was a divider. Indeed, if *Reservoir Dogs* changed Quentin Tarantino's life, *Pulp Fiction* changed the film industry.

As the budgets of mainstream movies had grown bigger, so had the risks, as major flops like *Hudson Hawk* and *The Last Action Hero* had recently evinced. But compared with the sheer profitability of *Pulp Fiction*, even the successes appeared relatively modest. Many upcoming independent filmmakers (such as Paul Thomas Anderson and David O Russell) were galvanized by Tarantino's ascension and the environment in which to make their movies suddenly flourished. Taking their cue from Disney's acquisition of Miramax, other studios started their own indie wings, such as Fox Searchlight and Paramount Classics, in the hope of producing their own *Pulp Fiction*.

Tarantino, the ultimate film-geek success story, revelled in the attention. But *Pulp Fiction* put him on a whole different level: one where he was far more exposed and deeply scrutinized than he had been after *Reservoir Dogs*. This time, the question of what he'd do next was far less easily answered.

OPPOSITE, TOP: Just as Keitel had come to the rescue of *Reservoir Dogs*, in *Pulp Fiction* he came to the rescue of Vincent and Jules.

OPPOSITE: Tim Roth got to keep his own accent for the minor-but-pivotal role of diner-robber Pumpkin.

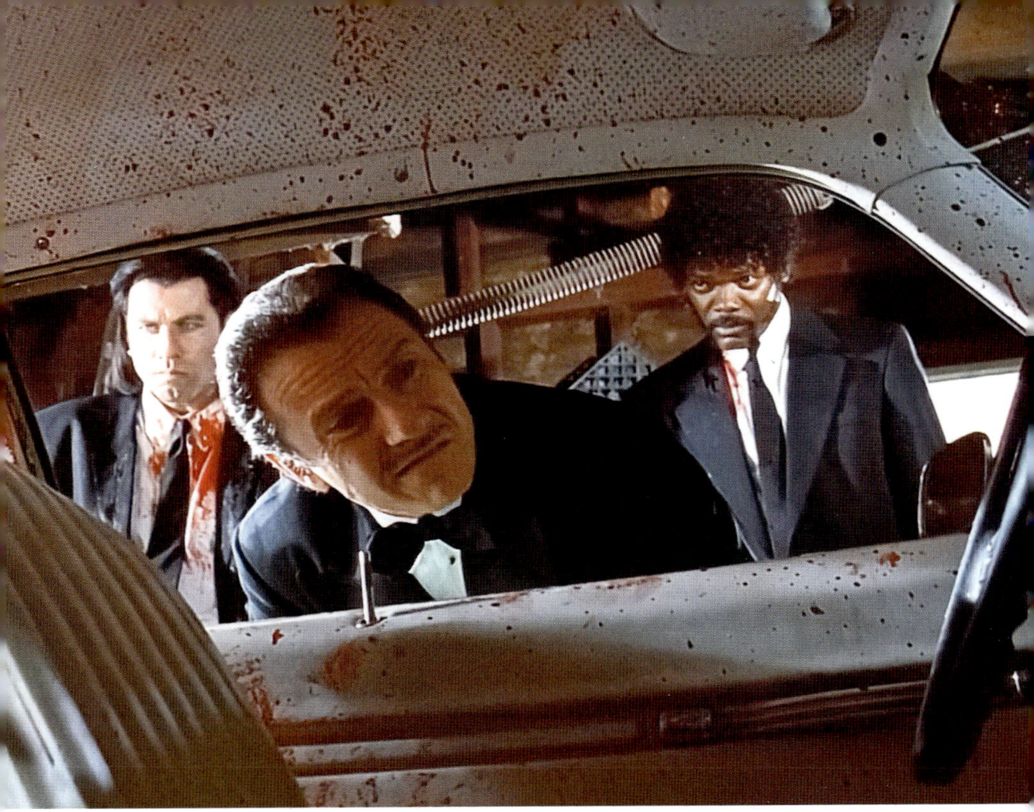

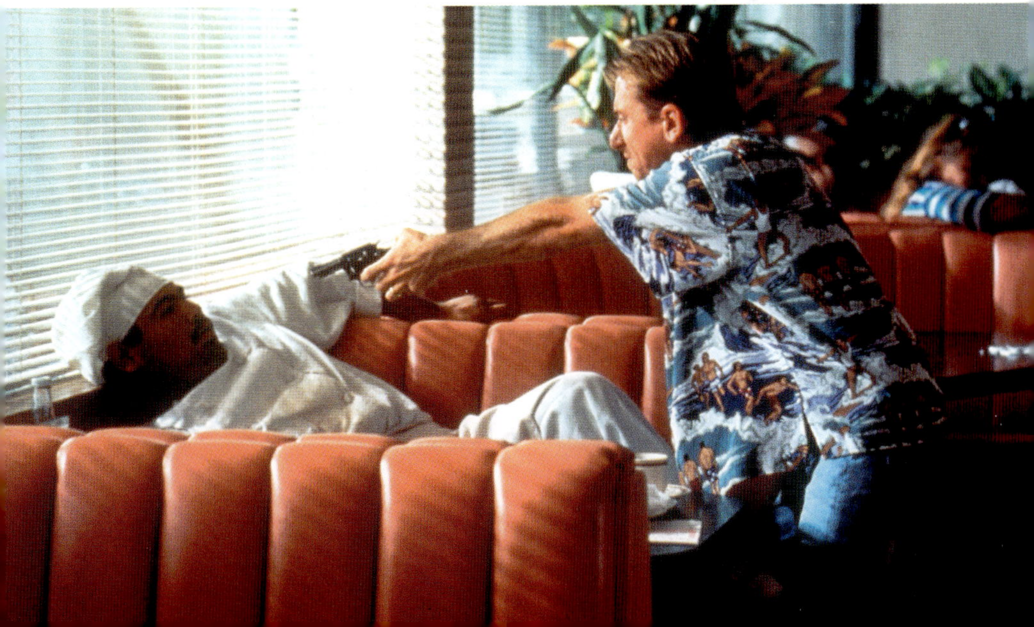

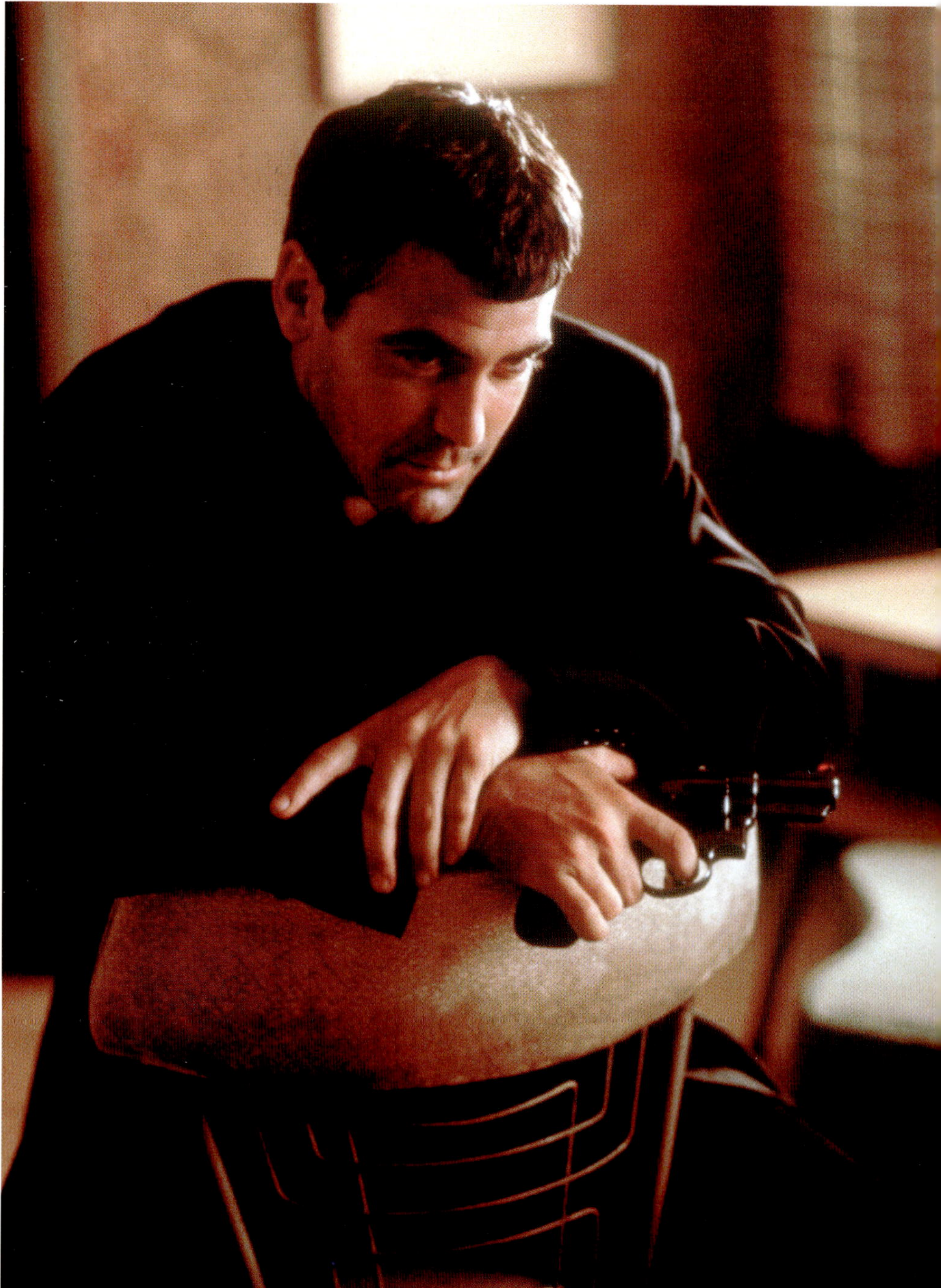

FOUR ROOMS
& FROM DUSK TILL DAWN
1995/1996

Between Tarantino's second and third feature films nestle a pair of projects that revealed his openness to collaboration, while also putting paid to the idea that anything he touched would turn to gold. Unlike *True Romance* and *Natural Born Killers*, these weren't simply writing projects that were picked up by other, more experienced directors. Both movies were very much shared with peers of Tarantino, and he was actively involved in their creation.

The first found its roots in the heady era of *Reservoir Dogs*, and the friendships he formed with other 'Class of '92' filmmakers at the Sundance Film Festival. He had since stayed in touch with Allison Anders and Alexandre Rockwell, and when the latter suggested at a dinner party that they make a movie together as a statement of their shared independent spirit, Tarantino was game.

The concept, as Rockwell outlined it, was to follow the misadventures of a hapless bellhop in a New York hotel on New Year's Eve, with a different story playing out in a different room, each tale directed by one of them, along with a pair of up-and-coming Texan auteurs, Richard Linklater (*Slacker, Dazed and Confused*) and Robert Rodriguez (*El Mariachi, Roadracers*). The movie was to be titled *Five Rooms*, and thanks to Tarantino's involvement, Miramax backed it, despite the fact that portmanteau pictures rarely went down well at the box office. Although, when Linklater withdrew from the project it was retitled *Four Rooms*.

Anders took the Honeymoon Suite, with first chapter 'The Missing Ingredient': a whimsical story about a coven of witches (including Valeria Golino, Ione Skye, Lili Taylor and Madonna) attempting to summon the goddess Diana (Amanda De Cadenet). This arcane ritual required the procurement of fresh semen, for which they turned to the bellhop, Ted.

This Jerry Lewis-inspired role went to Tim Roth, whose overactive, twitchy and shrill performance is virtually unbearable, especially during the first two chapters. After his seed has not

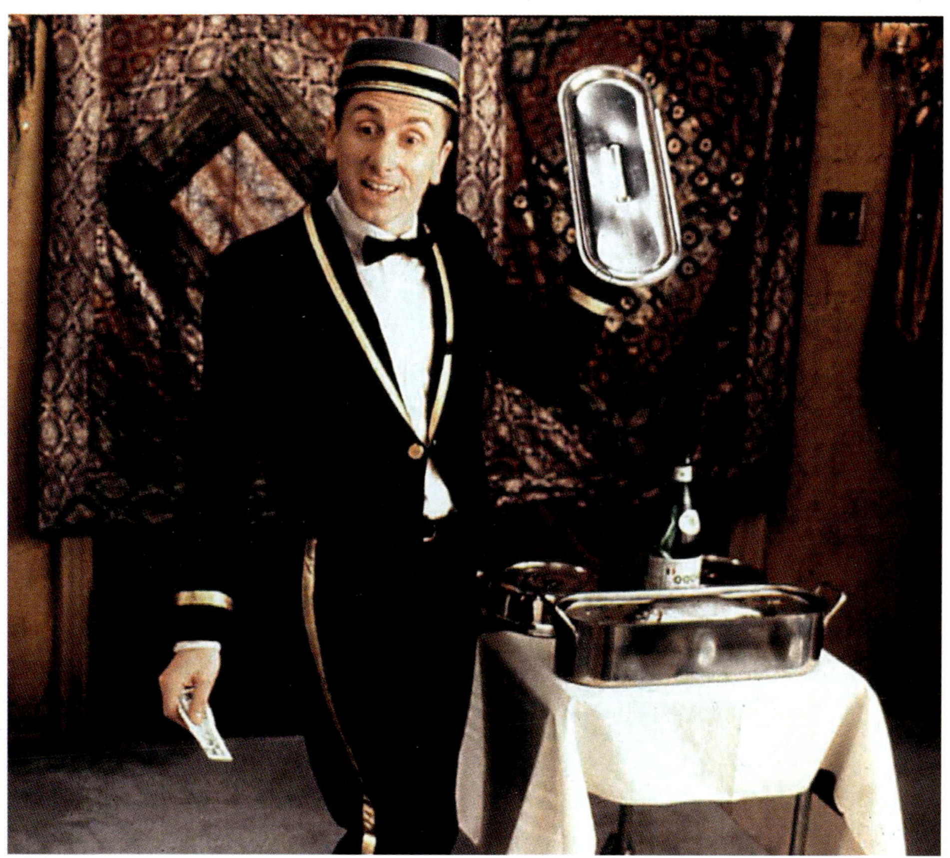

ABOVE: The role of bellhop Ted was originally intended for Steve Buscemi, but with his availability compromised it went to his fellow *Reservoir Dog* Tim Roth.

unpleasurably been extracted by Skye's witch, Ted finds himself in Rockwell's room for 'The Wrong Man', where he becomes embroiled in what may or may not be an unsettling sex game between a gun-wielding husband (David Proval) and his bound-and-gagged wife (Jennifer Beals).

Both Anders' and Rockwell's shorts feel perfunctory and pointless, which wasn't entirely their fault. During post-production,

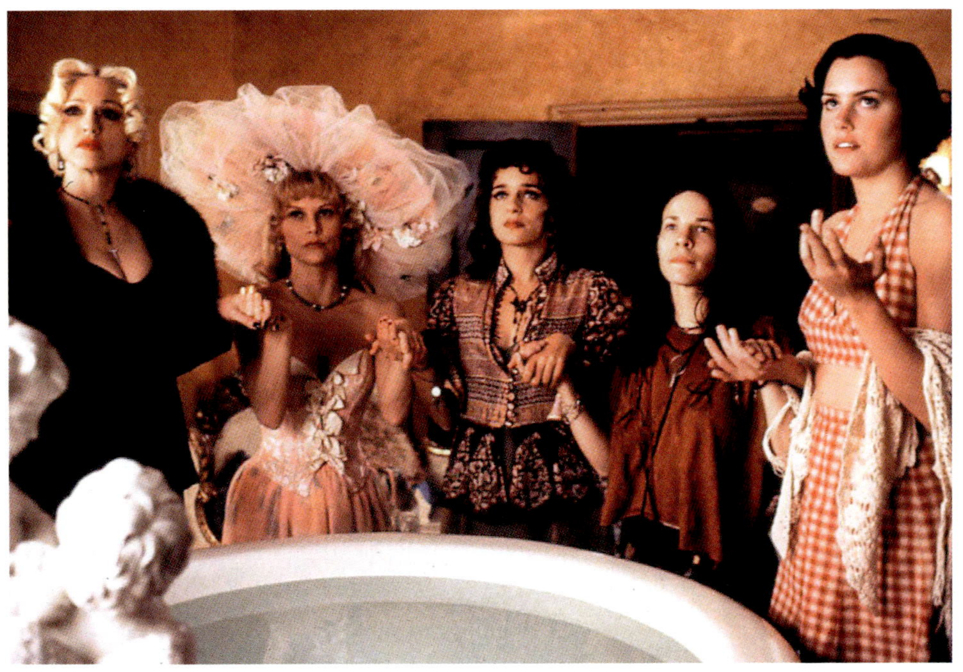

Harvey Weinstein insisted the film be cut down drastically from its original running time of 160 minutes, and as Tarantino was untouchable, the scissor blades were pointed squarely in their direction. Rodriguez only managed to survive such interference by cutting his entry, 'The Misbehavers', so tight it couldn't feasibly lose another second. Of the four shorts, his is the best: a naughty-scamp farce amplified to insane proportions after Ted is bribed to watch over two children by their fearsome father (Antonio Banderas). It ends with the pencil-moustached patriarch returning to find the room on fire, a 'T-and-A' movie on the TV, and Ted, with a syringe sticking out of his leg, clutching the foot of a decomposing prostitute.

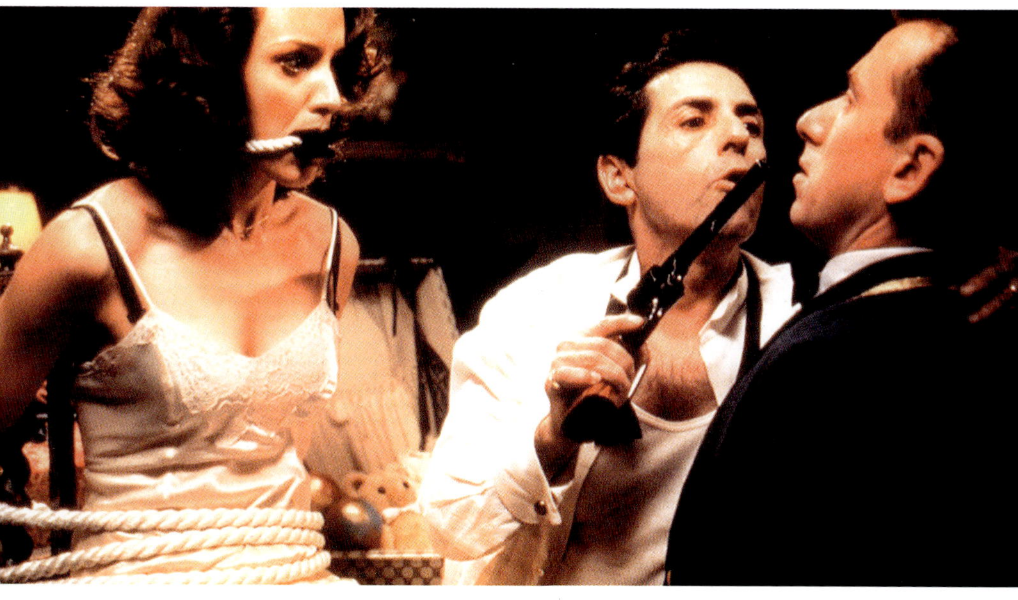

Perhaps unsurprisingly given *Pulp Fiction*'s astonishing success, the hotel's Penthouse was reserved for Tarantino, who self-referentially titled his segment 'The Man from Hollywood'.

The power imbalance between Tarantino and his fellow directors was clear. 'No one wanted to make a decision without Quentin's approval,' said Rockwell. This manifested not only in the length and 'main act' positioning of Tarantino's chapter, but also in the size of its pop-artish set which, the other directors wryly noted, was so big it could have accommodated all of theirs.

Tarantino was also the only *Four Rooms* contributor who cast himself in the movie, as Chester Rush, a film-star character conceived by Tarantino as being the worst version of himself, as if

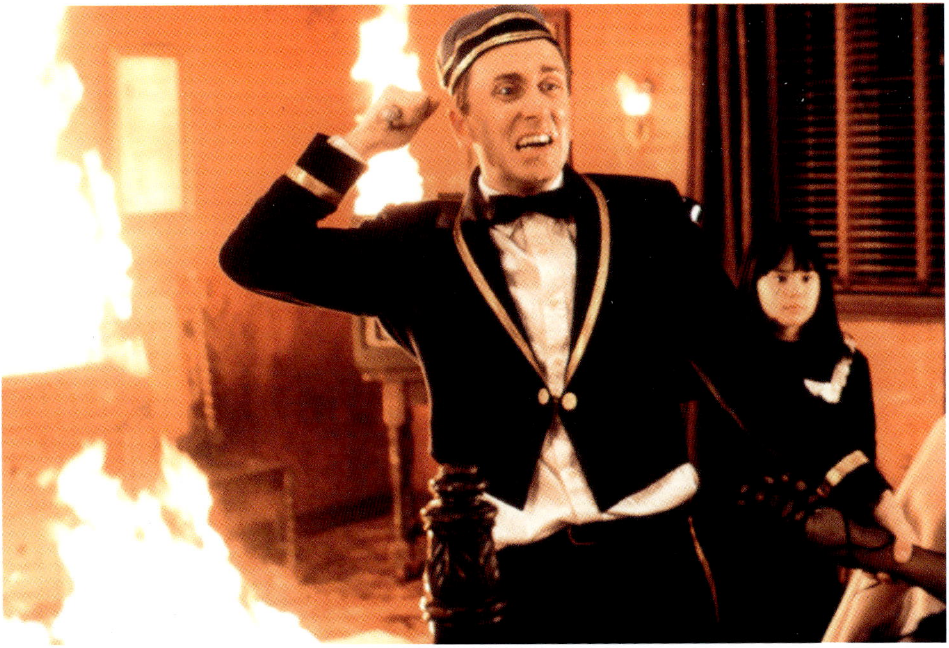

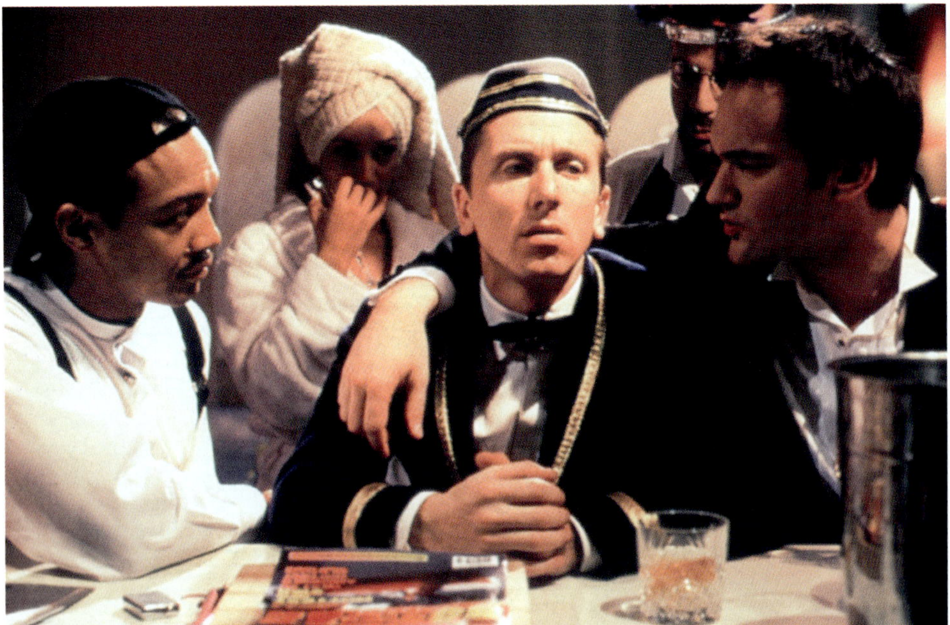

he could exorcize his ego by playing it up for comedy. He also pastiches his own movies by effectively replicating the ear-cutting and adrenaline-shot scenes from *Reservoir Dogs* and *Pulp Fiction*, respectively. Here, in a gag inspired by an episode of *Alfred Hitchcock Presents*, Ted must chop off the pinkie of Chester's friend Norman (Paul Calderón) if he loses a bet that his Zippo will light 10 times in a row.

Whereas *Dogs* and *Pulp* ramped up the tension before reaching their audience-shocking peaks, the joke here is that Ted's cleaver comes down almost instantly when Norman's lighter fails to light the very first time. Then the bloody fallout occurs off screen as the end credits roll. It's mischievously subversive, but the effect is dampened by the sheer self-indulgence of the whole affair – a flaw that is hardly helped by Bruce Willis' uncredited appearance as another of Chester's boozy pals.

The film was Tarantino's first unmitigated flop, its derisory reviews matched by its poor performance in cinemas. Even a fan audience primed by the anthology antics of *Pulp Fiction* didn't care for a portmanteau that was only one quarter Quentin, despite his presence overshadowing the other directors'. The whole experience tarnished the relationship between Tarantino, Anders and Rockwell, not to mention their dream of independent-spirited directorial unity. However, the friendship and mutual professional respect between Tarantino and Rodriguez remained intact. In fact, they were already planning another collaboration.

OPPOSITE, TOP: Tim Roth as Ted, not appreciating his new role as a babysitter in Robert Rodriguez's 'The Misbehavers'.

OPPOSITE: Beals and Roth join Paul Calderón, Bruce Willis and Tarantino himself for the director's self-referential segment, 'The Man From Hollywood'.

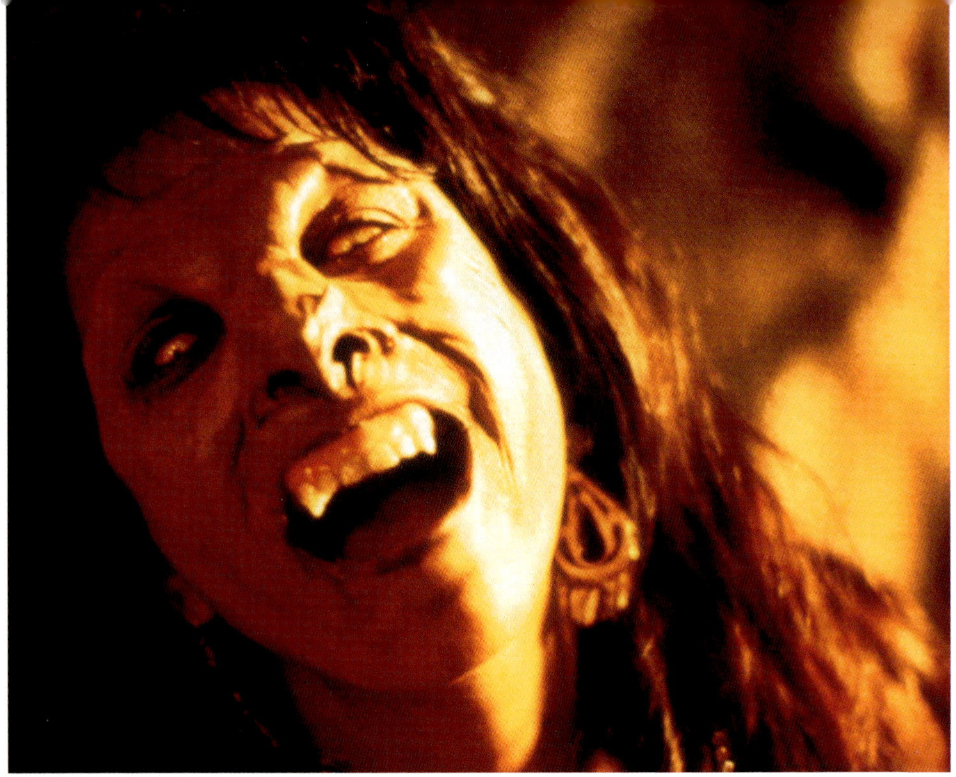

Since Tarantino wrote *From Dusk Till Dawn* for Robert Kurtzman back in 1990, the movie had been mired in Development Hell. The project's prospects improved with the success of *Reservoir Dogs* and *Pulp Fiction*, but the resultant craving for anything Tarantino-related was a mixed blessing for Kurtzman. The good news: there was fresh interest in his Mexican vampire movie. The bad news: it had become too hot a prospect for a first-time director. So, he decided to move on, and resigned himself to a 'story by' and producing credit. Meanwhile, his company KNB EFX – which had worked on both of Tarantino's films, from Marvin's excised ear in *Reservoir Dogs* to the other Marvin's blown-out brains in *Pulp Fiction* – would still oversee all the make-up and creature effects. Eventually, Miramax's horror/sci-fi brand Dimension Films backed the project with a substantial budget of $19 million, and *From Dusk Till Dawn* was raised from the dead.

The script, which started life as a seven-page outline that Kurtzman had put together with writer John Esposito, had always occupied a special place in Tarantino's heart. 'Even more than directing my first movie, writing *From Dusk Till Dawn* was the most exciting time in my life,' he said. It had enabled him to go from being someone who wrote in their spare time to doing it as their day job. 'There was no other jump that I have had in my life that was as big a jump as that.' Yet when the movie was revived, he decided not to direct it himself. Instead, that job would go to his newest best friend.

During the Toronto Film Festival in 1992, 24-year-old Texan guerrilla filmmaker Robert Rodriguez was videotaping the audience reaction to his high-octane Spanish-language debut film *El Mariachi*. Someone was laughing louder than anyone around them, he noticed. Then he recognized them as the director of *Reservoir Dogs* – a movie that had recently blown Rodriguez away. Rodriguez and Tarantino were both invited to panel discussions on movie violence, and felt an 'immediate kinship' as first-time filmmakers, Rodriguez said. 'Most first films that come out are more personal kind of dramas or something. But ours were just twisted genre pictures.'

Rodriguez grew up in San Antonio making home-video movies with his nine siblings and, as is now Hollywood legend, had partly funded the $7,000 *El Mariachi* by taking part in experimental drug trials. As well as directing, writing and producing, he also often acts as his own editor, cinematographer, composer and visual

OPPOSITE: One of the 'carnivorous banshee beasts' that populates the second half of *From Dusk Till Dawn*.

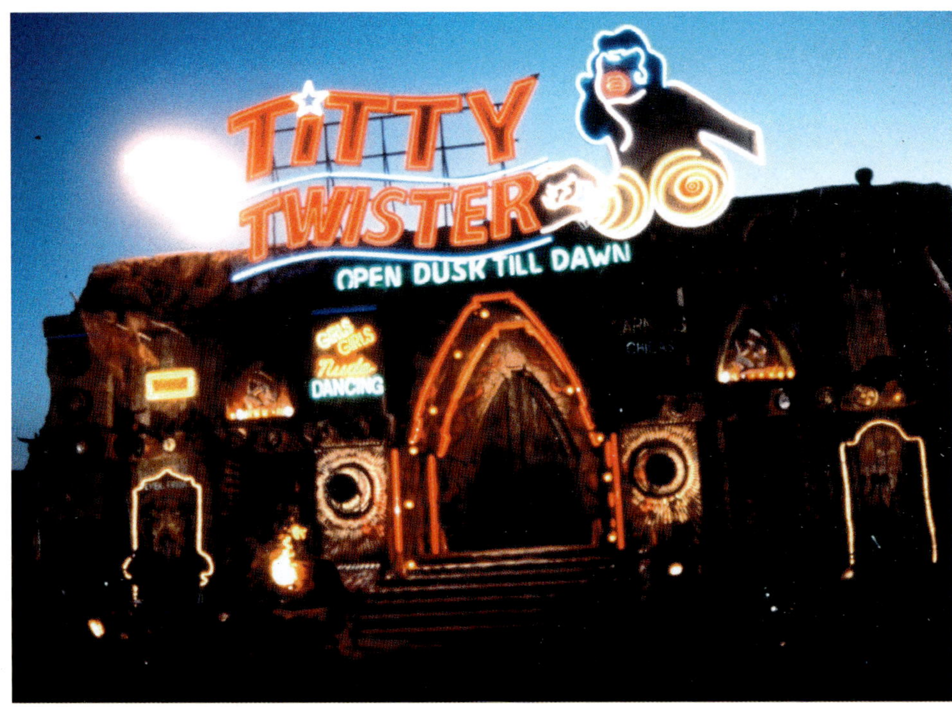

ABOVE: The neon-plastered exterior of the vamp-packed biker bar, where most of the insane action takes place.

effects supervisor. With an insatiable creative energy, Rodriguez is far more prolific than Tarantino, and even founded his own studio (Troublemaker) and TV channel (El Rey). But in terms of sheer movie-geek enthusiasm, his energy was easily matched.

So Tarantino knew Rodriguez would totally get *From Dusk Till Dawn*, and didn't hesitate to put the script under his nose while he was prepping *Pulp Fiction* in an office just two doors down from where Rodriguez was writing *Desperado*, his bigger-budget English-language re-do of *El Mariachi*. Rodriguez loved the way Tarantino's script started out as a real-world crime movie – about a pair of black-suited armed-robber brothers, Seth and Richie Gecko, who take a holidaying preacher and his children hostage

QT TV

On 11 May 1995, Tarantino made his small-screen directing debut with the 24th episode of NBC's hit medical drama *ER*. The idea had been George Clooney's, who suggested the guest spot to Tarantino while they were shooting *From Dusk Till Dawn* together. While the episode, titled 'Motherhood', wasn't written by or even specifically for Tarantino, it certainly had some QT DNA. *Pulp Fiction* bit-partners Angela Jones, Kathy Griffin and Alexis Arquette all appear; stars Sherry Stringfield and Julianna Margulies wear sunglasses, *Reservoir Dogs* style, for a rooftop break scene; and there is even a severed ear (cut from the head of a Latina gang member).

A decade later, Tarantino returned to TV to direct a double episode of *CSI: Crime Scene Investigation*, one of his favourite shows. Titled 'Grave Danger' (pictured), it involved investigator Nick Stokes (George Eads) being buried alive – just like The Bride (Uma Thurman) in *Kill Bill Volume 2* – and earned him an Emmy nomination.

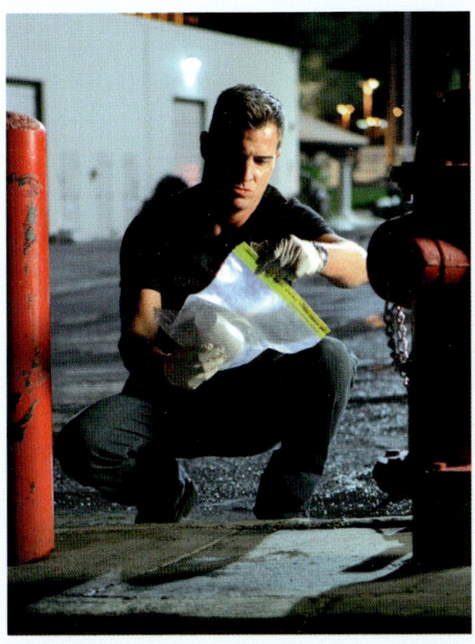

– before suddenly switching genres. 'You'd be turning the page and suddenly there were vampires,' he said. 'You were like, "Wait a minute. . ."'

It's an audacious, genre-blending device. Once all the characters arrive at a south-of-the-border biker bar and strip club named The Titty Twister, the movie pivots into a full-tilt blood-and-gore monster picture when the venue is revealed as a vampiric honey trap. The Geckos and their hostages are besieged by bloodsucking creatures Tarantino described as 'a bunch of carnivorous banshee beasts'. These weren't angst-ridden immortals struggling with the burdens of their afterlife, but 'just a bunch of monsters, and you should kill as many of them as you possibly can, because they're trying to kill you.'

And it all happens without even a hint of foreshadowing. 'You don't hear some radio saying, "There have been mysterious disappearances in Mexico!"' Tarantino pointed out. 'And then when [the vampires] show up, it's like whoosh! The audience, like the characters in the movie, can't believe what's in their lap and what they have to deal with.'

After Rodriguez and the pair agreed that Tarantino should take the role of nerdy-psycho brother Richie, Tarantino took back the script and rewrote it. He removed a speech where the preacher character Jacob quotes Ezekiel 25:17, because he'd since repurposed it for Jules in *Pulp Fiction*. And he added another 25 pages to the front half to further build up the tension and make the pivot feel even more surprising.

Interestingly, he also rewrote Richie to be less verbose, giving most of his quips to Seth, and reconfigured Richie as a sexual

OPPOSITE: Salma Hayek suppressed her fear of snakes to perform Santánico Pandemonium's crowdpleasing entrance.

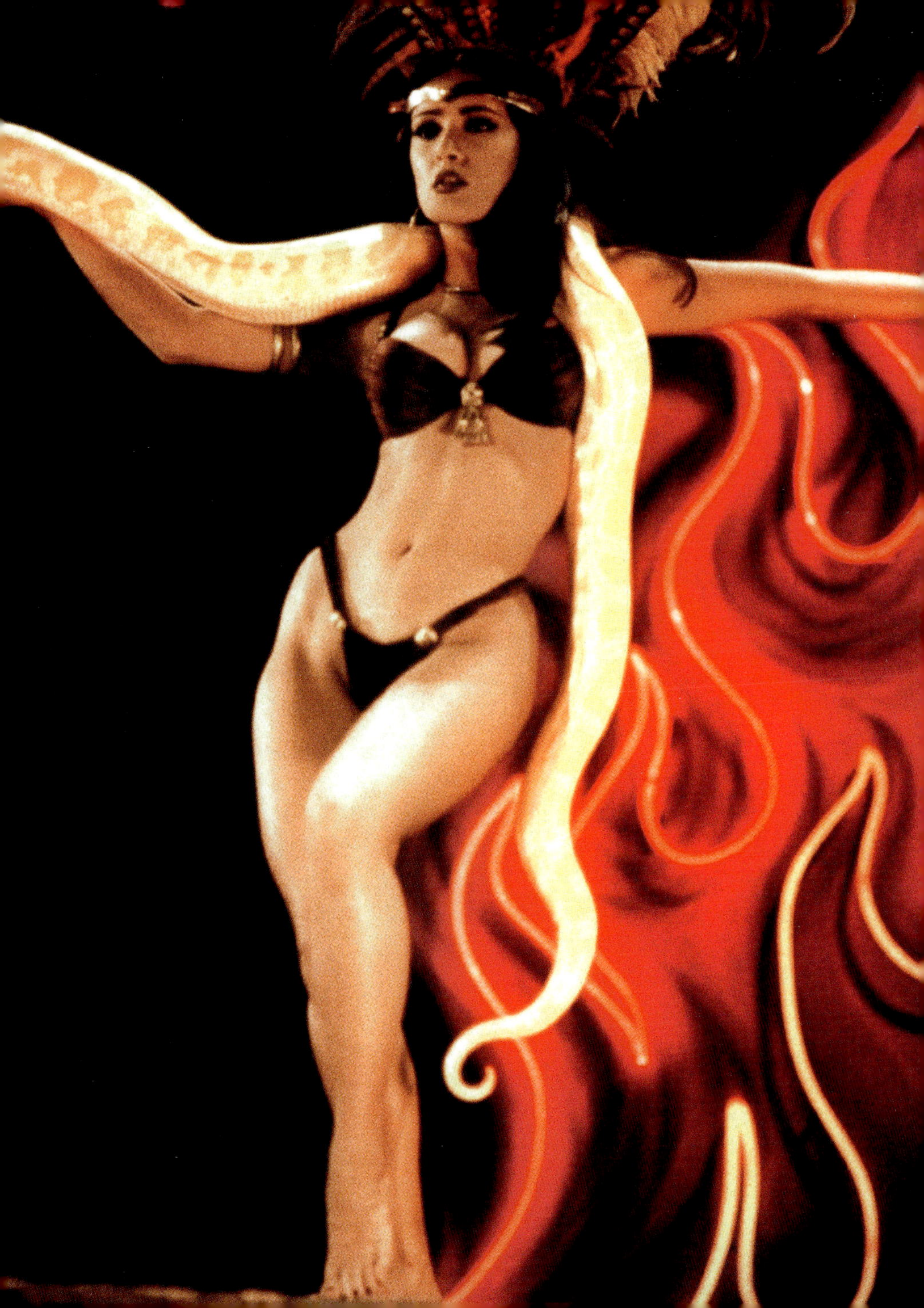

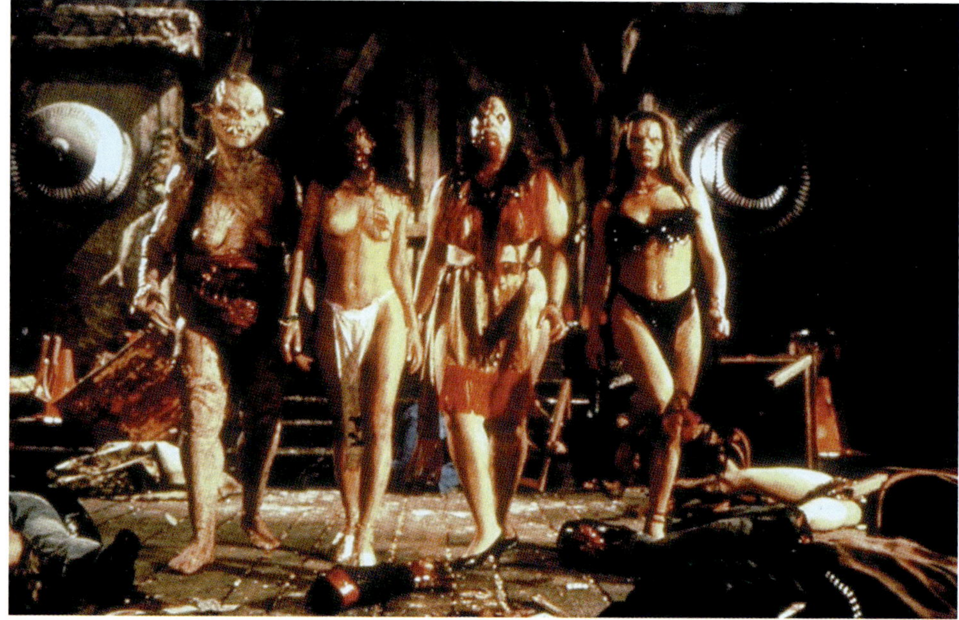

predator who rapes and murders their first hostage. This would even further distance the film's 'real-world' front half from its fantastical second half. For some critics it was a step too far, but Tarantino was unrepentant. 'It really roots Richie and Seth,' he said. 'They are not roguish good guys, right? No. They are the real deal.'

The role of Richie's brother, the charming but ruthless Seth, was the one Tarantino originally suggested to John Travolta but it was eventually taken by George Clooney, keen to step up to big-screen action after making his name in hospital drama *ER*, and even keener to play against his nice-guy image as suave paediatrics doc Doug Ross. Also playing against type was Tarantino regular Harvey Keitel, setting aside his tough-guy tendencies to portray

Jacob, the preacher who has lost his faith and is kidnapped by the Geckos, along with his two kids. Though, thanks to his calm and inherently steely nature, it often feels like he has more control over things than the brothers – especially after the carnage erupts.

As Jacob's teen daughter Kate, Rodriguez cast Juliette Lewis, whose experience playing Mallory Knox in *Natural Born Killers* certainly helped sell Kate's final-act transformation into a kick-ass vampire killer. And in the minor role of Texas Ranger Earl McGraw, killed by Richie in the opening scene, he cast one of Tarantino's favourite forgotten character actors, Michael Parks.

Rodriguez brought along some of his own regulars, too, namely Danny Trejo as a vamp barman, Cheech Marin in three different roles (Border Guard, Chet Pussy and Carlos), and *Desperado*'s Salma Hayek, who performs a memorable table dance draped in a python, as queen vamp Santánico Pandemonium. The sequence culminates with Hayek sticking her tequila-drenched toe in a gaping Tarantino's mouth.

Elsewhere, Rodriguez and Tarantino's movie-geekiness is borne out by the notable presence of make-up artist legend Tom Savini (*Friday The 13th, Dawn of the Dead*) as a biker with a flip-up crotch gun, and footballer-turned-blaxploitation legend Fred Williamson (*Hammer, Black Caesar*) as a Vietnam-vet trucker. While the plot gives no hint of the vampire mayhem to come, Savini and Williamson's presence at The Titty Twister may have tipped off the more film-savvy first-time viewers that the gritty hostage crime movie was about to handbrake-turn into lurid exploitation territory.

With creature make-up that transforms Hayek into a snake-like monster, gore effects that include a guitar improbably made out of human body parts, and a sequence in which Savini transforms into a giant rat monster, *From Dusk Till Dawn* proved a challenging show for KNB EFX. 'This has been absolutely the

A vampire franchise

From Dusk Till Dawn spawned two sequels, made simultaneously and released in 1999. *Texas Blood Money* was produced by Tarantino and Lawrence Bender (who'd also produced the original), and directed by their old friend Scott Spiegel. This was largely a re-tread that involved another criminal gang encountering the Titty Twister bloodsuckers. The second, *The Hangman's Daughter*, was a prequel based on a story by Rodriguez and written by his cousin Álvaro. Directed by P J Pesce, it was set in 1913 and told the origin story of Santánico Pandemonium (Ara Celi). Both films were made under the Dimension Films banner and were aimed squarely at the direct-to-video market.

hardest movie we've ever done,' said Greg Nicotero during an on-set interview. 'I don't think I've been more than five feet away from Robert for the entire six, seven weeks that we've been shooting, because he's so creative.'

Though Rodriguez and Tarantino certainly enjoyed the bloody and explosive experience, their movie was not to everyone's tastes. *From Dusk Till Dawn*, sniffed David Hunter of *The Hollywood Reporter*, 'pushes the envelope but fails to make any lasting impression except revulsion at the spectacle of acclaimed independent filmmakers wasting their talents on such trash.' Yet in contrast, *Variety*'s Todd McCarthy praised it as a 'deliciously trashy, exuberantly vulgar, lavishly appointed exploitation picture'. While the film is certainly scrappy and unpolished, it is buoyed by its subversive wit and an unapologetically juvenile sense of fun.

From Dusk Till Dawn was a modest hit, making just under $60 million worldwide, and revealing to Hollywood the strength of Clooney's big-screen-star presence. Plus, with its unhinged midpoint twist, it hinted at a future development in Tarantino's own career, which would shift him away from the genre he had made his name in. The garish B-pics and exploitation movies that fuelled the two-in-one film's monstrous second half would inspire him further: first with *Kill Bill* and then with *Grindhouse* – another Rodriguez collaboration, which double-billed Tarantino's *Death Proof* with Rodriguez's *Planet Terror*. Not for nothing did Rodriguez, in 2017, describe *From Dusk Till Dawn* as his and Tarantino's 'first Grindhouse double feature'.

But Tarantino wasn't quite done with the crime genre yet. In fact, with his next movie, he would explore it more deeply than he ever had before.

BELOW: Kate (Juliette Lewis), Jacob (Harvey Keitel) and Seth (George Clooney) go into vampire-killer mode.

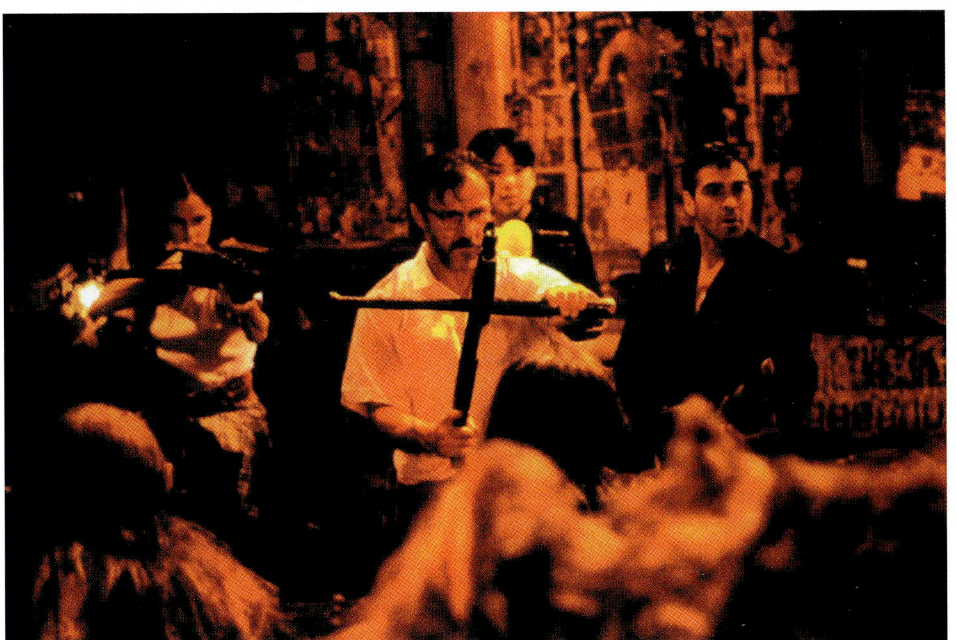

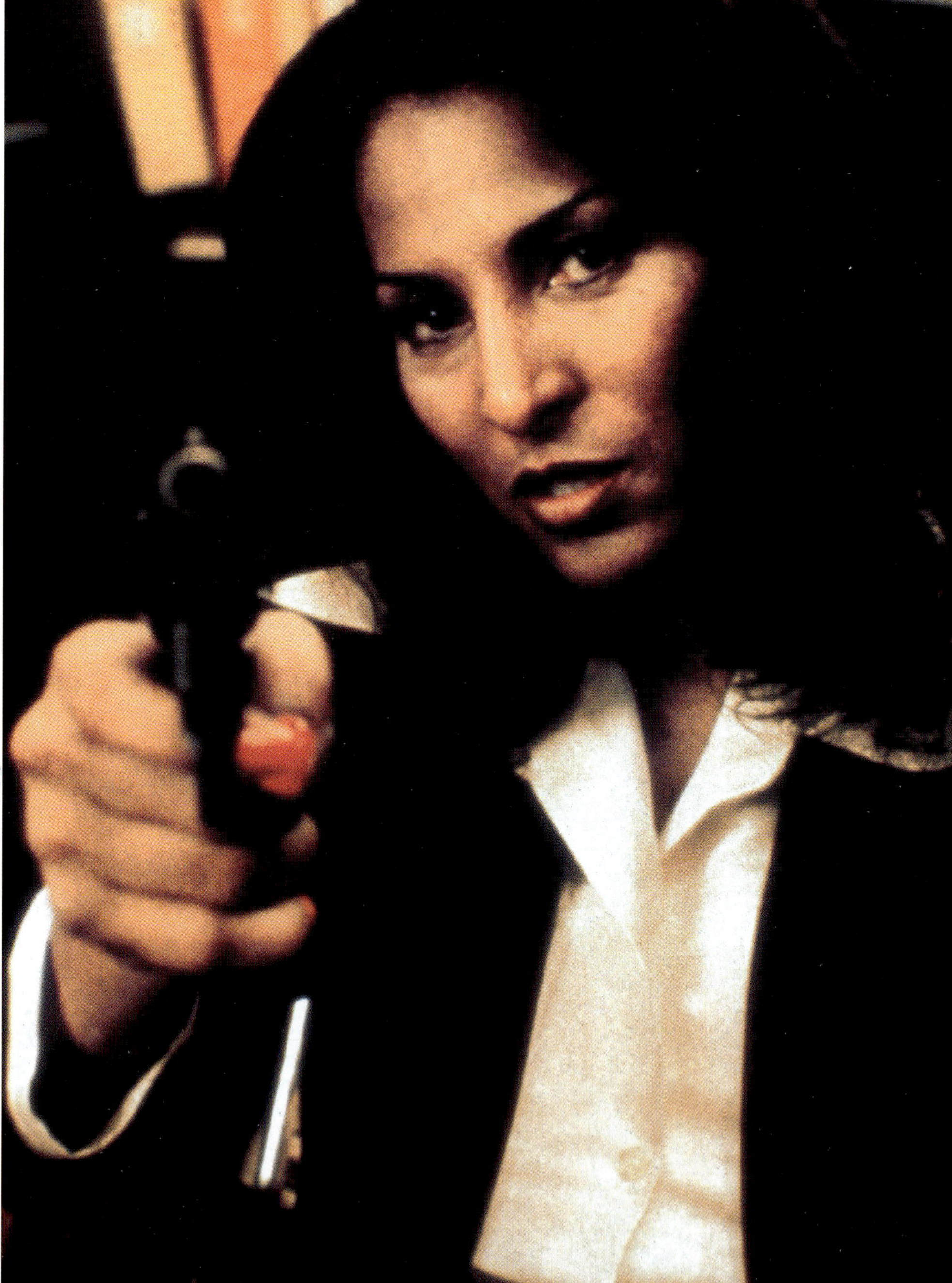

'Fuck you and your chill pill!'

JACKIE BROWN
1997

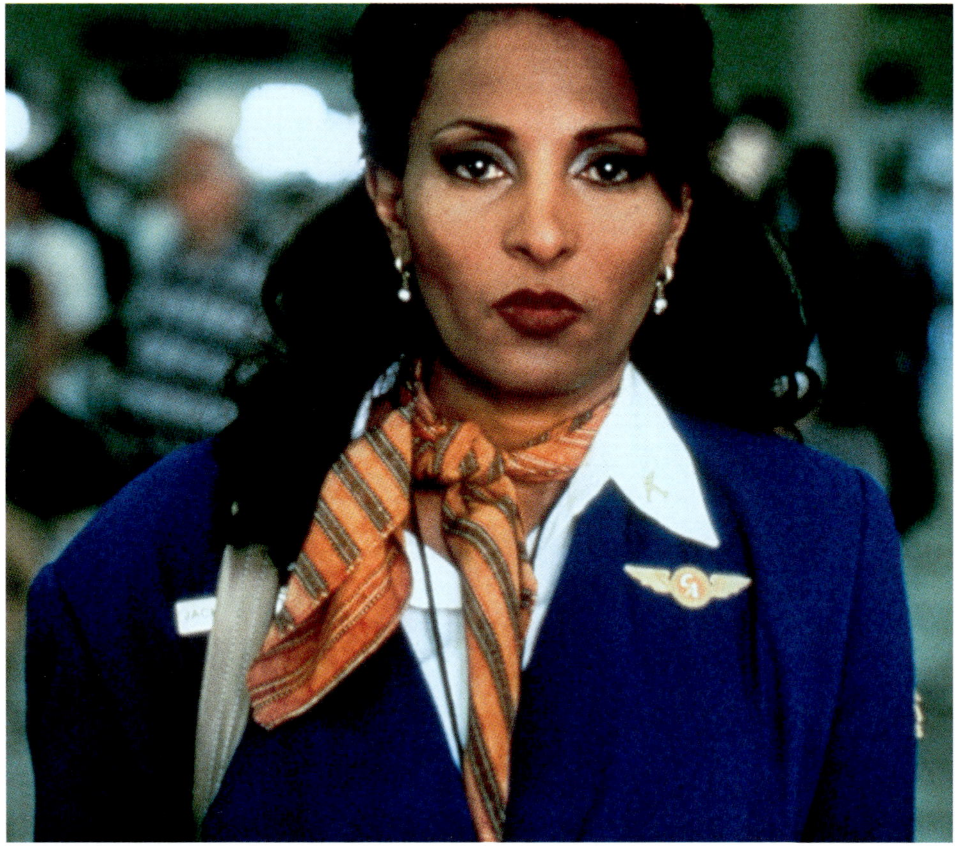

As the years following *Pulp Fiction* passed, it started to look like Tarantino might already be a spent force as a movie director. He was keeping busy and visible with his various acting gigs and TV work but the wait for his next movie grew longer and longer. Could it be that *Pulp Fiction* was impossible to follow? Or just that its success had sapped his creative impetus?

When Tarantino did finally deliver his third picture in late 1997, he insisted there had been no struggle to surmount his own tower of precocious achievement. He was never going to be a 'movie a year' guy, he insisted. Once he was done with the long 'express train' of *Pulp Fiction* publicity, he simply took what he considered a well-deserved year off. Then he started on his new script, a process that took another year. He denied that, during this process, *Pulp Fiction* weighed heavily on his mind as the gargantuan achievement he'd never surpass. With one qualification: 'The only thing I knew was I didn't want to out-epic myself. I wanted to do a smaller film. More character based. I wanted to go *underneath Pulp Fiction.*'

Jackie Brown was a change of pace and style for Tarantino. Not only was it a smaller film, it was also lighter on trash-culture references and violence, with a mostly linear narrative, and didn't feature a single person in a cool black suit. 'This movie doesn't take place in my universe,' he said. *Jackie Brown* is calmer and more mature than his previous offerings, featuring long-in-the-tooth characters who have seen better days and are just trying to make their remaining days that much more comfortable. It's the kind of movie you might have expected from a filmmaker later in their life and career, not a 34-year-old on their third feature. It was also a first (and a last) for Tarantino: a direct, wholesale adaptation of someone else's material.

Tarantino first suggested he might tackle a novel adaptation while promoting *Pulp Fiction*. 'I'm a little concerned about my voice getting old hat,' he admitted. 'So what I'm thinking I might end up doing now is taking a novel and adapting it. That still requires me to write; still requires me to put it in my voice. But it's also coming from somewhere else.'

That said, 'somewhere else' wasn't far from where Tarantino already was. Elmore Leonard was one of his biggest influences.

OPPOSITE: Blaxploitation star Pam Grier as world-weary air hostess Jackie Brown.

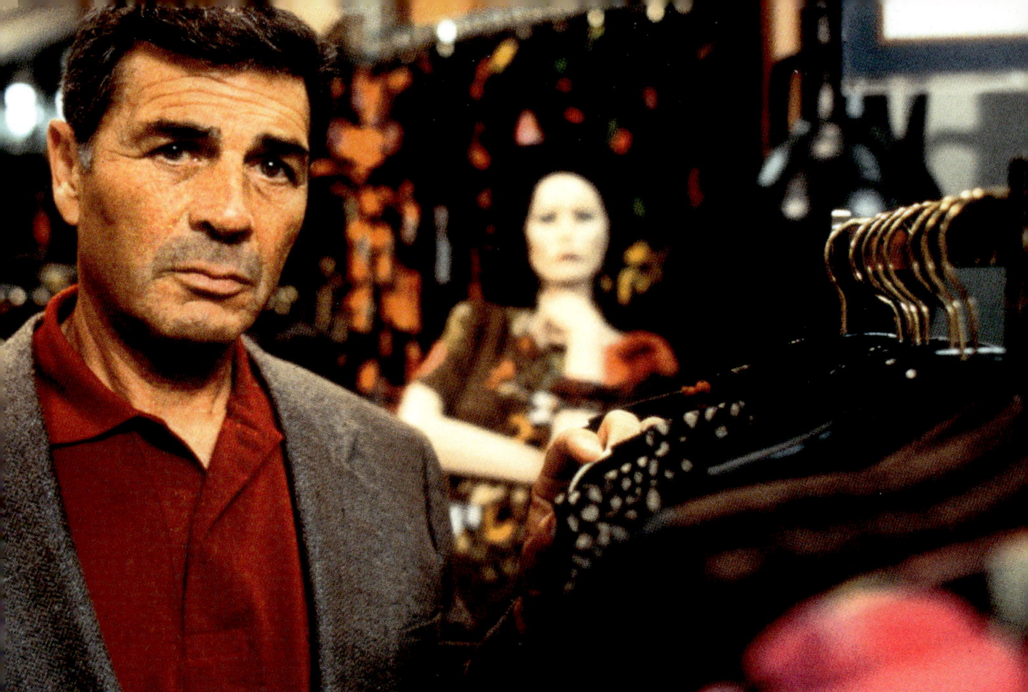

He'd read the veteran pulp novelist's books since his early teens and would always adapt them in his head, even making lists of people he'd like to cast. He considered *True Romance* as 'my version of an Elmore Leonard novel in script form,' while Leonard's infection of the crime genre with the mess of real life had inspired both *Reservoir Dogs* and *Pulp Fiction*. 'He showed me that characters can go off on tangents and those tangents are just as valid as anything else. I like the way real people talk. Leonard opened my eyes to the dramatic possibilities of everyday speech.'

Tarantino first read Leonard's *Rum Punch* as a galley while he was preparing *Pulp Fiction*, but couldn't commit to optioning it, so he reluctantly let it go. By the time he was finished with his anthology movie, the book had been published, but it was thankfully still available and, on a re-read, he said, 'I fell in love with it the exact same way I did a couple years before.' That's when he knew *Rum Punch* would be his next movie.

But he wasn't so in awe of Leonard's prose that he didn't mess with it. He relocated the story from South Florida to his home turf (Los Angeles' South Bay), he changed the title to match the lead character, and he made her Black. In both book and movie, *Jackie Brown* is a tough and resourceful air stewardess in her mid-40s who, after becoming pinned between the small-time gunrunner she smuggles money for and the sting-operating cops who have caught her, resolves to outmanoeuvre them all and keep the cash herself, with the help of an ageing bail-bondsman who falls for her. Despite the character being written as white, on reading and re-reading the book, Tarantino couldn't imagine anyone better fitting the role, with its compelling blend of world-weariness, strength, cool and pluck, than Pam Grier.

Then 47 years old, Grier was the star of some of Tarantino's favourite blaxploitation movies, primarily 1973's *Coffy*. He'd auditioned her for the part of Jody, Lance's wife, in *Pulp Fiction*, but realized he could never imagine Eric Stoltz telling her to shut up. Now he had a part that was an ideal fit. While approaching Grier, Tarantino felt he should make it clear to her this wasn't simply stunt casting, as some had said of Travolta. 'This is about you being the perfect actress to play this role. . . It's not because you won some Seventies revival contest.'

He did confess to being nervous telling Leonard about all his changes and held off making the call until just before production, in May 1997. This amused the then-71-year-old novelist, who was well used to his work being adapted. 'That's all right,' he told Tarantino. 'Do what you want. You're the filmmaker!' According to Tarantino, Leonard also told him that not only did he think *Jackie Brown* was the best adaptation of his work he'd ever read,

The return of Ray Nicolette

Around six months after *Jackie Brown*'s release, Michael Keaton
unexpectedly reprised his role of Ray Nicolette (pictured below)
with a surprise cameo in another Elmore Leonard adaptation: Steven
Soderbergh's *Out of Sight*, starring George Clooney and Jennifer Lopez.
The idea originated with *Out of Sight* producer Stacey Sher of Jersey
Films, who had worked with Tarantino on *Pulp Fiction*. Given his own
love for characters crossing over between movies, Tarantino backed
the idea and convinced Miramax, who held the rights to the character,
to let Universal Pictures have Nicolette for free. He even invited an
equally enthusiastic Soderbergh to the *Jackie Brown* editing suite so he
could watch all of Keaton's scenes.

Both directors saw it as a tribute to Leonard, implying that the
author's universe was so cogent, it could connect two different movies
made by two different directors for two different studios. 'They put
their conglomerate bullshit aside and actually let something artistic
happen,' Tarantino said. 'So that was really kind of cool.'

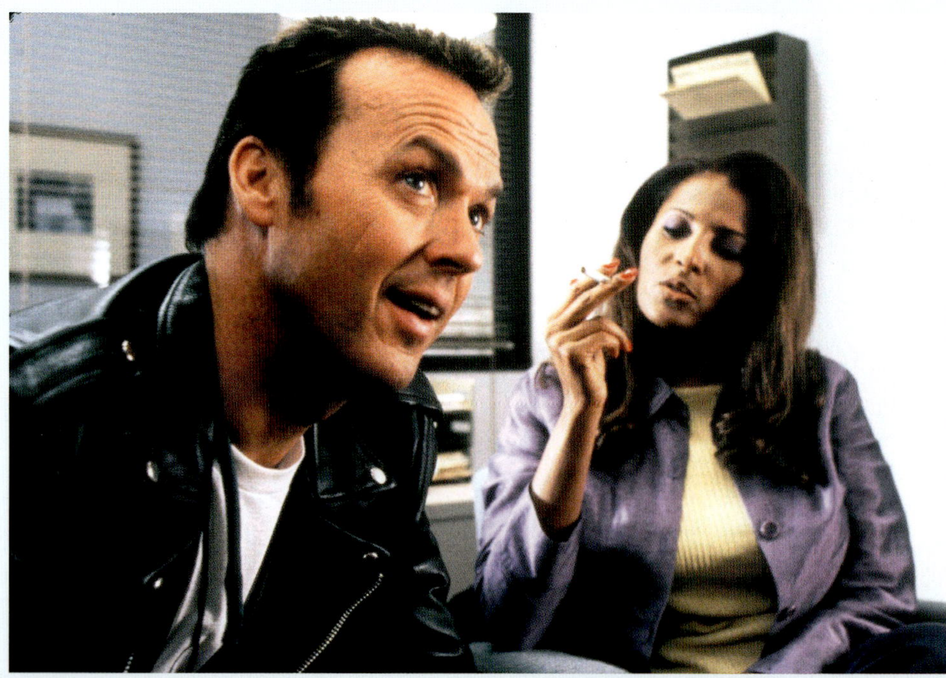

but that 'it was maybe the best script he'd ever read.' That, Tarantino said, 'made me feel really good.'

Tarantino surrounded Grier with a tight ensemble that showed he'd lost none of his allure to great actors, despite his extended absence. Samuel L Jackson strengthened his bond with the director by taking the role of Ordell Robbie, the intimidatingly laidback gunrunner who, in an early scene, memorably persuades one of his employees – played by stand-up star Chris Tucker – to climb in the trunk of his car before he shoots him to death. Heavyweight actor Robert De Niro accepted Tarantino's invitation to play Ordell's schlubby ex-con associate Louis Gara. Former Batman Michael Keaton took the relatively minor role of ATF agent Ray Nicolette. And to play stoner beach-girl Melanie, Tarantino brought in Bridget Fonda, daughter of Peter *'Easy Rider'* Fonda.

For the key role of Max Cherry, the director chose someone who could, like Grier, be seen as Seventies stunt casting. Robert Forster had long been on Tarantino's radar, having impressed him in the TV show *Banyon*, and in movies like *Medium Cool* (1969) and *Alligator* (1980). But it wasn't until *Jackie Brown* that he found the perfect combination of character and actor.

The relationship between Jackie and Max is what truly marks *Jackie Brown* out from Tarantino's other films. It's a believable, touching and gently kindled romance that, without ever making a point of it, reminded audiences that falling in love isn't exclusively the domain of the young. You see this in Max's first sight of Jackie when he picks her up from jail, as she makes the long walk from the building to the gate; it's as if a light has switched on somewhere inside him. And the way he latches on to her music taste, constantly playing 'Didn't I Blow Your Mind This Time' by soul band The Delfonics, is schoolboy-crush sweet. When they finally kiss at the end, Tarantino proudly pointed out that their 'combined age is

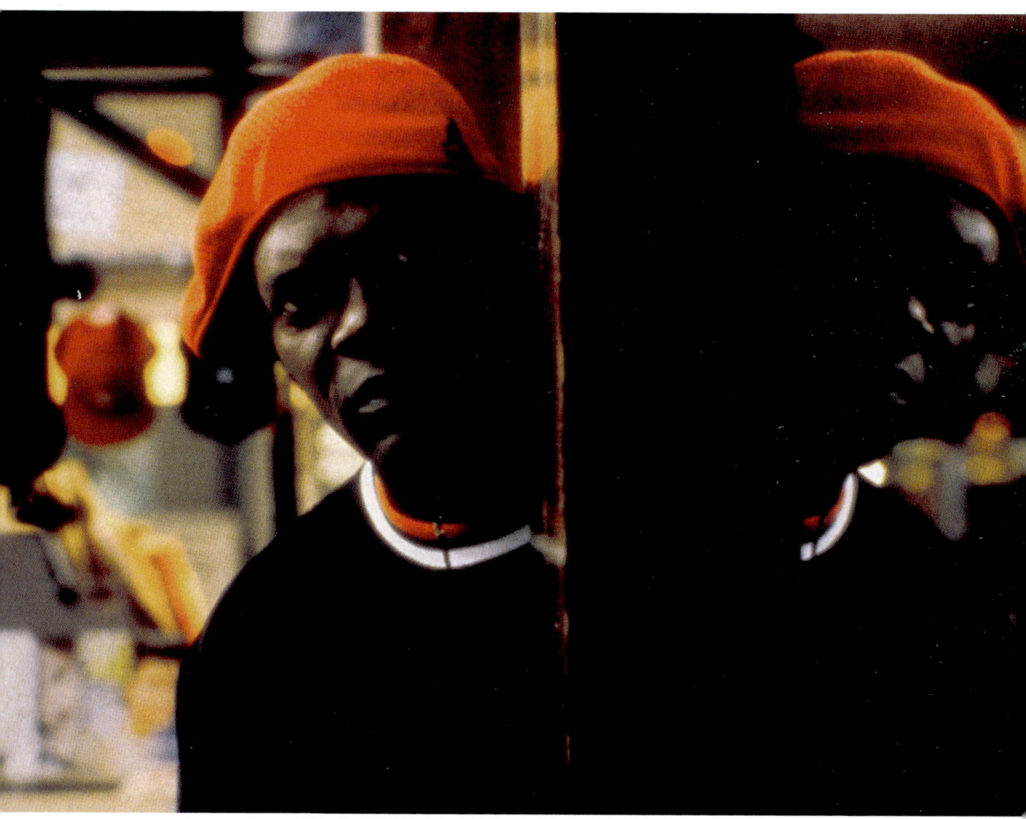

ABOVE: Samuel L Jackson was heavily involved in crafting
the look of gunrunner Ordell Robbie, basing his long hair and
Fu Manchu beard on the kung fu movies he loved.

over 100', making it a rarity in Hollywood movies. 'I've talked to
some younger people that didn't like it at all,' he said. '"It's like
watching my grandparents kiss!" And it's like, "Well, I didn't make it
for you then."'

The question of who Tarantino *did* make *Jackie Brown* for hung over
its release. While the film grossed almost $75 million against a budget
of $12 million, it did not come close to matching the commercial or

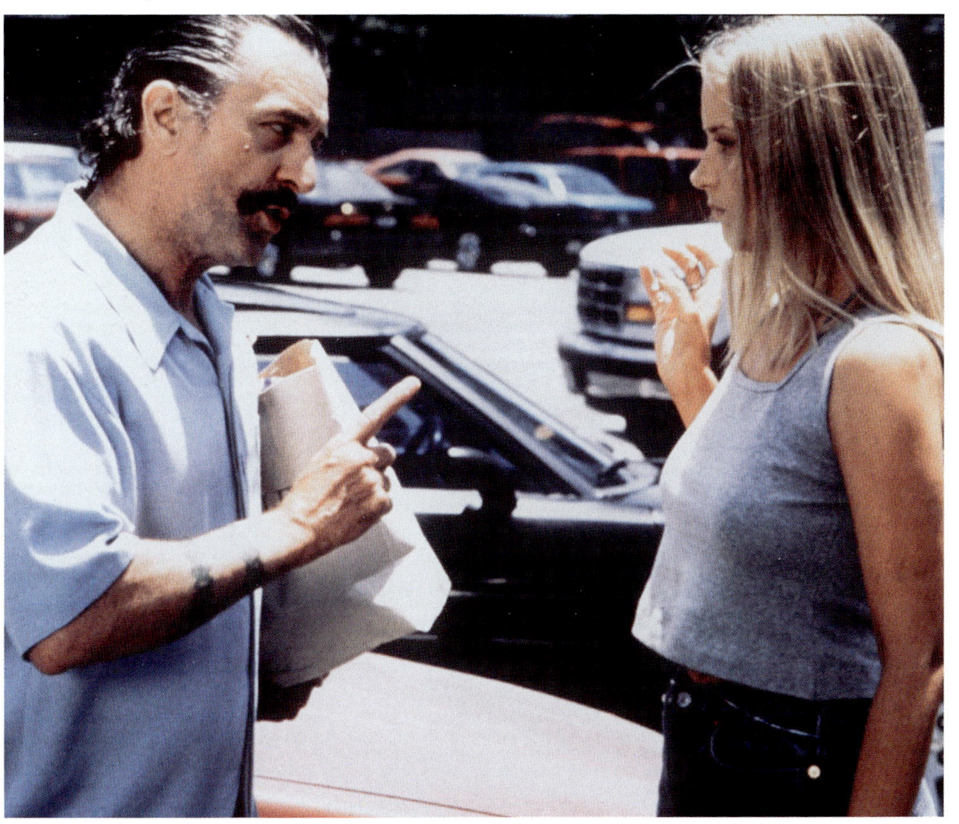

ABOVE: Bridget Fonda's character Melanie suffers one of the most shocking deaths in any Tarantino movie when Louis, needled by her teasing, suddenly shoots her in a parking lot.

cultural impact of *Pulp Fiction*, and was compared unfavourably with it. *Jackie Brown* was 'slower, talkier, more sluggish' wrote Janet Maslin in *The New York Times*. 'For all its enthusiasm, this film isn't sharp enough to afford all the time it wastes on small talk, long drives, trips to the mall and favourite songs played on car radios.'

While the film did receive positive reviews, some of which applauded Tarantino for his apparent newfound restraint and sensitivity, there was an overwhelming sense of the film being a little underwhelming, especially to fans expecting the next *Pulp Fiction*. The movie's languorous pacing and generous length were taken as overindulgence, but for Tarantino, the movie needed to be structured that way: you need to spend time chilling with the characters and getting to know them before the money-heist plot kicks in during the film's second half.

Interestingly, once Jackie's plan to make off with Ordell's half-a-million dollars is in action, Tarantino reverts a little to non-linear form, repeatedly rewinding events to present them from different characters' perspectives, revealing a little more with each replay. All that time spent observing the characters earlier in the movie pays off. Rarely do movie heists feel so character-driven, shifting through gears that feel emotional rather than mechanical.

For once, at least, Tarantino wasn't being attacked for his depiction of violence or drugs. However, the tenor of his dialogue drew some flak, with his repeated use of the n-word once again attracting scrutiny. For director Spike Lee, enough was enough. He called Tarantino out, finding the 'excessive use of the word disturbing', and describing the director as 'ignorant'. Lee accepted that some of his own movies had also used the word, but insisted the difference here was 'the volume'. Also, he added, 'I think as an African American I have more of a right to use that word.' Tarantino, however, was 'infatuated' with it. 'What does he want to be made,' Lee asked, 'an honorary Black man?'

As much as it was his tribute to Elmore Leonard, *Jackie Brown* was the product of Tarantino's love for, and identification with, Black culture. And he wasn't afraid of saying this in interviews. 'I grew up surrounded in the Seventies by Black culture, probably the greatest time of Black culture in this nation's history,' he told talk-show host Charlie Rose in late 1997. 'I went to an all-Black school for a long period of time,' he continued, while relating how many of his mother's boyfriends had been Black, and her best

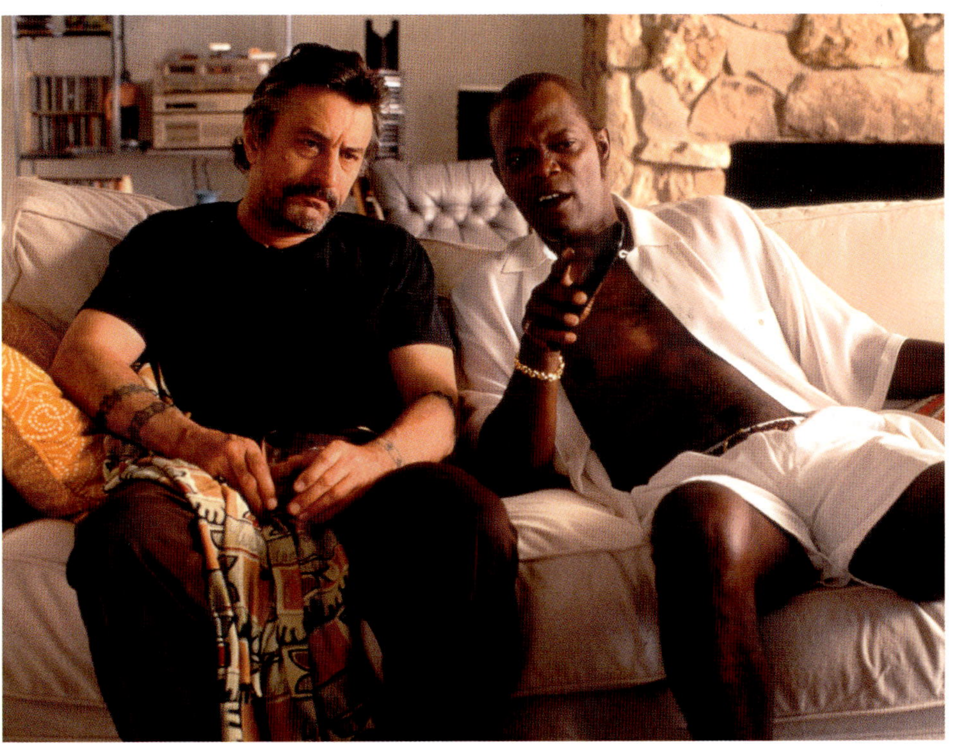

ABOVE: Robert De Niro as Louis Gara, a role with little dialogue that confirmed De Niro's astonishing capability to convey so much with even the subtlest of gestures.

friend Jackie too. He wasn't just a 'visitor' to Black culture. 'It's part of me,' he said. 'We all have different parts of us and one part of me is Black, as far as my upbringing and affinities go. That's my heart, just a shade of me, it's not all of me.'

Unsurprisingly, he didn't appreciate Lee's comments. 'If he believes in his heart of hearts that I'm a racist, that's one thing, okay?' Tarantino said. 'If he doesn't believe that, it's simply about me being a writer. And as a writer, I demand the right to write any character in the world that I want to write. And to say that I can't do that because I'm white, but the Hughes brothers [Albert and

Allen, directors of *Menace II Society*] can do that because they're Black. . .I do not accept that.'

Tarantino dismissed Lee's attack as 'just bald-faced promotion', and never backed down or apologized for his use for the n-word. Nor did he shy away from it. As counted by the *Dallas Observer* in 2019, it would be used 110 times in *Django Unchained* and 47 times in *The Hateful Eight*.

The reception to *Jackie Brown* got to Tarantino. Aside from the attacks on the language, the movie's reception was relatively muted, with approving nods replacing the rapturous applause of 1994. It was not exactly showered with awards; Robert Forster's Oscar nomination for Best Supporting Actor was the only one it received. (Grier at the very least should also have received one, Tarantino believed.)

But the film was a conscious effort by Tarantino to do something different, both tonally and visually. And it worked. It's his most sober and romantic picture, and has improved with age. On the film's 25th anniversary re-release, critic Peter Bradshaw praised it as a 'stone-cold liquid nitrogen classic'. But the director could obviously not appreciate that at the time, and even in hindsight, he has distanced himself from the film, claiming he was never truly as invested in it as his others. 'I lost my stamina in the last quarter of the last lap of *Jackie Brown*,' he reflected in 2008. 'Part of the reason was I wasn't taking something I created from scratch and turning it into a full project. When I finished the edit and got my cut the way I wanted, I was emotionally done. I believe people could say it's my best movie, but there's a slight once-removed quality, located somewhere in my balls where that doesn't live.'

Tarantino felt an overwhelming sense from his fans that they found the film a little underwhelming, not Tarantino-esque enough. If they wanted extreme violence, dark laughs and trash-culture references, his next movie would certainly deliver. But they would have to wait a very long time to get it.

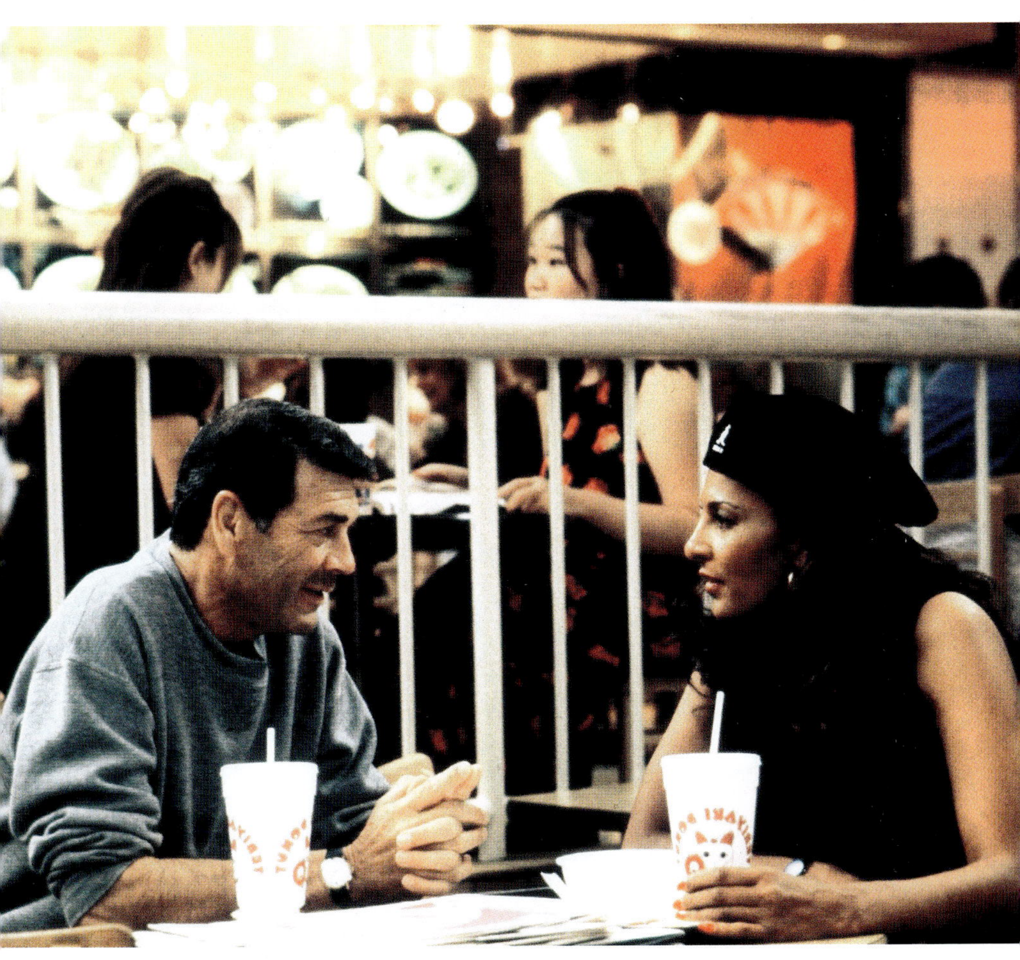

BELOW: Tarantino was proud of the fact that the combined age of *Jackie Brown*'s romantic leads was over 100.

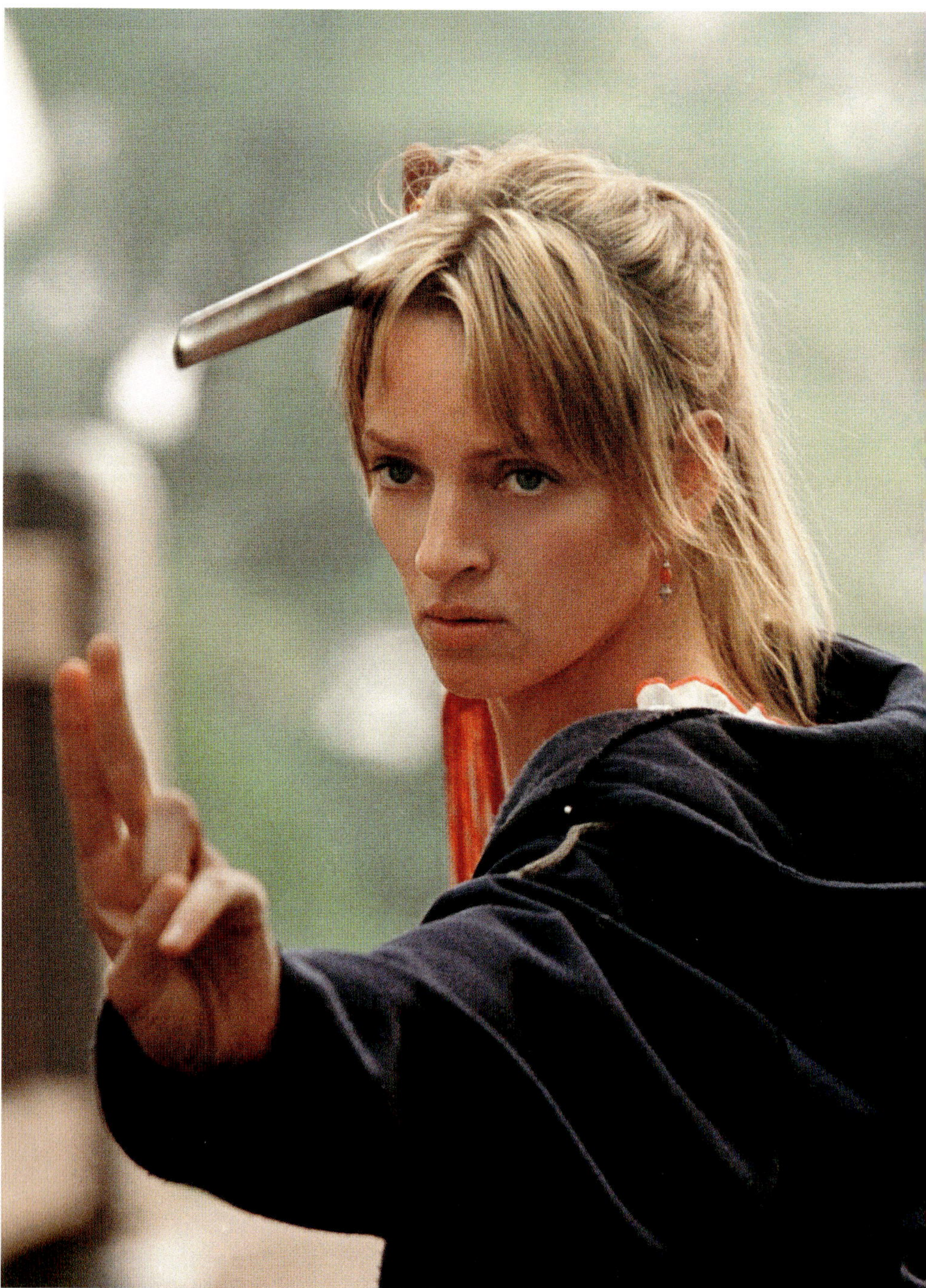

'Revenge is never a straight line.
It's a forest.'

KILL BILL
2003–04

According to Tarantino, Uma Thurman told him during the *Pulp Fiction* shoot that she was considering quitting acting. This was a 'damn shame,' he thought. So, firstly, he resolved to make sure she'd be as happy as possible on his shoot. Then, during an end-of-week wind-down in a faux British pub called the Daily Pint in Santa Monica, he tempted Thurman to stay in the game with the promise of a future collaboration.

Tarantino laid out an idea for an old-school exploitation revenge movie, along the lines of a 1973 Swedish XXX-rated pic he loved, *They Call Her One Eye*. 'Of all the revenge movies I've seen, that is definitely the roughest,' he said. While that movie's main character, Frigga (Christina Lindberg), would ultimately provide the visual inspiration for *Kill Bill*'s eyepatch-wearing villain Elle Driver (Daryl Hannah), Tarantino's 'roaring rampage of revenge' would star Thurman as the deadliest woman in the world, hunting down her former partners in the Deadly Viper Assassination Squad (DiVAS). The opening scene, he outlined, would show her beaten and bloody, looking up at the people who just killed all her loved ones. Enthused, Thurman suggested a cool embellishment: the camera pulls back to reveal she's wearing a bridal gown. 'That's when she became The Bride,' said Tarantino, and over the next few days he scribbled out the first 30 pages of the script, titled *Kill Bill*. For the rest of the shoot, he and Thurman kept brainstorming the concept, fresh ideas pinging back and forth between them.

After *Pulp Fiction*, Thurman obviously did not quit. But it would be another decade before she reunited with Tarantino, and The Bride finally got to see some rough-revenge action.

The gap between *Jackie Brown* and *Kill Bill* would be Tarantino's biggest hiatus yet: a six-year stretch of perplexing directorial inactivity that, like the last break, left an information vacuum that only rumour could fill. Had he burned out? Was he too grievously wounded by the *Jackie Brown* response? Or was he paralyzed by indecision over what to do next? After all, in various interviews he'd promised a prison-set Western, a British heist movie and a *Pulp Fiction* prequel.

On his eventual return, Tarantino gave a familiarly dismissive explanation for his extended sabbatical. He'd been stricken by 'writer-itis'. Having directed someone else's material with his last

BELOW: Gogo Yubari (Chiaki Kuriyama), O-Ren Ishii (Lucy Liu) and Sofie Fatale (Julie Dreyfus) in the House of Blue Leaves.

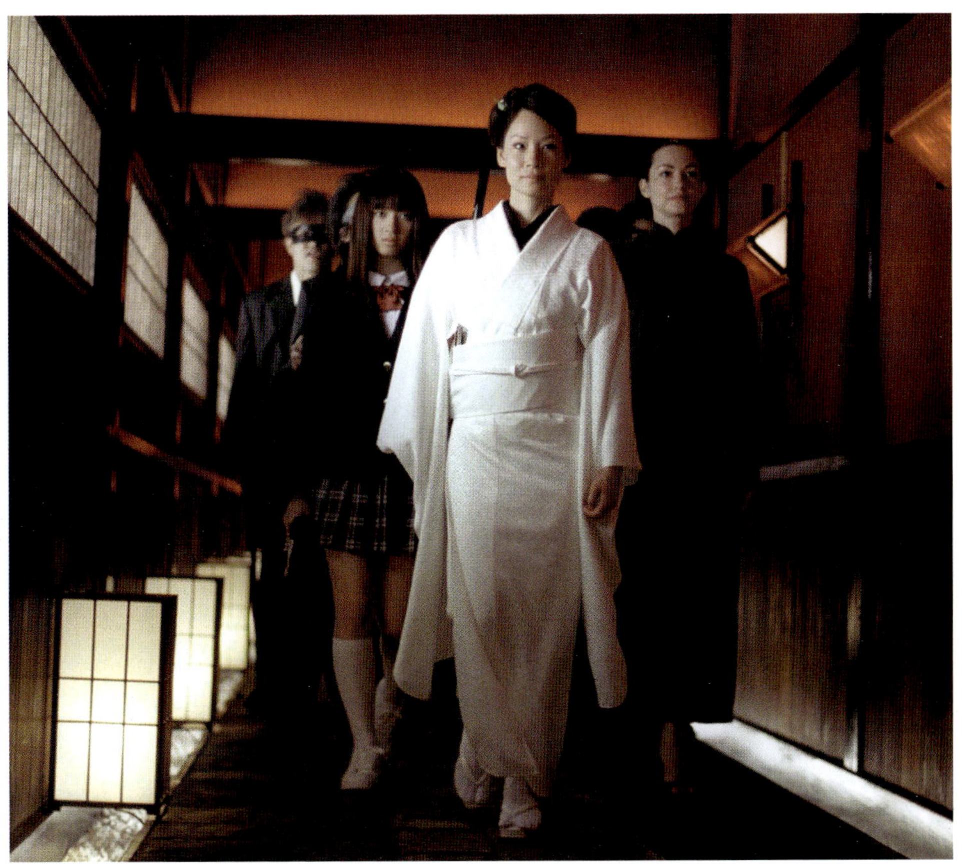

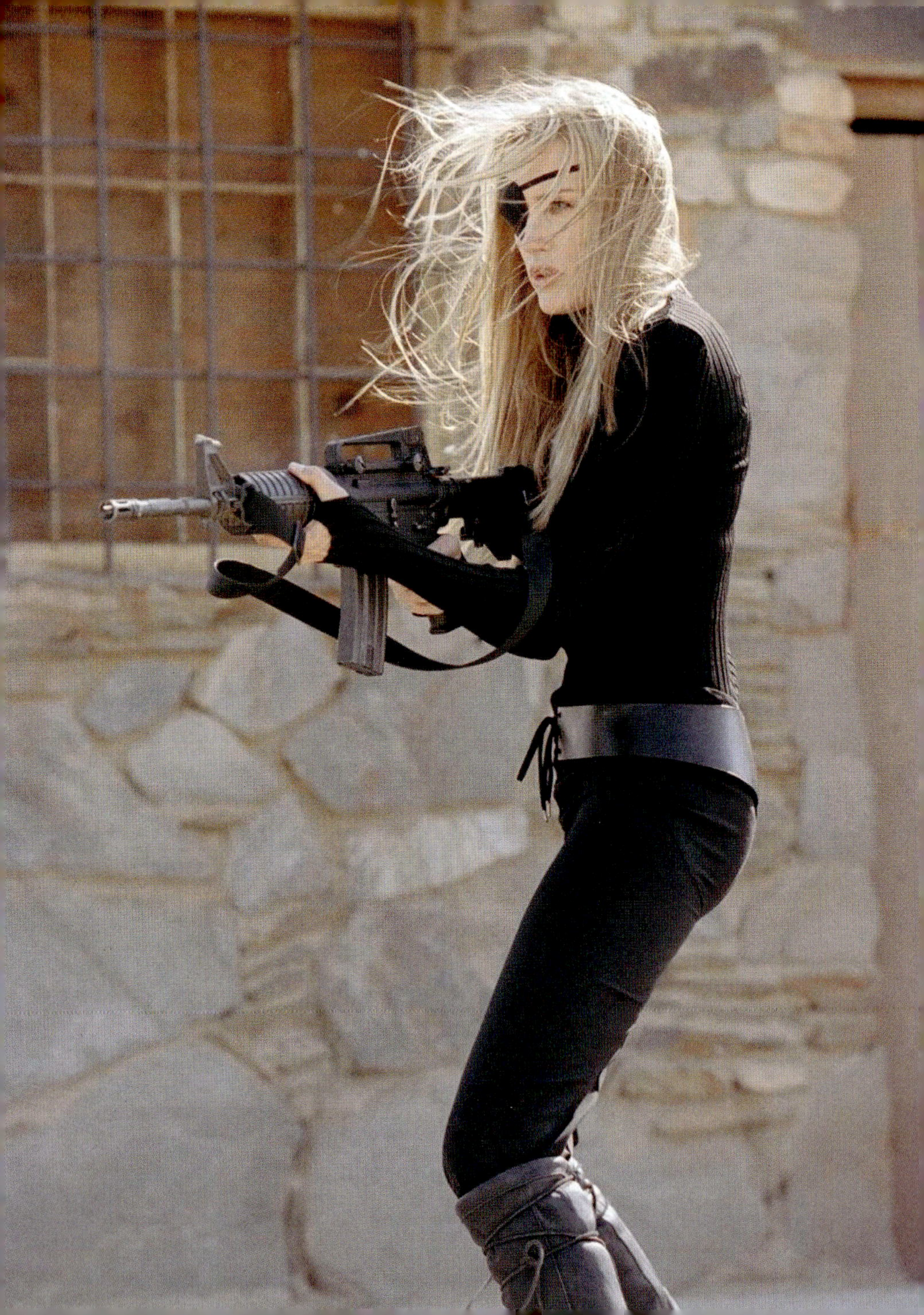

movie, he claimed it was time for the writer in him to take charge. And, apparently, take him prisoner. The writing project that had consumed him was a men-on-a-mission World War II epic titled, in unspellchecked Quentinese, *Inglourious Basterds* – after the 1978 Enzo G Castellari movie *The Inglorious Bastards*, whose poster boasted, 'Whatever the Dirty Dozen did, they do it dirtier!' However, where Castellari's film was a tight, gritty 99 minutes, Tarantino's script was a novelistic sprawl containing enough material to fill three different war films.

It took a fateful meeting with Thurman to snap him out of it. On 25 March 2000, he bumped into her for the first time in years at the Miramax Oscar party. Still keen to become The Bride, she reminded him of his promise in 1994, and wondered if *Kill Bill* would ever happen. That night, he went home and pulled those 30 pages out of a drawer. On re-reading them, he thought, 'This is some funny shit. This would be really good.' Realizing he needed to cleanse his creative palate, he set the interminable *Inglourious Basterds* aside and decided to make *Kill Bill* instead. Tarantino promised Thurman he'd have it written by her birthday, at the end of April. Which would be no problem for a lean, mean, 90-minute revenge flick, he guessed. But it actually took him 15 months to complete, as this script also turned into a massive epic, over 200 pages long. He just couldn't help himself.

It couldn't merely be a revenge movie, it had to be all the revenge movies he loved rolled into one, drawing from all the different genres that used a retributive plot engine: spaghetti Westerns, Yakuza thrillers, samurai movies and kung fu actioners. As the script grew, Italian *giallo* and Brian De Palma tributes were

OPPOSITE: Daryl Hannah as eye-patched DiVA Elle Driver, whose look was inspired by Christina Lindberg in Swedish revenge pic *They Call Her One Eye*.

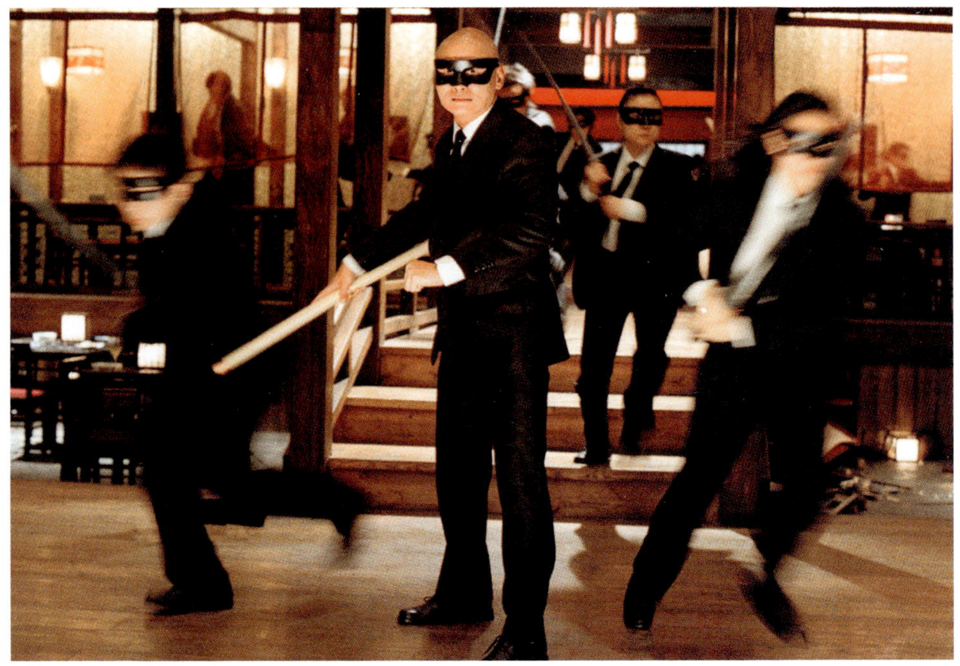

ABOVE: Hong Kong star Gordon Liu as Crazy 88 boss Johnny Mo, the first of his two appearances in *Kill Bill*.

also thrown into the gritty mix. But the film would be action-driven, giving Tarantino the opportunity to work with some of his favourite martial-arts legends.

Sonny Chiba was given the role of sword master Hattori Hanzo – a fresh version of a character he'd played across several seasons of Japanese TV show *Shadow Warriors*. Veteran Shaw Brothers star Gordon Liu was gifted the twin roles of Johnny Mo, the Kato-masked, *Reservoir Dogs*-suited leader of criminal-warrior gang The Crazy 88, and wispy-white-bearded kung fu mentor Pai Mei. The role of Bill, meanwhile, went to David Carradine, the one-time lead of Seventies Old-West-meets-East TV show *Kung Fu*.

The remaining DiVAS would be filled by a typically Tarantino combo of current stars (Vivica A Fox and Lucy Liu as Vernita Green and O-Ren Ishii, respectively), an old chum (Michael Madsen, providing one of his finest performances as one of *Kill Bill*'s most sympathetic characters) and another actor given a comeback shot: Hannah, who relished Elle Driver's all-out malevolence. Meanwhile, Tarantino favourites Samuel L Jackson and Michael Parks were given minor roles. Tarantino's shoo-in for The Bride, however, proved a little harder to cast than he'd expected.

By the time he finally delivered his doorstopper script to Thurman, she was pregnant with her and then-husband Ethan Hawke's first child. After briefly considering recasting the role, Tarantino decided the film simply couldn't be made without her, and delayed the shoot to accommodate her. With that final delay out of the way, the movie that 'Q and U' had dreamed up all those years earlier was finally coming together.

Tarantino had always believed action directors to be the greatest of all directors, so the whole idea on the *Kill Bill* shoot, he said, was to test the limits of his talent. As such, it was a deeply different production experience to any of his previous movies: an intense and physically exacting nine-month shoot that took in China, Hong Kong, Japan and Mexico, as well as the United States, going vastly over schedule and $16 million over its $39 million budget. Primarily based in the Beijing Film Studio and using Hong Kong fight coordinators supervised by Yuen Woo-ping (*Iron Monkey, The Matrix, Crouching Tiger, Hidden Dragon*), it was a baptism of fire for Tarantino as an action director.

'We didn't know what the fuck we were doing,' he admitted. 'Other people do storyboards and shit, but we didn't do any of that crap.' His script detailed key action sequences, such as the fierce front-room melee between The Bride and Vernita Green, which opens *Kill Bill Volume 1* and the magnificent mass brawl at the House of Blue Leaves that concludes it. But there were numerous discussions, amendments and embellishments that were further extended by the need for multiple translators (Chinese to English, Japanese to English, Chinese to Japanese). One action sequence scheduled for three days took eight weeks. But to Tarantino this was a point of pride rather than failure. 'In Hong Kong and China, they say, "Fuck the schedule." You're done when you're done.'

And the movie itself wasn't getting any shorter. It even included a bloody anime segment, directed by Kazuto Nakazawa, to provide the back story of crime lord O-Ren. During production, Tarantino convinced himself that he and editor Sally Menke would figure out a way to cut it all down and avoid the film from running at four hours, but he was spared an editing-room headache by producer Harvey Weinstein, who suggested dividing *Kill Bill* into two parts.

The film, Tarantino saw, was already structured to handle the division. The first part would end with the show-stopping, limb-hacking 'Showdown at House of Blue Leaves', having set up the characters and mythology in a lithe and relatively dialogue-light action-focused movie. It would also accentuate *Kill Bill*'s Eastern influences, while the second part would dig into its Western roots – and the characters. If *Kill Bill Volume 1* was a kaleidoscope of violence, then *Kill Bill Volume 2* was, to quote David Carradine, 'the inside look at the mind and heart of violent people.'

Volume 2, released six months after *Volume 1*, ends with a final confrontation that is more verbal than physical. When The Bride – whose previously bleeped-out name is finally revealed as Beatrix Kiddo – learns she has a living daughter, it turns borderline mawkish in its final moments. This wasn't unintentional. 'I think *Kill Bill Volume 2* is pretty sweet,' said Tarantino. 'It's quite emotional

OPPOSITE: Gordon Liu as Pai Mei, the second of his two *Kill Bill* roles, and a villain Tarantino brought back from various Shaw Brothers pictures.

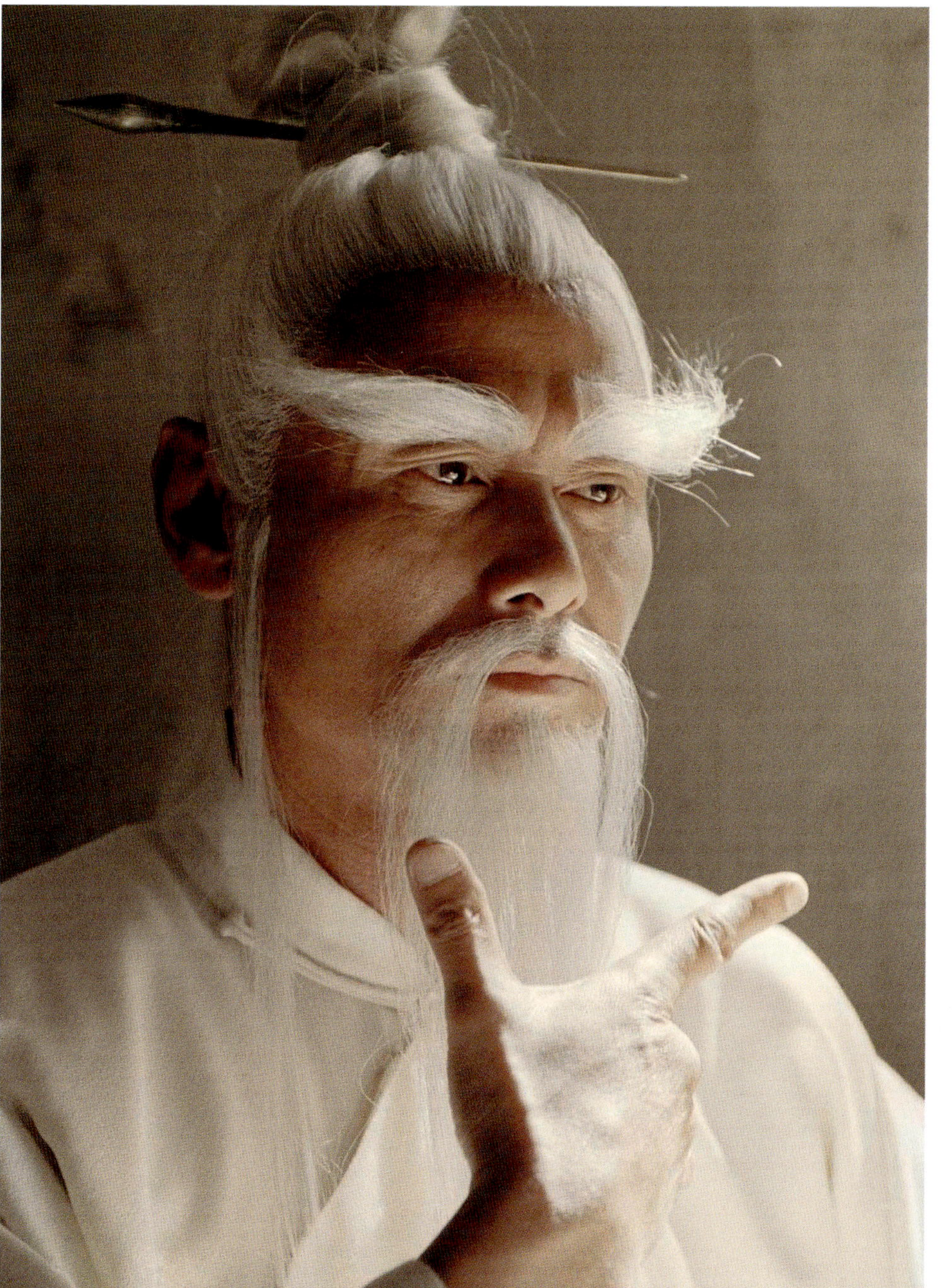

and moving.' Although, it still delivers a strong dose of action, via
the flashback training sequences with Liu's Pai Mei, and a smash-
mouth trailer-trashing confrontation between Elle Driver and The
Bride that Tarantino dubbed 'the war of the blonde gargantuans'.

While the shoot was tough for Tarantino, it was hell on his lead
'blonde gargantuan'. 'He couldn't have written me a more
challenging, difficult part,' said Thurman, who underwent three
months of training before cameras rolled. David Carradine was
impressed by his co-star. 'I've never seen anybody work as hard,'
he said. 'I mean, this has got to be the hardest picture that anybody
has ever done. She's just a trouper through it.'

A tarnished legacy

The worst hardship Thurman suffered while shooting *Kill Bill* took
place near the end of the shoot, in Mexico, during a scene that wasn't
even designated as a stunt. They needed to film The Bride driving to
confront her ex-boss (and ex-lover) in a convertible Karmann Ghia.
Thurman was not a confident driver, and said she'd rather not do it.
But with no stunt double available Tarantino convinced her it would
be fine: all she needed to do was drive along a straight stretch of road
at around 40mph, fast enough to dramatically whip her hair around.
However, the road was more sandy and less straight than anticipated,
and during the take Thurman went into a spin, which sent the car
slamming into a tree. She suffered permanent neck and knee injuries.
It was, said the director years later, 'one of the biggest regrets of my
life. A trust was broken.' Publicly, Thurman supported both the movie
and Tarantino as her director, while the details of the crash were
suppressed until 2018. But privately the incident fractured the bond
between 'Q' and 'U', and Tarantino would consider the legacy of the
film, and what they achieved with it, 'tarnished'.

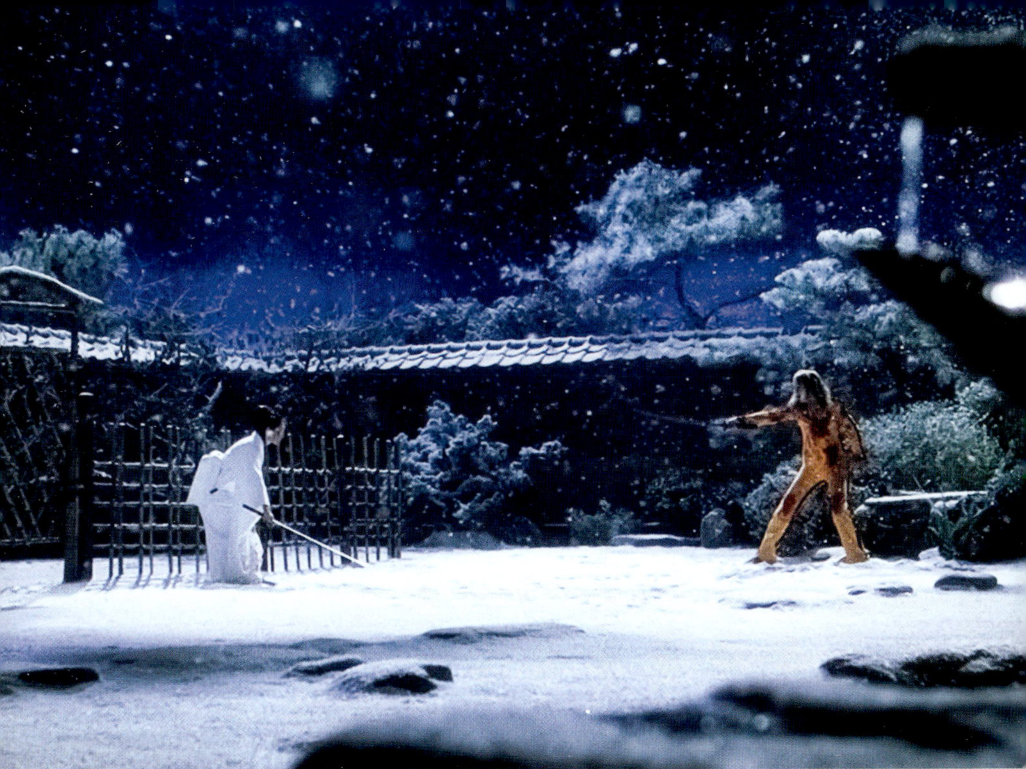

ABOVE: The Bride's (Uma Thurman) final showdown with
Yakuza boss O-Ren Ishii (Lucy Liu).

It wasn't simply the physical exertion of the fight sequences
that pushed and punished Thurman, or nailing the steely, enigmatic
specifics of the character. In the spectacular fight scene with
the ball-and-chain-wielding schoolgirl bodyguard Gogo Yubari
(Chiaki Kuriyama), Thurman had to be throttled with a chain.
According to Tarantino, Thurman herself suggested she be choked
for real – for a few seconds, in close-up. And, not wanting to trust
anyone else with the job, it was he who pulled on the choking chain.

Both volumes were hits, making just over $180 million and $150
million respectively. Tarantino's long absence from directing
hadn't at all damaged his career. In fact, it made the movie more of

an event, accentuated by its division into two halves, hyping up an audience already primed for cinematic cliff-hangers by the *Lord of the Rings* and *Matrix* movies.

Kill Bill took Tarantino into new, challenging territory as a filmmaker, and not simply in terms of choreographing and executing action. With the assistance of a new cinematographer, veteran Oscar-winner Robert Richardson (a regular collaborator with Martin Scorsese and Oliver Stone – with whom he made *Natural Born Killers*), the movie was also his most visually ludic and audacious yet. The tracking-shot introduction to the extravagant House of Blue Leaves set, for example, outdoes

The movie universe

Despite the background presence of Red Apple cigarettes (as smoked in *Pulp Fiction*, *Four Rooms*, *The Hateful Eight* and *Once Upon A Time. . .in Hollywood*), *Kill Bill* does not take place in the same world as those movies. Not exactly. In 2016, Tarantino confirmed that there are two levels to his connected cinematic universe: the 'realer than real' universe that contains *Pulp Fiction*, *Reservoir Dogs* and *True Romance*, among others, and the 'movie universe', which contains *Kill Bill* and *From Dusk Till Dawn*. 'So basically, when the characters of *Reservoir Dogs* or *Pulp Fiction* go to the movies, *Kill Bill* is what they go see.'

Which raises the question: does Uma Thurman play The Bride in the Tarantinoverse? Or does Mia Wallace, star of the *Fox Force Five* pilot that partly inspired *Kill Bill*? If the former, does that mean Thurman exists in Tarantino's world, alongside Mia Wallace? The filmmaker hasn't elaborated, but his universe-layering distinction does make a lot of sense, in terms of explaining why, in *Kill Bill*, Japanese airlines allow samurai swords in hand baggage, and in *From Dusk Till Dawn* vampires exist.

Vincent and Mia's arrival at Jack Rabbit Slim's in *Pulp Fiction* by suddenly gliding up into the air and taking a top-down view. It required six hours of rehearsal and 17 takes, during which a crane had to be rolled in through removable sidewalls so Steadicam operator Larry McConkey could step onto it. Richardson and Tarantino proved a good team, and the director of photography would return to shoot all but one of Tarantino's following movies.

BELOW: Tarantino was inspired to cast Chiaki Kuriyama as Gogo after seeing her in Kinji Fukasaku's dystopian thriller *Battle Royale*, one of his favourite films.

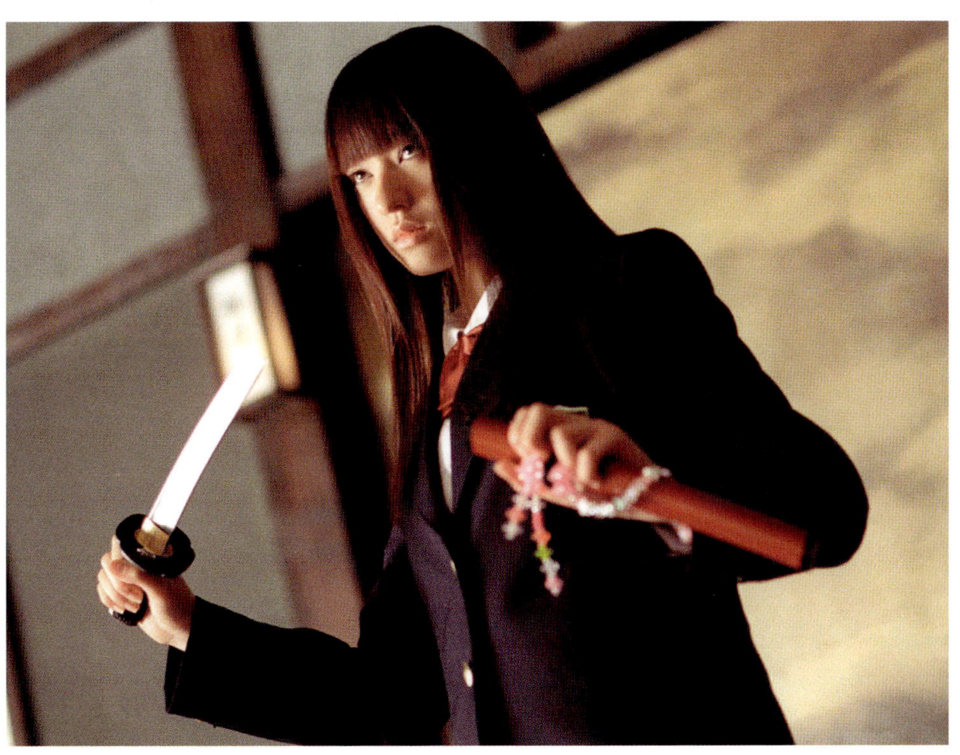

Though *Kill Bill* took Tarantino out of the States for the first time and tested his limits, it still felt recognizable to his fans. It chopped up the narrative into chapters, messed with the chronology (O-Ren is the second DiVA we see The Bride kill, but she's actually the first on her list), and featured trunk shots, bare female feet and Tarantino's fictional Red Apple cigarettes. It also went all-out with the references. The Bride's yellow-and-black motorcycle leathers and jump suit in *Volume 1*, for example, match the duds worn by Bruce Lee in 1978's *Game of Death*.

It delivered some fantastic, deep-cut needle drops, too, such as Tomoyasu Hotei's bombastic instrumental rock anthem 'Battle Without Honour or Humanity', and Santa Esmeralda's epic flamenco cover version of Nina Simone's 'Don't Let Me Be Misunderstood', which plays over the snowy garden confrontation between O-Ren and The Bride. Tarantino developed a new magpie habit of snatching musical cues from other movies and TV shows, such as British psycho-thriller *Twisted Nerve* (scored by Bernard Hermann), crime drama *Ironside* (Quincy Jones), and spaghetti Western masterpiece *The Good, The Bad and the Ugly* (Ennio Morricone, whose work is liberally plundered by *Kill Bill*, and would be many times more in Tarantino's future films).

From its soundtrack to its visual style, the positive response to *Kill Bill* couldn't have been more different to *Jackie Brown*'s reception. It affirmed Tarantino's decision, conscious or otherwise, to run in the other direction from his last film's sober maturity and go crazy in the grindhouse. And in the grindhouse he would stay for his next project, which was, in its own way, no less audacious or ambitious.

OPPOSITE: Previous to playing DiVAS boss Bill, David Carradine was best known for being Caine in TV show *Kung Fu* – which was referred to by Jules in *Pulp Fiction*.

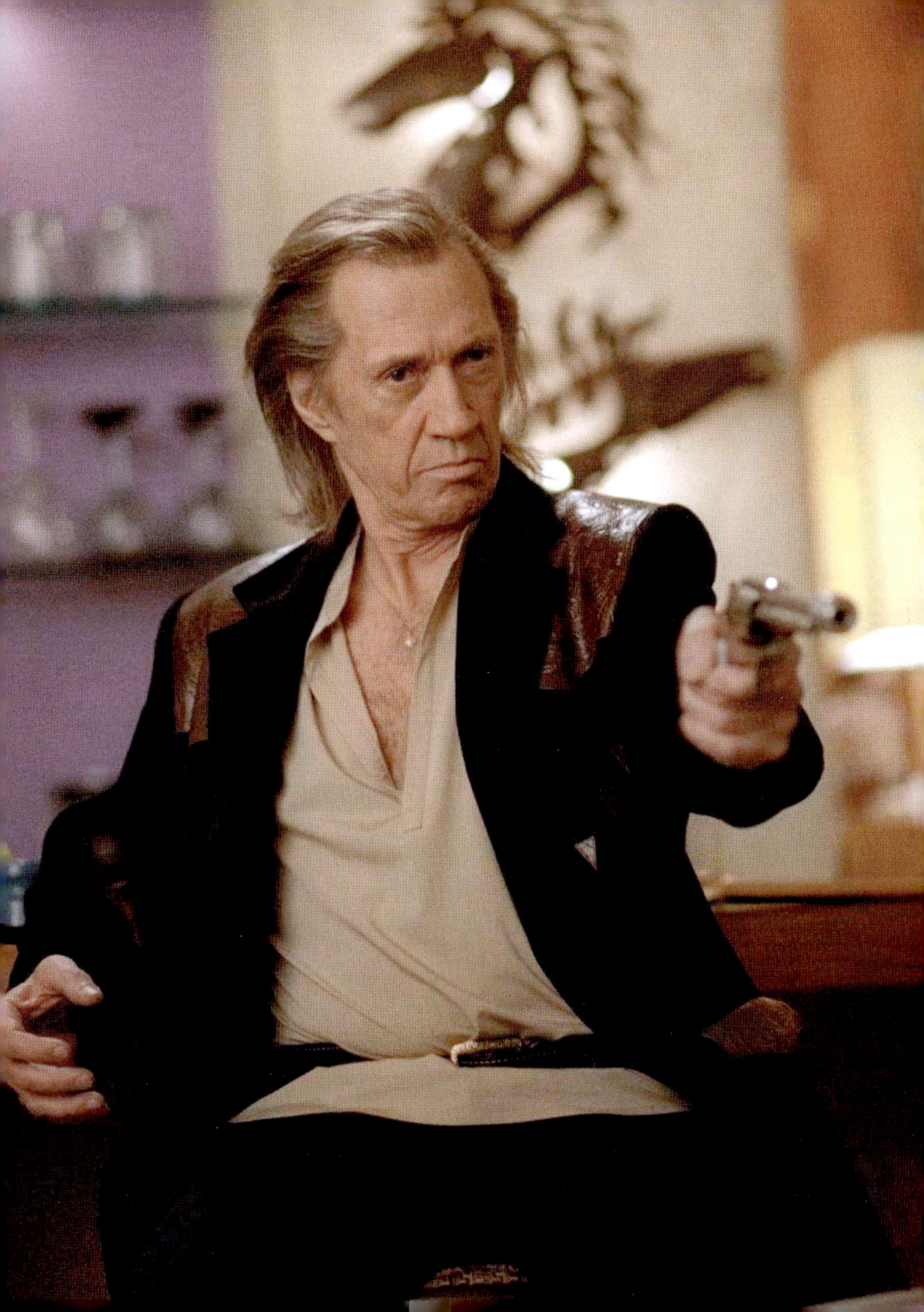

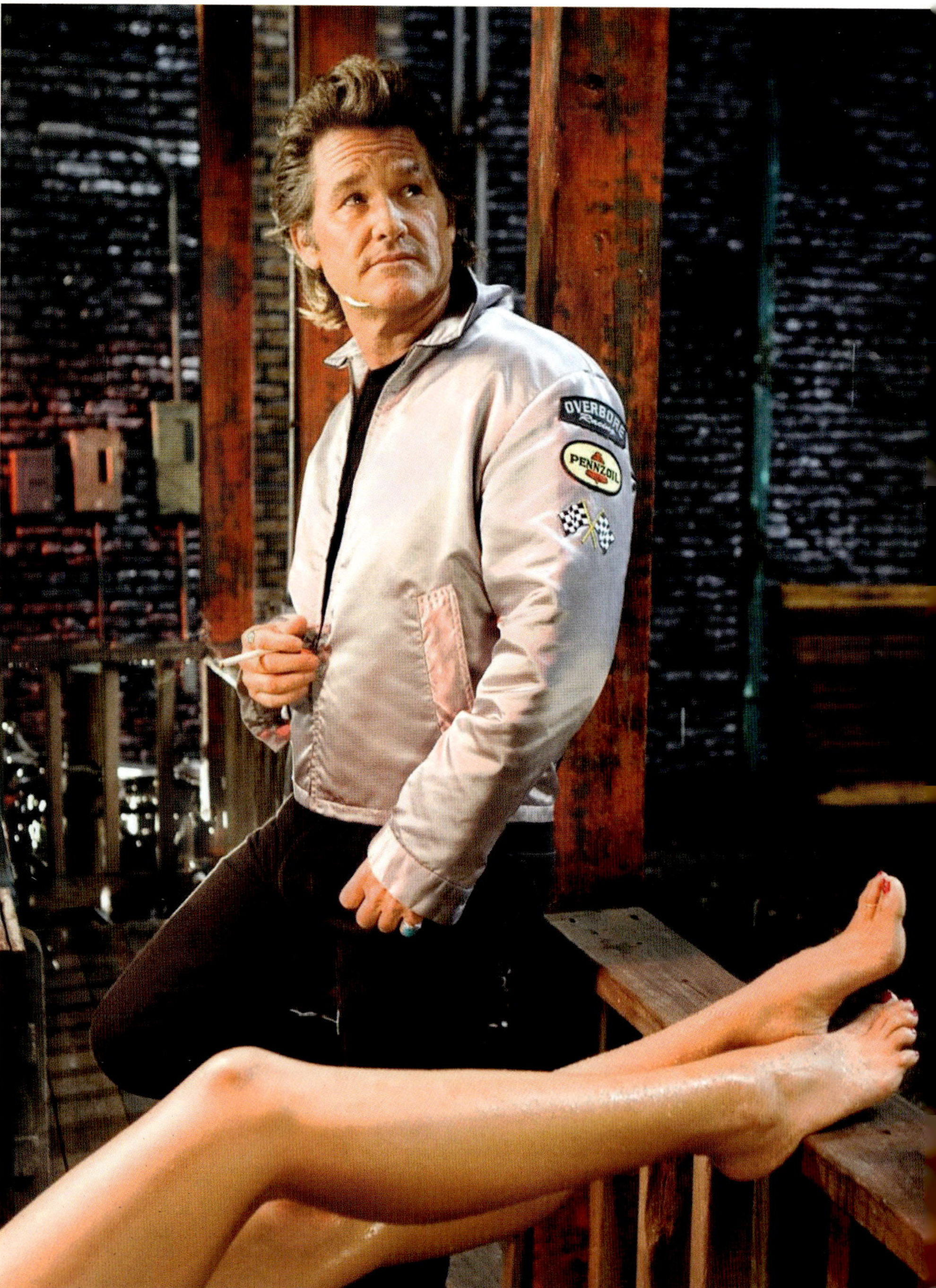

OVERBORE
PENNZOIL

GRINDHOUSE/
DEATH PROOF
2007

Movie night chez Tarantino was never a simple matter of putting on a DVD and hitting the couch. For the benefit of his guests, the filmmaker would delve into one of his carefully climate-controlled storage vaults and pluck out a couple of old 16mm or 35mm prints. They might be scratched and patchy from months of being bundled from theatre to theatre across the States, or even have a missing reel, causing odd narrative lurches. But they were the real deal: original exploitation flicks – cheerleader movies, perhaps, or chop-socky spectacles, or lurid Italian horrors – that Tarantino would complement with a curated selection of original trailers.

During the previous decade, he had broadened the audience for his ever-growing print collection with a yearly 'QT Fest' in Austin, Texas, where he was joined by his compadre Robert Rodriguez. These nights, whether at home or in an Austin theatre, were his tribute to the bygone days of double and triple features in old, dilapidated cinemas. Or, as *Variety* coined the term, grindhouses.

One evening in Hollywood, just as Tarantino was preparing to dive back into wrangling *Inglourious Basterds*, his intended follow-up to *Kill Bill*, Rodriguez visited. As he walked into the living room, Rodriguez spotted a one-sheet for the double bill of hot-rod drama *Dragstrip Girl* and Roger Corman's *Rock All Night*, both released by American Independent Pictures in 1957. He revealed that he had that very same poster, and as he spoke, an idea struck him. He and Tarantino could do their very own double feature. They could take a movie each, thus creating a custom-made 'Tarantino movie night' for the whole world to enjoy, complete with fake trailers, a deliberately scuzzed-up visual style, and even a missing reel in each movie. Plus, they could both work out of Rodriguez's Troublemaker Studios in Austin, which would make it relatively quick and easy. Tarantino loved the idea, and instantly had a title in mind: *Grindhouse*.

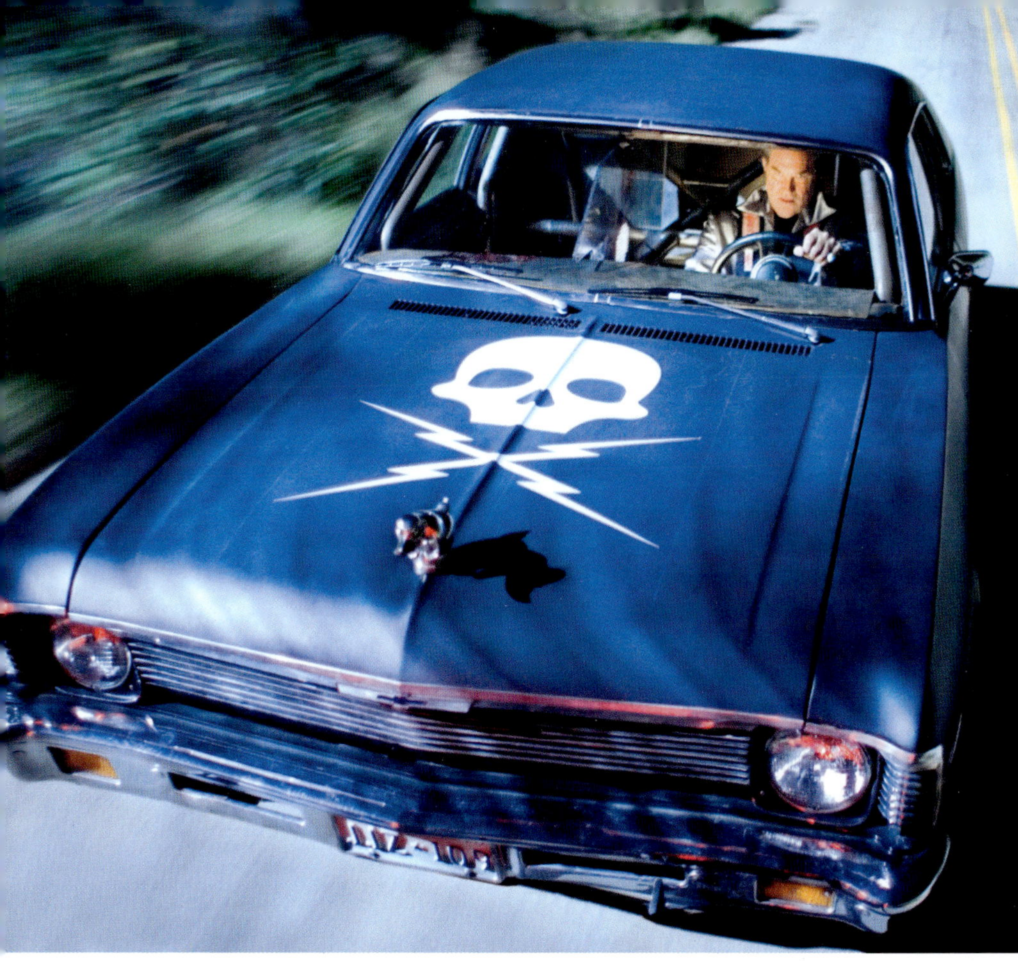

ABOVE: Kurt Russell as Stuntman Mike, a slasher villain with a 330-horsepower difference.

Rodriguez already had a zombie-movie script in progress titled *Planet Terror*, so the theme for *Grindhouse* was to be horror. This suited Tarantino, as he'd recently binged on slasher films. Watching killer after killer stalk and murder nubile teens, he'd noticed how the films were structurally similar, and thought it would be fun to treat the genre just like he'd treated the heist movie in *Reservoir Dogs*, presenting his 'own crazy cockamamie version' of a slasher.

Tarantino's concept for his half of the double bill was rooted in a conversation he'd had years earlier about, of all things, his Volvo. Following the success of *Pulp Fiction*, he'd bought one of the Swedish cars – the brand reputed to be the best for road safety – after developing anxiety about dying in a car crash. On telling this to a fellow movie-biz person, they informed him that any car can be made 'death-proof' by a stunt team for around $10,000. This sparked the creation of Stuntman Mike: a grizzled old-school stunt performer who uses his muscle car to murder attractive young women. 'What if he had a death-proof car that he could get into any crash he wanted, and it would be a sexual, rapist-like experience, but he is going to survive the crash because of his car?' Tarantino asked himself. 'Wow, I have never seen that movie before.' A movie that, Rodriguez pointed out, had its title built in.

So, what started out as a slasher film became a slasher/car-chase hybrid, with Tarantino now drawing inspiration from tarmac-tearing capers like the Burt Reynolds-starring *White Lightning* and 1971 cult classic *Vanishing Point*, whose iconic white Dodge Challenger 440 Magnum appears as *Death Proof*'s hero car. During an uncharacteristically swift screenwriting process (around four months), he further messed with genre expectations by teasing one character, Butterfly (played by *CSI: NY* star Vanessa Ferlito), as the film's 'final girl' – the archetypal savvy survivor – during an extended character-hang-out sequence in an Austin bar that was heavily influenced, he said, by his own time hanging out with 'different posses of female friends'. But at the film's mid-point she is brutally killed off, along with her best friends (Sydney Tamiia Poitier and Jordan Ladd), in a gore-spraying head-on collision orchestrated by Stuntman Mike (Kurt Russell, a genre-movie veteran whom Tarantino was desperate to see back as the kind of 'badass' he'd played back in his Eighties heyday).

The story then jumps forward 14 months to a new location – Lebanon, Tennessee – where Mike stalks four fresh victims, played by Rosario Dawson, Mary Elizabeth Winstead, Tracie Thoms and New Zealander Zoë Bell , a previously unknown stunt performer who had doubled Uma Thurman in *Kill Bill*, and befriended Tarantino during that shoot. After tormenting the girls on the road, with Bell clinging onto the bonnet of the aforementioned Dodge Challenger in an astonishing stunt, they turn the tables on Mike, who suddenly, amusingly becomes a 'crying bitch', as Tarantino

BELOW: Sidney Poitier's daughter Sydney Tamiia Poitier
(left) stars as DJ Jungle Julia, one of Stuntman Mike's victims.

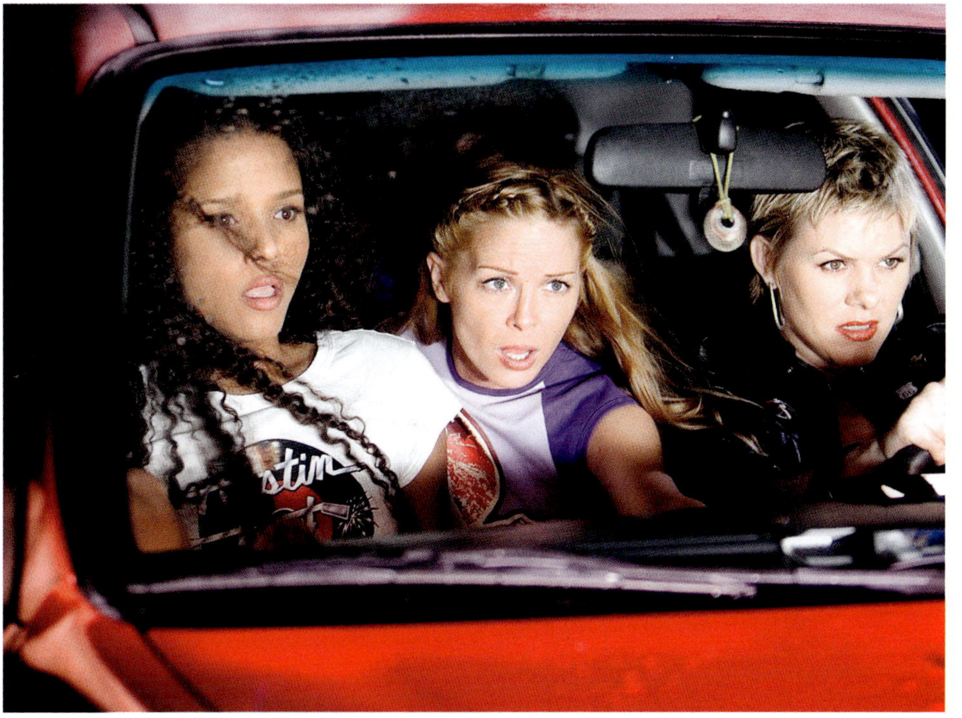

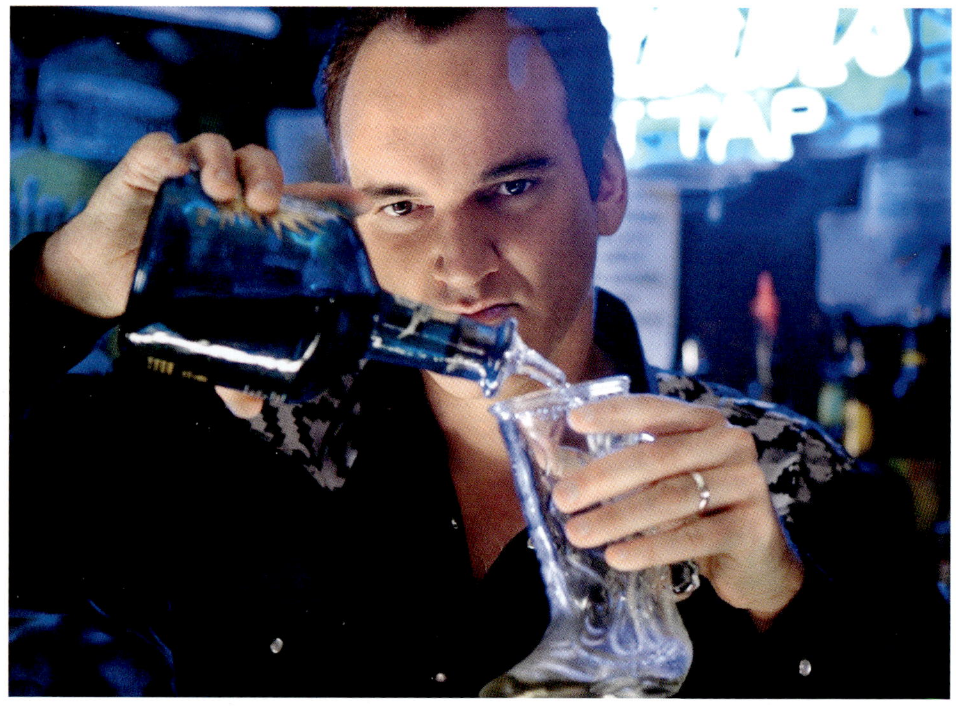

ABOVE: Tarantino as *Death Proof* barman Warren, pouring –
yes – a 'tasty beverage'.

put it, when they chase him down, run him off the road and beat
him to a bloody pulp. In its final act, *Death Proof* goes from a
slasher with a vehicular twist to a full-on female revenge movie in
the spirit of *Kill Bill*, except with cars instead of katanas.

Despite his enthusiasm while conceiving and shooting *Death
Proof*, Tarantino would come to consider it his weakest movie.
Though, this being Tarantino, that wasn't the same thing as
thinking he'd made a bad film. 'I want to go out with a terrific
filmography,' he said in 2012. '*Death Proof* has got to be the worst
movie I ever make. And for a left-handed movie, that wasn't so
bad, all right? If that's the worst I ever get, I'm good.'

Tarantino, Special Guest Director

Between *Kill Bill Volume 2* and *Grindhouse*, Tarantino and Rodriguez
enjoyed another brief collaboration. Rodriguez was co-directing his
2005 comic-book adaptation *Sin City* with its creator Frank Miller,
using digital techniques to preserve Miller's starkly black-and-white
ultra-noir on the screen. Knowing Tarantino was committed to
shooting on film, Rodriguez wanted to show his friend how it felt
to shoot digital and work with actors in a green-screen environment.
So, he selected a juicy scene for Tarantino to come in and guest direct.

The sequence involves private eye Dwight (Clive Owen) driving the
body of corrupt cop Jackie Boy (Benicio Del Toro) to a tar pit. During
the increasingly intense drive, his anxieties take the voice of Jackie Boy
himself, who has seemingly come alive to goad him. Tarantino loved
the scene and brought his own visual ideas, adding the different
coloured lights that pass through the otherwise black-and-white
sequence. Rodriguez said he'd wanted the scene to have 'a different
tone', and was delighted that Tarantino gave it his own stamp.

It is certainly uneven and oddly paced, testing patience with its
long and largely inconsequential dialogue scenes, which feel less
about getting to know the characters than simply spending time
with them. There's also a leering quality to *Death Proof*, with the
camera (operated by Tarantino himself) lingering on barely-
covered female posteriors and many bare feet. This may be a
knowing reference to the film's exploitation origins, while also
consciously subjecting the viewer to Stuntman Mike's predatory
male-gaze point of view, but it doesn't do Tarantino any favours.

Death Proof is also egregiously self-referential. DJ Jungle Julia
(Poitier) appears on a series of billboards, which include her
striking Mia Wallace's *Pulp Fiction* poster pose and wearing *Kill Bill*
yellow and black. Abernathy's (Rosario Dawson) ring tone is the
sinister whistle from *Twisted Nerve*, as heard in *Kill Bill Volume 1*.

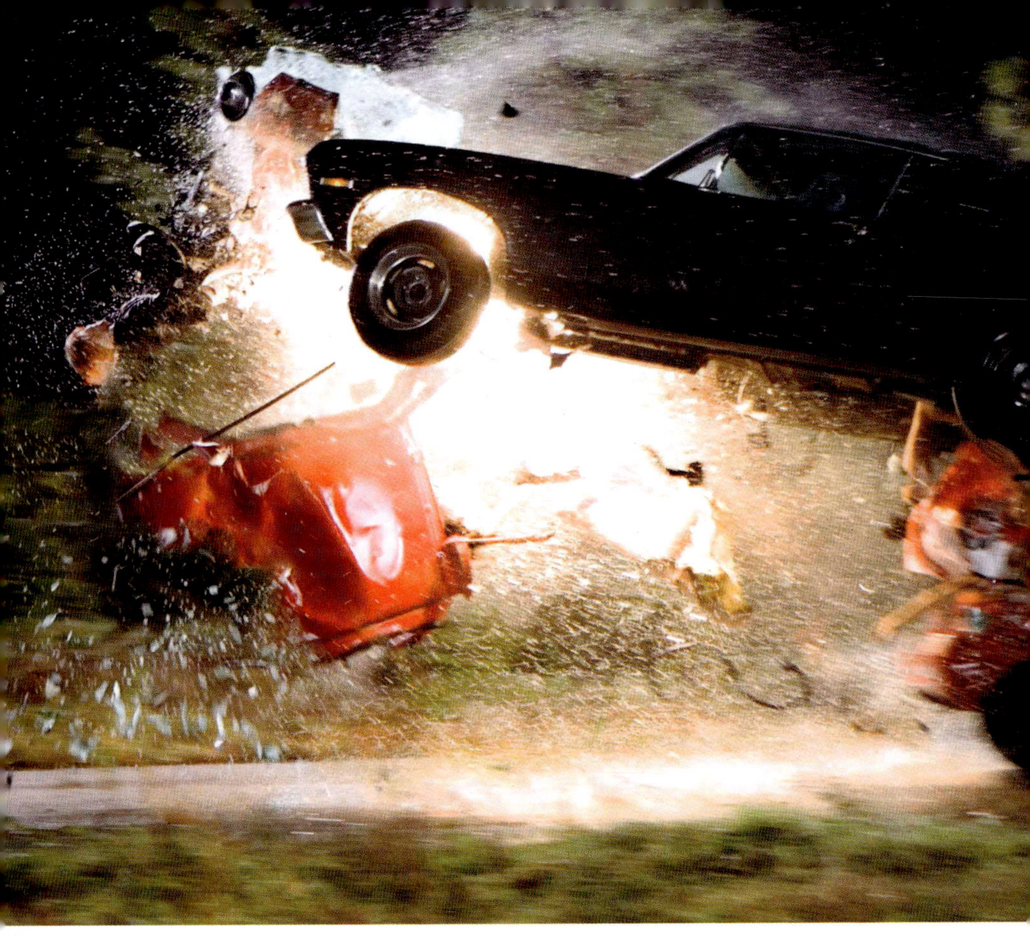

And Quentin himself turns up in the role of barman Warren, apparently with the sole purpose of using the QT-trope phrase 'tasty beverage'. . .twice. One could see it as providing Easter-egg treats for his fans, but it does feel a little like Tarantino is suggesting he's gone from referencing pop culture to becoming pop culture.

Still, considering it was made when CG-assisted mayhem had become the norm, the movie does excel in its done-for-real road carnage, with seasoned stunt performers like Tracy Dashnaw, Terry Leonard and Buddy Joe Hooker behind the vintage wheels. Tarantino wanted his film to feature 'real cars doing real shit at full

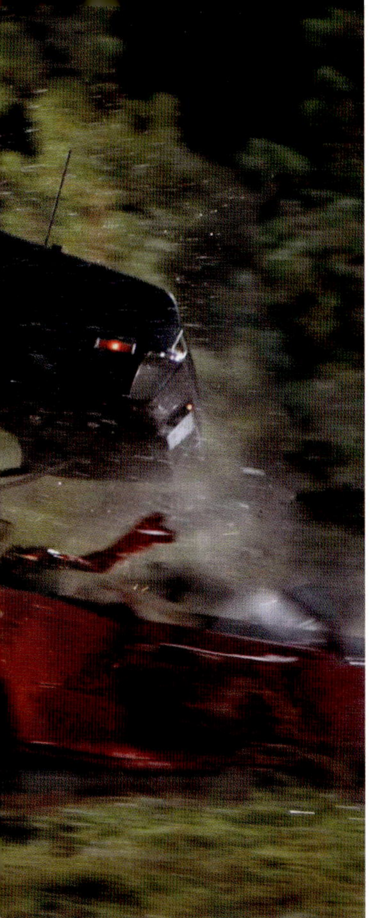

fucking speed,' and that is certainly what he and stunt coordinator Jeff Dashnaw delivered with vehicles like Stuntman Mike's 1970 Chevy Nova and later his 1969 Dodge Charger (both featuring the angry duck hood ornament from Sam Peckinpah's trucker movie *Convoy*). The trouble was, when *Grindhouse* opened in US cinemas in April 2007, there was barely anybody watching.

When Rodriguez and Tarantino dreamed up their intentionally tawdry double feature, with its fake-damaged picture quality, missing reels, sloppy editing and ersatz trailers, they assumed it would have an eager home-turf audience who were in on the joke. They also convinced Harvey and Bob Weinstein, who had put over $50 million into the trashy concept and needed a hit, having bitterly parted ways with Disney and Miramax – the company they founded – and set up anew as The Weinstein Company in Spring 2005.

'Me and Robert felt that people [in the US] had a little more of a concept of the history of double features and exploitation movies,' Tarantino admitted 12 years later. 'No, they didn't. At all. They had no idea what they were watching. It meant nothing to them, what we were doing. So that was a case of being a little too cool for school.'

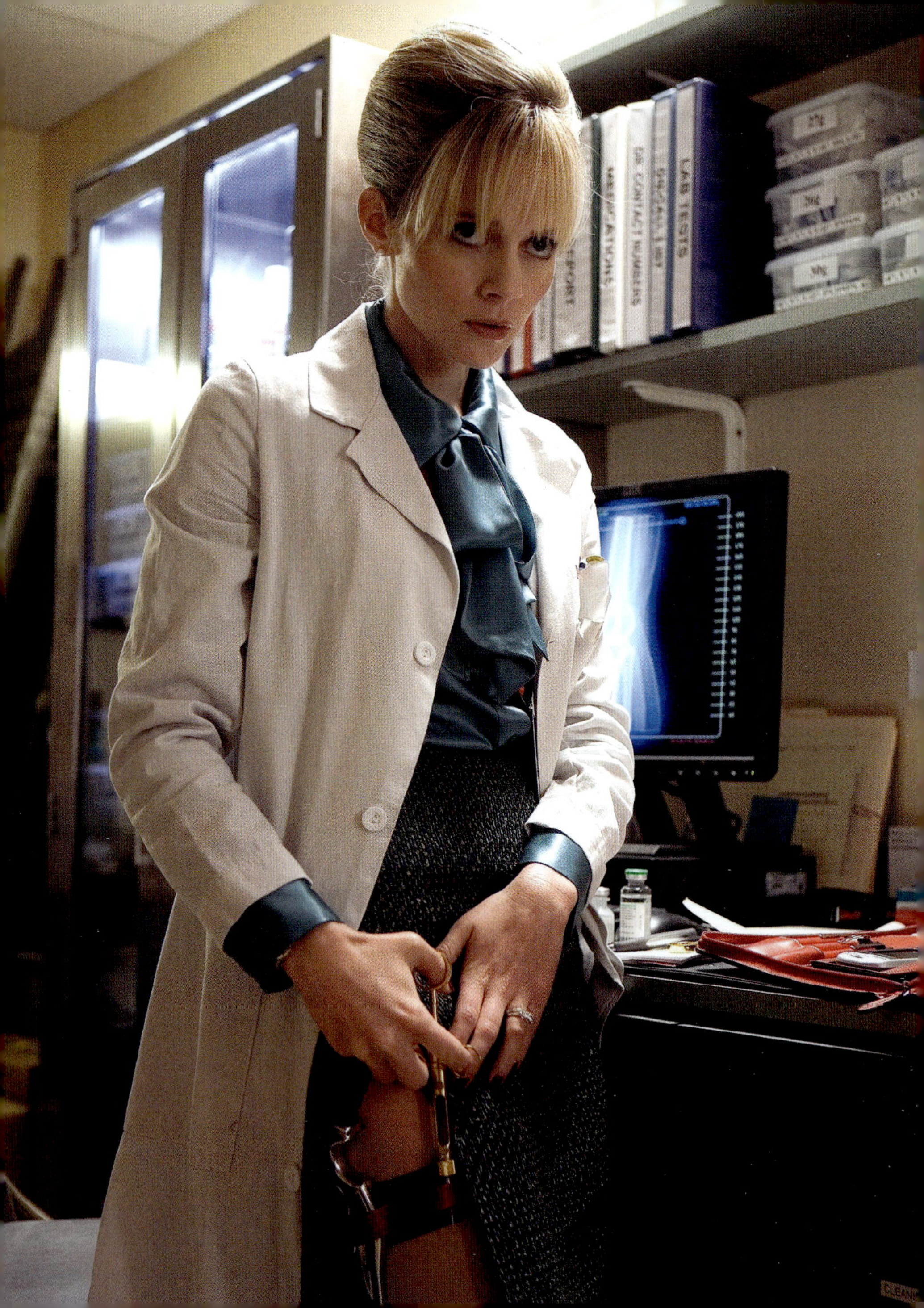
REPORT
DR CONTACT NUMBERS
KEEP A LIST
LAB TESTS

The film was a colossal flop, grossing only half of its budget. It was, Tarantino said, 'a bit of a shock to my confidence.'

Consequently, *Grindhouse* was withdrawn from distribution, and plans to release it in certain overseas markets (including the UK) were cancelled. Instead, longer versions of *Planet Terror* and *Death Proof* were put out separately, restoring all the material that Tarantino and Rodriguez had cut to make their double bill a relatively tight three hours. It was a rational commercial decision, but also a shame as it essentially invalidated each movie's raison d'être and left it exposed to scrutiny of a different tenor. Both *Death Proof* and *Planet Terror* (a John Carpenter-esque sci-fi horror with added gross-out elements and Tarantino on bit-part duties as 'Rapist #1', complete with a melting penis) had more charm as a shoulder-to-shoulder duo, with their considerably shorter running time. The fake trailers that nestled between them were also lost in the recalibration, despite being one of *Grindhouse*'s biggest treats.

Originally, Rodriguez and Tarantino had planned to make the trailers themselves, but in the end, Rodriguez provided only one, for a 'Mexploitation' action film starring Danny Trejo, titled *Machete*. (Which retrospectively turned out to be a real trailer: Rodriguez made *Machete* as a feature in 2010, and even did a sequel, *Machete Kills*.) The other trailers were provided by volunteer contributors eager to get in on the grungy fun. *Hostel* director Eli Roth (who appears in *Death Proof*) provided a trailer for *Thanksgiving*, a holiday-themed slasher that also evolved into a real Roth feature in 2023; while heavy metal musician-turned-

OPPOSITE: Marly Shelton as the syringe-wielding Dr Dakota Block in Robert Rodriguez's *Planet Terror*. Dr Block also makes a short guest appearance alongside Tarantino favourite Michael Parks in *Death Proof*.

horror-director Rob Zombie provided the brilliantly titled *Werewolf Women of the SS*. The best of the bunch was Edgar Wright's *Don't*, a haunted-house flick with an all-British cast (including singer Katie Melua) who never say anything, the conceit being that a US grindhouse distributor wouldn't want its audience realizing it was a UK production until they're actually watching the movie. There was also a fifth trailer added to a few Canadian prints, after Canadian first-time director Jason Eisener won a fake trailer contest organized by Rodriguez at the 2007 SXSW Festival. Titled *Hobo With a Shotgun*, that too was adapted into a full-length movie, which was released in 2011 and starred Rutger Hauer.

Unfortunately for Tarantino, even when *Death Proof* was released individually as a 127-minute standalone movie, it didn't perform well, grossing only $31 million worldwide. When it opened in the UK, he, along with a group of British friends that included producer Nira Park and directors Edgar Wright and Joe Cornish, snuck into a West End screening to see how it was going down. 'We walk in the theatre and there's about 13 people in there. On the opening 8.30 show,' Tarantino recalled. 'That was a rather humbling experience.' But, he added, 'we sat down and watched it and had a good time.' Like he once said, he made movies for himself, and everyone else was invited. If they didn't accept? Their loss.

As it happened, it was the last time so few would show up.

A RODRIGUEZ/TARANTINO DOUBLE FEATURE
GRINDHOUSE
THE LAST HOPE FOR HUMANITY... RESTS ON A HIGH-POWER MACHINE GUN!
PLANET TERROR
QUENTIN TARANTINO and ROBERT RODRIGUEZ are back!
But this time they're BACK to BACK!
Plus
These 8 women are about to meet 1 diabolical man!
KURT RUSSELL is "DEATH PROOF"
See!
TWO GREAT MOVIES FOR THE PRICE OF ONE!
TOGETHER IN ONE SMASH EXPLOSIVE SHOW
APRIL 6, 2007
TROUBLEMAKER STUDIOS
DIMENSION FILMS

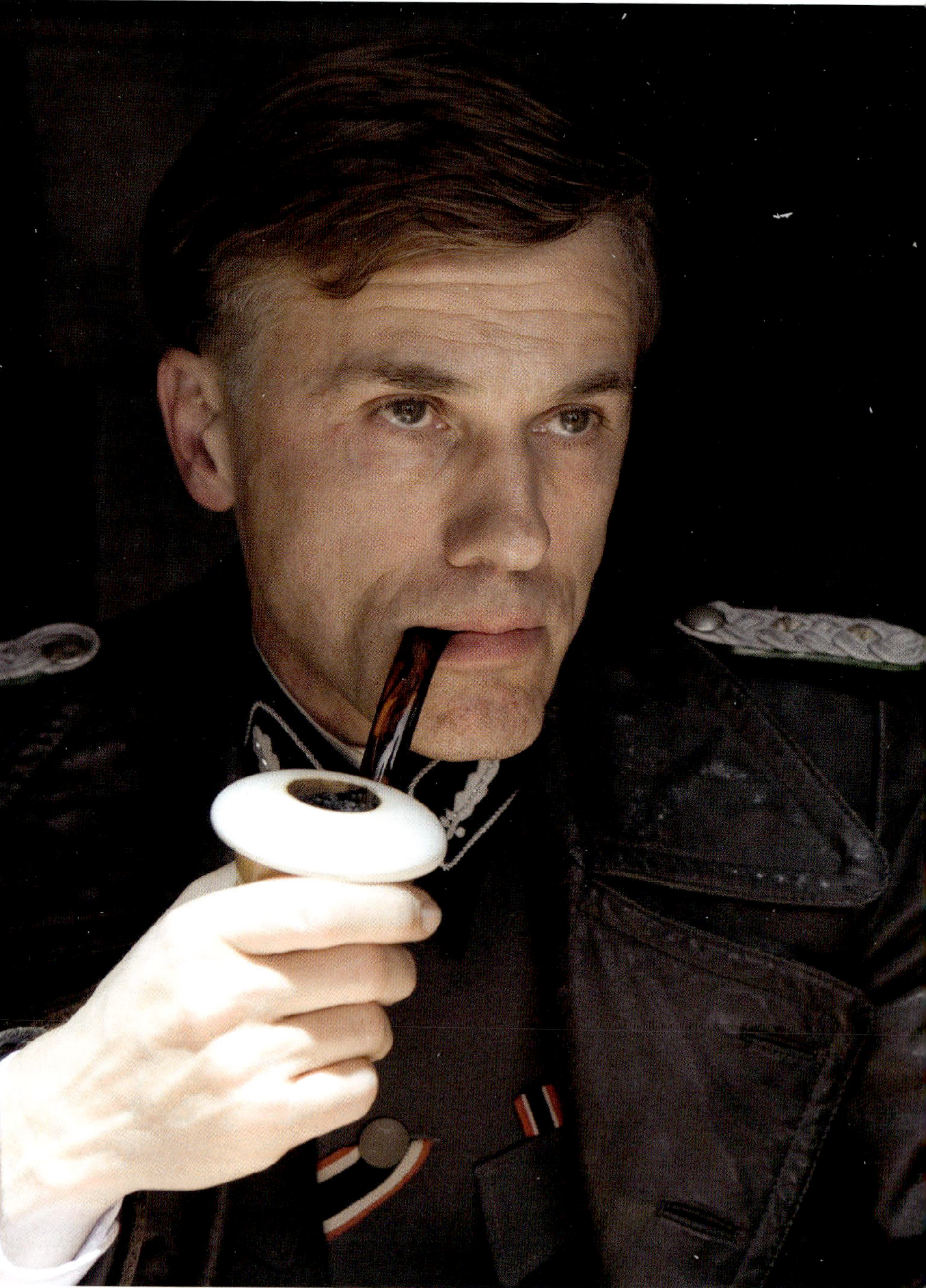

INGLOURIOUS BASTERDS
2009

The problem with Hollywood World War II movies, thought Tarantino, was they just weren't fun anymore. For the previous 30 years they had been, for the most part, gravely serious dramas, usually focused on the Holocaust and the victims of the war. He missed the robust, rip-roaring adventures of the Sixties: men-on-a-mission pictures like *The Dirty Dozen* and *Where Eagles Dare*, or PoW-breakout classic *The Great Escape*. Movies, he said, where 'there was no crime in telling a thrilling story.'

Tarantino had been wrestling with his own men-on-a-mission movie since 1998, but as it turned out, the final incarnation of *Inglourious Basterds* (he's refused to reveal the reason for the title's deliberate misspelling) would be less of a men-on-a-mission movie than Tarantino had originally intended. And, while it would certainly be more humorous than other recent World War II pictures (uncomfortably so, for some commentators), it would also turn out to be the director's most important film since *Pulp Fiction*. One that would propel him along a whole new trajectory. Contemporary culture wasn't enough of a plaything for Tarantino anymore. Now, he'd be messing with history.

In January 2008, Tarantino decided to take one more crack at his unwieldy, novelistic sprawl of a script to see if he could reshape it into something he could feasibly shoot as a movie. He kept only the opening two chapters, the first of which introduced Hans Landa – the charming, articulate and terrifying Austrian SS officer known as the 'Jew Hunter' – and French-Jewish avenger Shosanna Dreyfus, who escapes Landa's clutches after an intense interrogation scene at a dairy farm culminates with the murder of her entire family. Tarantino also, of course, retained the Basterds – a squad of Jewish-American soldiers under hillbilly commando Lieutenant Aldo Raine, aka 'Aldo the Apache' – who are dropped behind enemy lines in 1944 Vichy France to terrorize the Germans

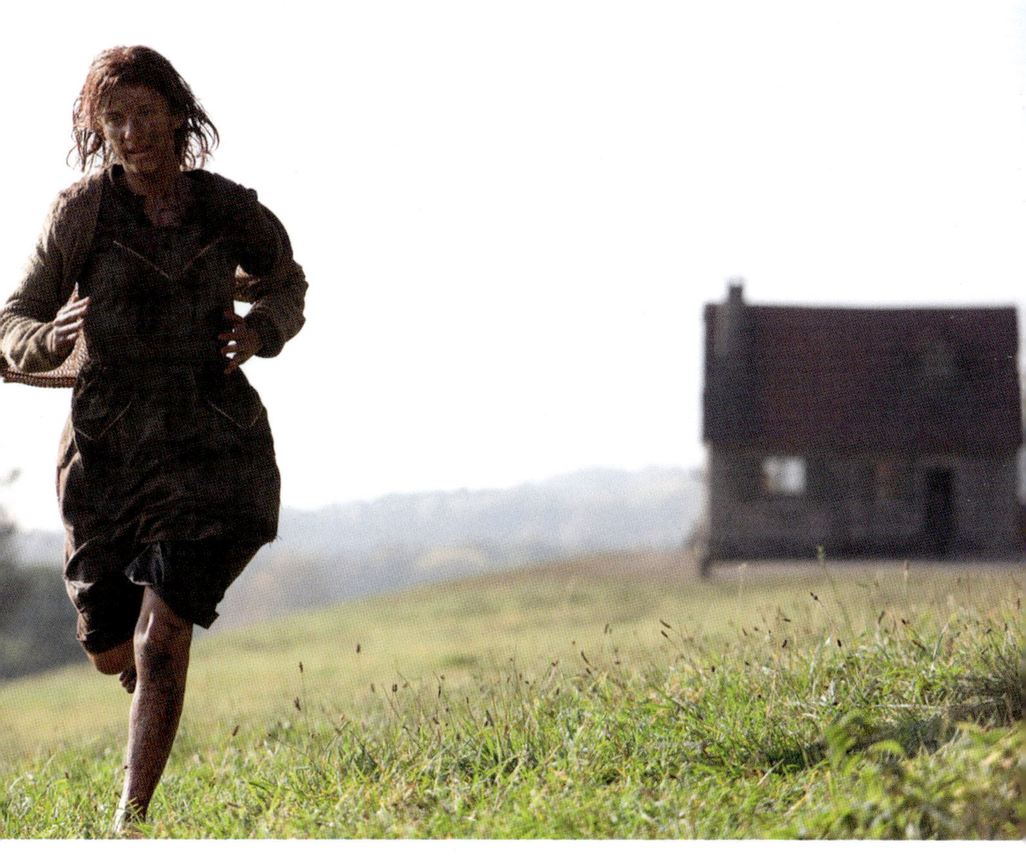

by scalping every man they kill. 'Holocaust movies always have Jews as victims,' said Tarantino. 'I want to see something different. Let's see Germans that are scared of Jews.'

Shosanna, meanwhile, is a resourceful survivor who prevails by keeping her cool in tricky situations. The key to her retribution is the Parisian cinema she inherits. It becomes the venue for the high-profile premiere of *Nation's Pride*, a Nazi propaganda film about a 'heroic' German sharpshooter, and therefore both the

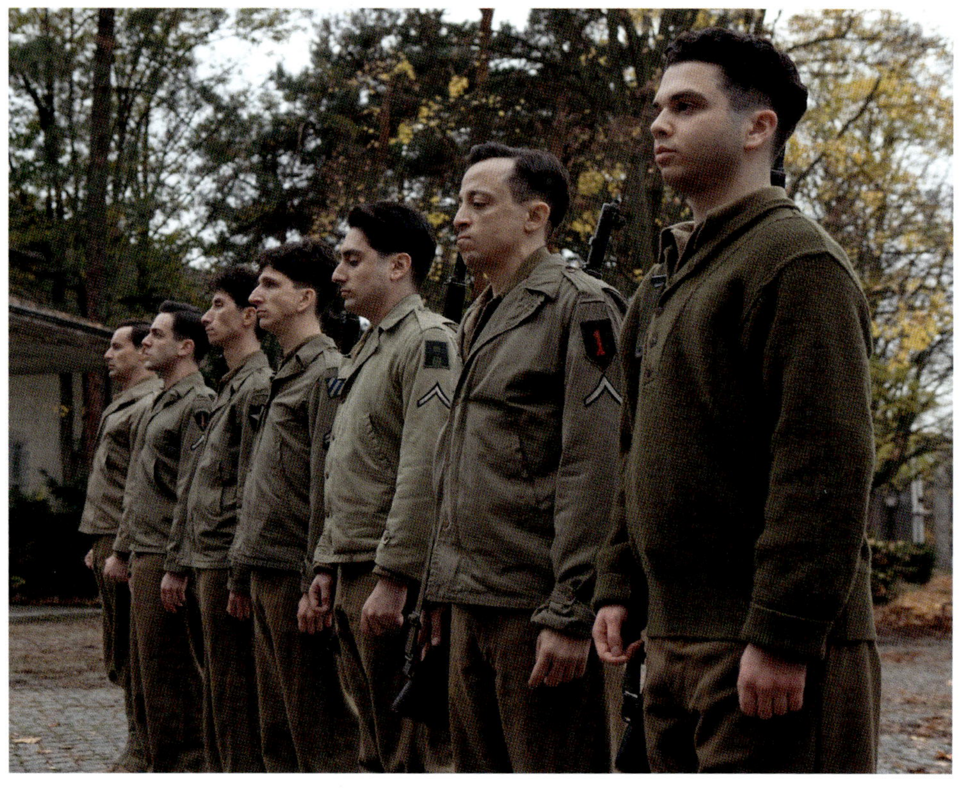

ABOVE: New recruits for the Basterds, a troop of Jewish avengers notably lacking in big-name actors.

ultimate target of the Basterds' campaign and the focus of Shosanna's revenge.

Tarantino shifted from watching Sixties and Seventies men-on-a-mission movies to films made during the conflict, by both sides. He heavily researched German wartime cinema, and became fascinated by Joseph Goebbels' role as a studio head: Goebbels, he learned, had his hand in nearly 800 films. While writing a scene between Shosanna and the aforementioned fictional sharpshooter, Frederick Zoller (who plays himself in the film based on his exploits), Tarantino had the characters discussing

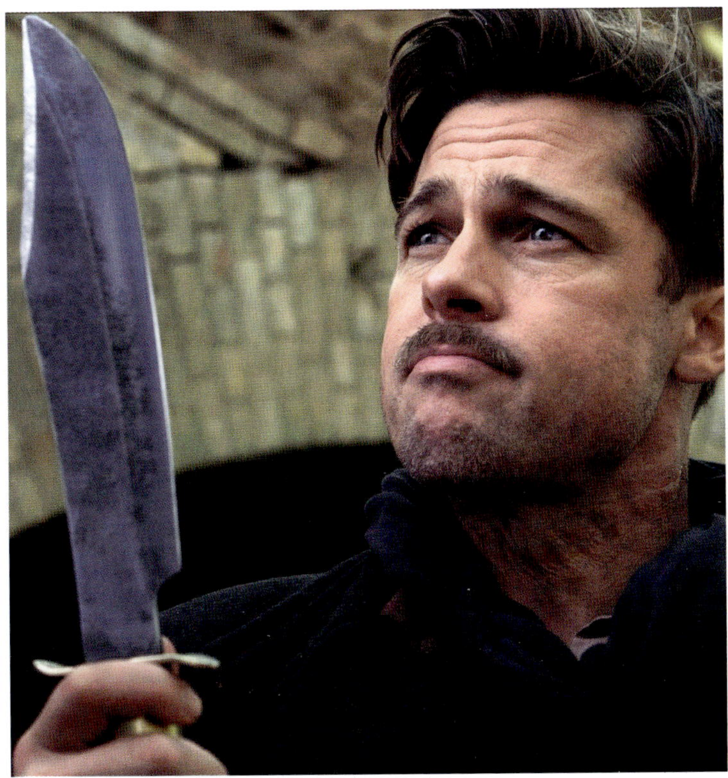

ABOVE: ...Other than Brad Pitt, of course, who played their commanding officer, Lt Aldo Raine.

G W Pabst and Leni Riefenstahl. When he put his pen down, it hit him: 'Man, I go to do a World War II movie and it ends up being a love letter to cinema!'

Partly as a result of the movie becoming less of a men-on-a-mission narrative, and partly because he wanted the Basterds to be authentically Jewish, Tarantino chose not to stack the titular hit squad with stars. The two biggest names among them were B J Novak from workplace sitcom *The Office* and Tarantino's friend and one-time mentee Eli Roth, whom he gave the role of Donnie

Donowitz, 'the Bear-Jew', who bludgeons Nazis to death with a Louisville Slugger. (Roth was also his 'Jewish fact-checker' during the rewrite.) However, Tarantino did alight on a bona fide A-lister for the part of their ruthless leader, Aldo Raine, a gruff warrior who likes to carve swastikas into the foreheads of those he doesn't kill, and for whom the phrase 'war crime' has little meaning when you're dealing with Nazis. 'I never feel like I need a star,' said Tarantino of his decision to cast Brad Pitt, one of Hollywood's biggest names. 'Brad is an actor I treated just like the other actors, who happens to be this huge movie star. But he is such perfect casting for this character that if Brad Pitt wasn't famous, I'd have lobbied for him to have this role.'

For the numerous non-American characters, Tarantino was determined to cast actors who could play their own nationality, and therefore converse in their native language. German and French performers speaking accented English felt too 'quaint', he said. This decision led Tarantino to a strong ensemble of European actors with varying degrees of overseas fame. Among the most recognizable were Diane Kruger, German star of the *National Treasure* movies, as actor-spy Bridget von Hammersmark; German-Irish actor Michael Fassbender as English film critic turned commando Archie Hicox, whose oddly accented German becomes a tense plot point during the film's excruciatingly suspenseful fourth chapter 'Operation Kino'; and Daniel Brühl, who took the role of the repellently entitled Zoller. For Shosanna, Tarantino found Mélanie Laurent, a 25-year-old Parisian who had been acting since she was 16.

The most crucial role, however, was Landa, the lead villain. The diabolically intelligent SS officer had emerged not merely as Tarantino's favourite character in the film, but also, he maintained, 'one of the greatest characters I have ever written and one of the greatest characters I will ever write.' Early on, he'd imagined

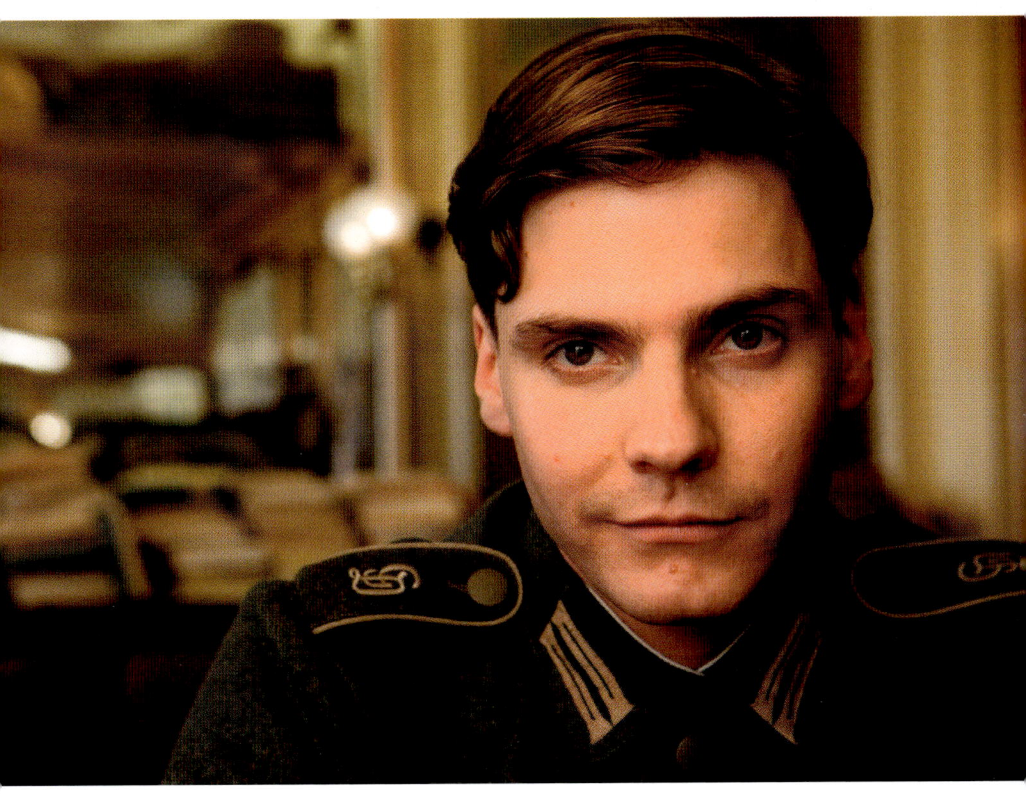

ABOVE: Daniel Brühl as German sharpshooter-turned-film-star Frederick Zoller, Tarantino's Nazi answer to Audie Murphy.

Leonardo DiCaprio in the role. But by the time he was ready to cast, he realized he needed an actor whose native language was German and could speak fluent English, French and Italian.

As the German auditions continued and no such actor presented himself, Tarantino started to worry. Had he written a character – one whose every scene was crucial – that was unplayable? He was running out of time. On the Tuesday of a week that was scheduled to end with distributor Universal Pictures officially picking up the production, Tarantino decided that if he

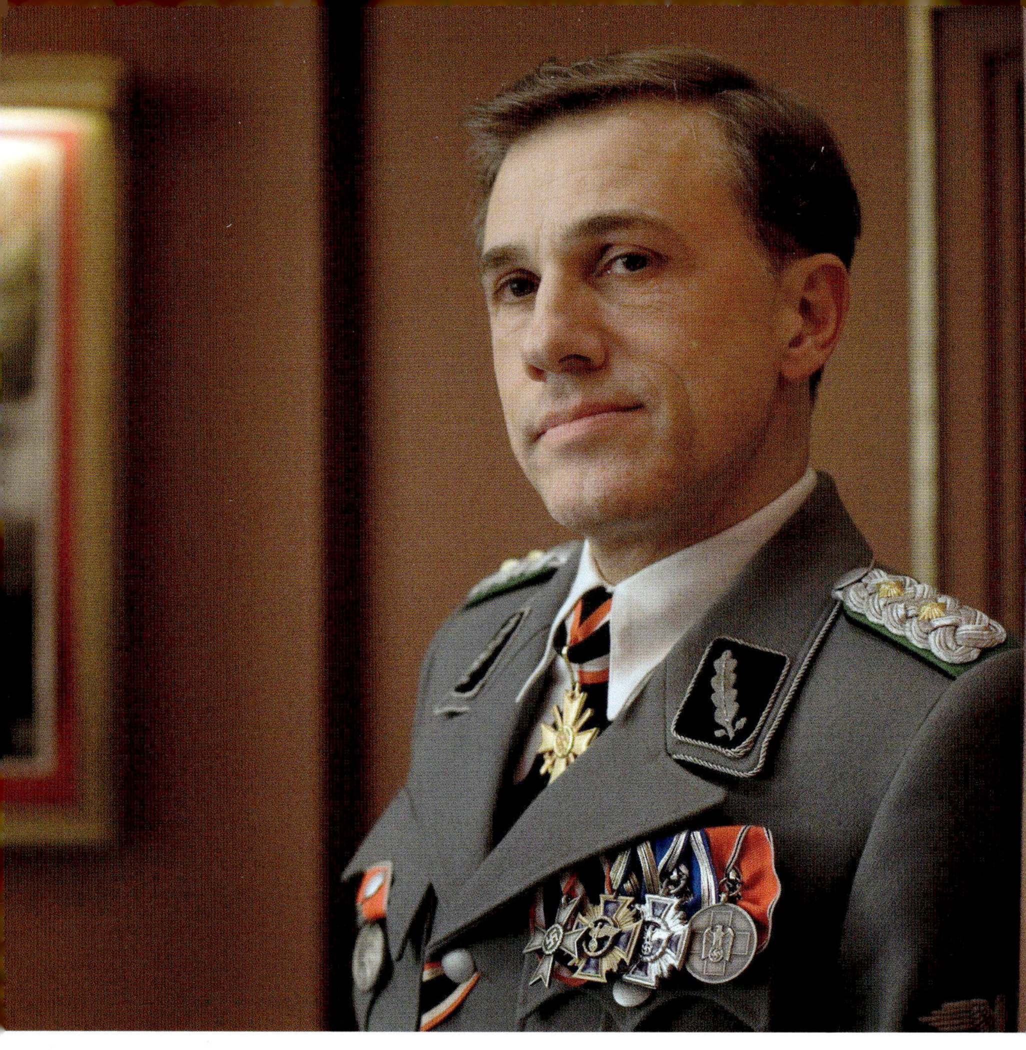

didn't have his Landa by Thursday, he would pull the plug. He called Lawrence Bender, German casting director Simone Bär and his agent Mike Simpson and told them, 'I just don't want to make the movie if we can't find the perfect Landa.'

Rather than panic, Bender calmly told Tarantino that, in that case, they'd spend the next two days doing nothing but searching for their Landa. If they still didn't find him, they would call it a day.

On Wednesday, just 24 hours before the plug-pulling deadline, an Austrian-born TV actor came in to read. Tarantino had never heard of him. Indeed, his English-speaking roles didn't get more prominent than the part of the villainous 'Weak Moustache' in 'The League of Hirsute Gentlemen', a sketch in 1995 British TV comedy series *The All New Alexei Sayle Show*. But, recalled Tarantino, 'the minute he read the first big sequence, me and Lawrence just looked at each other and we knew we were making the movie.'

Christoph Waltz is a revelation in *Inglourious Basterds*. With his sinister, crisp demeanour and verbosely theatrical sleuthing, he dominates every scene he appears in, whether talking a French farmer (Denis Ménochet) into betraying the Jewish neighbours hidden beneath his floorboards, or eloquently negotiating his surrender in a surprising final-act turnaround.

At the 2009 Cannes Film Festival, during his trilingual acceptance speech for the Best Actor award (almost a year before he won the Best Supporting Actor Oscar), Waltz told Tarantino: 'You gave me my vocation back'. This was in response to a comment the director had made earlier during the festival, where the film had its world premiere. In a statement that was no less true, Tarantino said that when Waltz came in and read for Landa, 'he gave me my movie back.'

Having spent 10 years writing *Inglourious Basterds*, Tarantino shot the $70 million movie in only 10 weeks – the same amount of time it took to make the $9 million *Pulp Fiction* back in 1994. The aim was to have it ready in time for Cannes, which he would pull off with aplomb with the considerable help of editor Sally Menke, who sadly died the following year, making this their final collaboration.

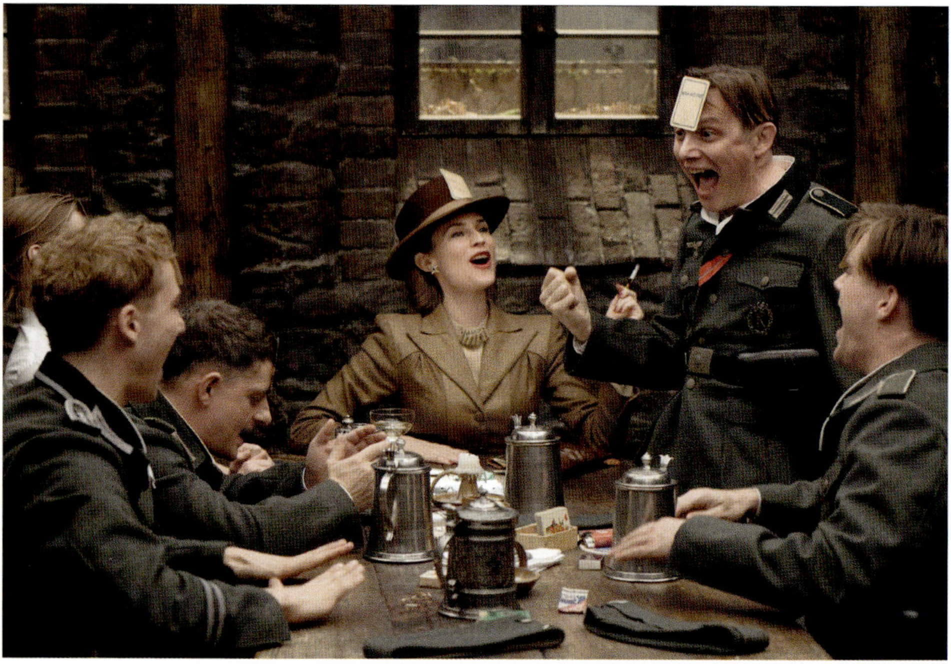

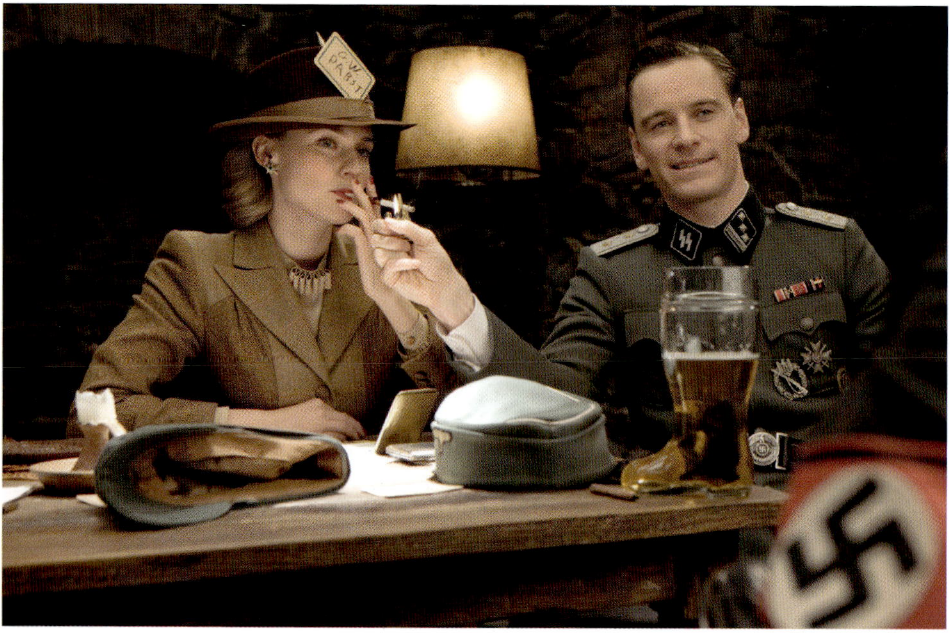

G. W.
PABST

As Roth recalled, *Inglourious Basterds* was 'like a military operation. Quentin was like a general on set. He was very serious and focused. We were there to make a movie for the love of movies, and the fun came in getting our shots right.'

As with *Kill Bill*, Tarantino chose to make his film primarily outside of the United States and based the production in Studio Babelsberg near Berlin. Despite some location work around Germany and in Paris, the film was mostly shot on stage, with its three extended, dialogue-driven set-pieces taking place in interiors: the opening scene in the LaPadite farm, the cellar-bar rendezvous in the 'Operation Kino' chapter and the climactic blow-out at the *Nation's Pride* premiere.

This gave the film a different texture to other action war movies, and defied any expectations, stoked by its men-on-a-mission promise, that it would be a battle-driven affair. 'I wasn't interested in dealing with American and German soldiers on battlefields fighting each other,' Tarantino said. 'I was more interested in the human dramas that can happen.' He focused on slowly building suspense through dialogue before allowing the pressure to burst into sudden violence, as it does with the Landa-ordered slaughter of the Dreyfus family at the end of Chapter One.

For the mid-movie 'Operation Kino' segment, he pushed things further than he ever had before. Here, Hicox and two of the Basterds meet von Hammersmark in a bar that not only turns out to be located underground (making backup access difficult), but is also unexpectedly filled with German troops, celebrating one of their number becoming a father. As they play a Guess Who?

drinking game, the incumbent Germans' intrusions on Hicox and von Hammersmark's conversation shift from drunkenly impolite, to worrisome, to deadly. Especially when the oddness of Hicox's accent becomes a topic of discussion that is joined by a previously unseen SS officer (August Diehl).

To Tarantino, the scene worked like 'a reduced *Reservoir Dogs*, but with Nazis and in German'. After writing it, even he couldn't quite believe how long it was. 'Jesus Christ,' he thought, 'it's 25 fucking minutes! Can I just stop the movie and have a 25-minute scene in a basement, like this little one-act play?' Then he remembered a criticism, levelled at him after *Pulp Fiction*, that he was too enamoured of minutia to ever become a master of suspense. Now he could prove them wrong. 'The length is making [the scene] more suspenseful,' he realized. Tarantino compared the suspense with a rubber band that's stretching tighter and tighter as the scene plays out. 'The longer I stretch the rubber band and dare it to break, the more you're waiting for it to break and the more unnerving it is,' he said. 'And then – snap!'

When it snaps in the La Louisiane bar, the scene ends with a flurry of gunfire that leaves only one character, von Hammersmark, living. But when the band snaps in the final act, as the Basterds infiltrate the premiere and Shosanna executes her plan to burn her cinema down using a pile of nitrate film hidden behind the screen, it results in an almighty, history-changing conflagration.

By this point Shosanna has been unexpectedly and disappointingly shot to death by Zoller. But she appears on the screen in a previously filmed segment spliced into *Nation's Pride*, shimmering and spectral, and tells the panicking audience: 'You are all going to die, and I want you to look deep into the face of the Jew that is going to do it!'

The symbolic power of the scene, which also features Roth's Donowitz and his fellow Basterd Omar (Omar Doom) firing indiscriminately into the premiere audience with machine-guns, was hardly lost on the film's own viewers. Here was a Jewish person using the literal power of film to incinerate Nazis. 'Via these film prints and via her cinema, Shosanna is intending to put the Nazis in an oven and create her own final solution,' said Tarantino. Except in a twist that few saw coming, she and the Basterds were killing not only random fictional Nazis, but the leadership of the Third Reich: Goebbels, Hermann Göring, Martin Bormann and Adolf Hitler – the first real people to appear as characters in a Tarantino film (along with Winston Churchill in the briefing scene). In one explosive swoop, Shosanna and co were ending the war a year early.

The further adventures of Hans Landa

After *Inglourious Basterds*, Tarantino could never quite get Hans Landa out of his head. Years later, he would reveal he'd imagined what life would be like for Landa during his post-war retirement in Nantucket. He'd wear a wig to cover up his swastika scar, and he'd also, rather horribly, be known as a hero, due to his involvement in bringing down Adolf Hitler. 'I do like the idea of writing a series of Hans Landa mysteries,' said Tarantino in 2019. 'So it's, like, 20 years after World War II and a murder happens on the island, and he's the detective [who] figures out who the murderer is.' In all seriousness, Tarantino pointed out, it wouldn't really be something he'd ever write. . . At least, not until he's much older.

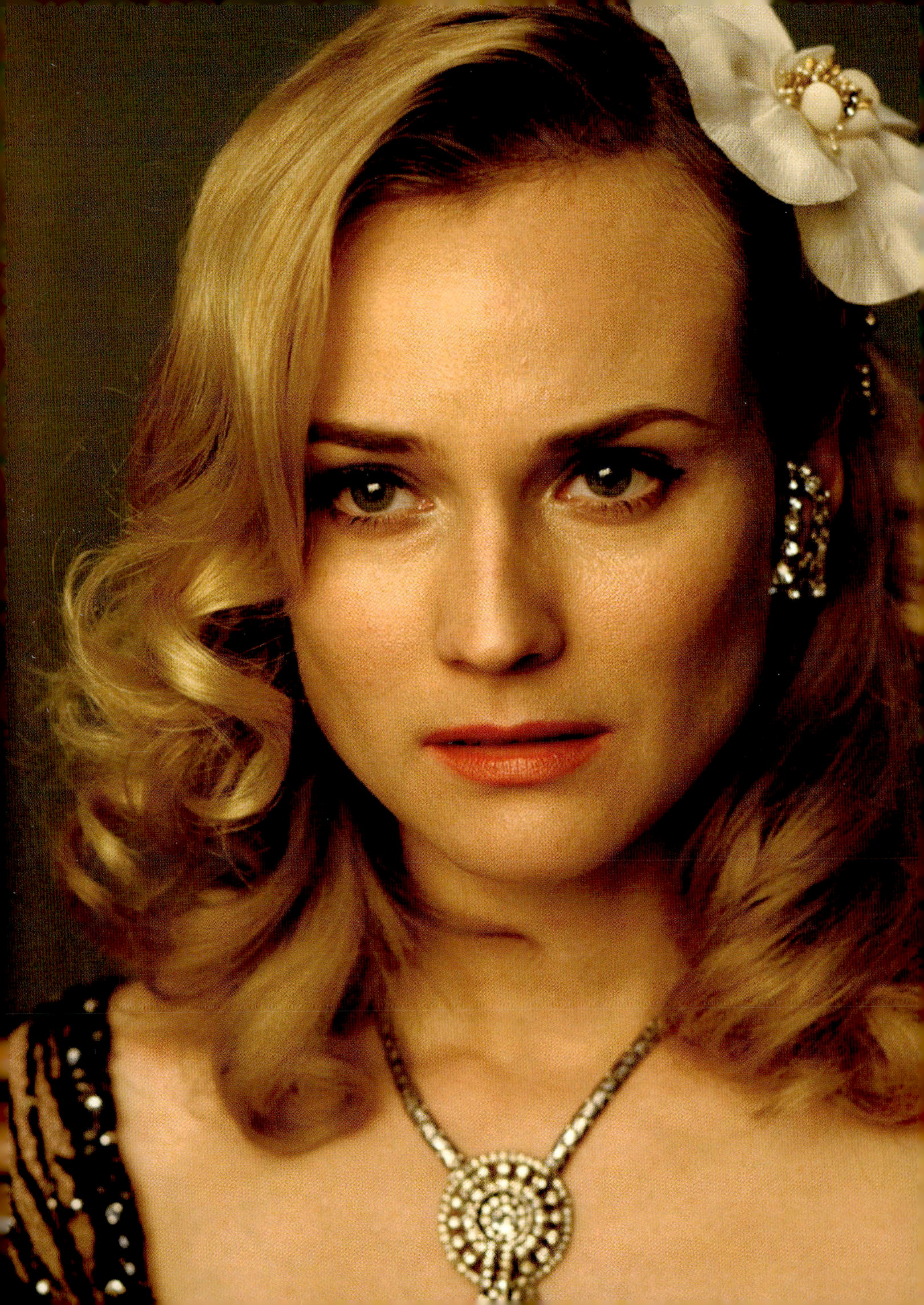

Tarantino had not intended to rewrite history when he started on *Inglourious Basterds*. That came from his characters, he explained. Usually, he let them follow their own paths, and ignored the 'roadblocks' of narrative convention that other writers would usually place in front of their characters. But for the first time in his career, his creations were meeting a roadblock he felt he couldn't remove: history. How could Donny Donowitz shoot Hitler and his cronies to death in a Parisian cinema in 1944 when everyone knew Hitler took his own life in a bunker a year later? Then Tarantino looked at it from Donny, Aldo, Shosanna and Landa's points of view. 'My characters don't know they're part of history,' he saw. 'My characters don't know there are things they can't do.' So why stop them? 'My characters have changed the course of the war. That didn't actually happen because my characters didn't exist. But if they had existed, everything that happens in *Inglourious Basterds* is quite possible.'

Tarantino's counter-factual audacity did not go down well with some critics. David Denby of *The New Yorker* described the movie as 'ridiculous and appallingly insensitive – a Louisville Slugger applied to the head of anyone who has ever taken the Nazis, the war or the Resistance seriously.' Many commentators took issue with the way the film portrayed Jews being as brutal and sadistic as the Nazis in an atrocity-committing free-for-all. Others simply found Tarantino's morally simplistic, violence-fuelled alternative reality offensive.

In response, Tarantino shrugged that he was simply being true to his characters. 'It is a method,' he said. 'I actually make it a point not to apply morality to my [characters].' While he confessed to setting up 'this nice little fantasy, masturbatory kind of thing of

OPPOSITE: Diane Kruger as German actress/Allied spy Bridget von Hammersmark, moments before her brutal death at Landa's hands.

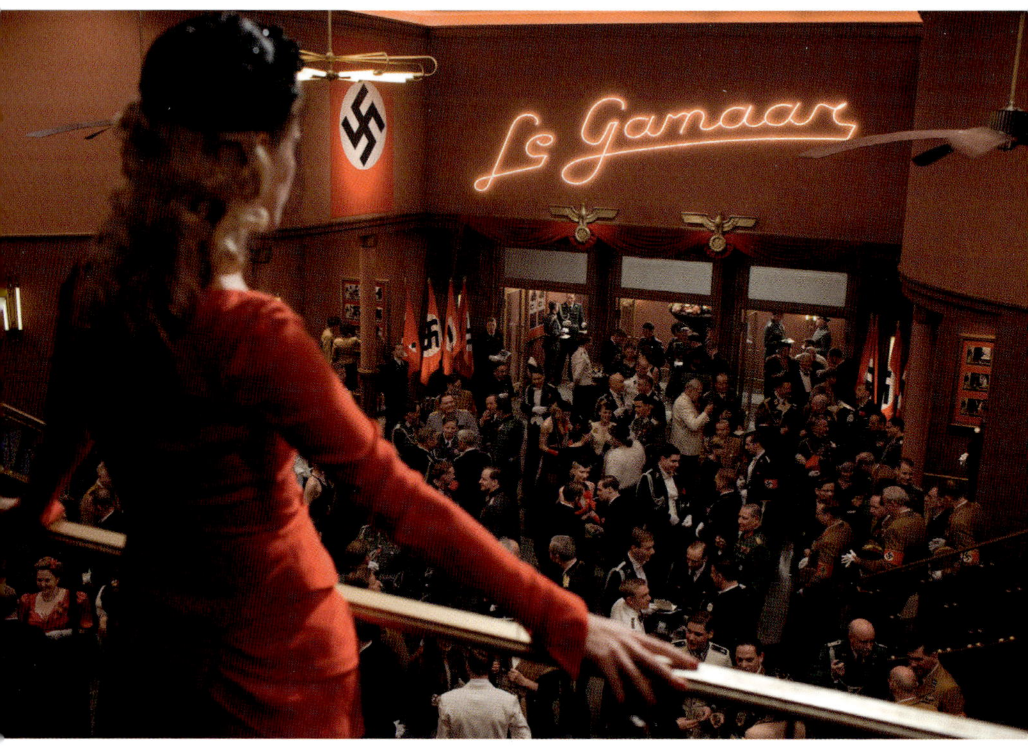

OPPOSITE: Shosanna looks over the crowd at the *Nation's Pride* premiere, hours before she'll have them all burned to death.

Jews turning the tables on the Nazis,' he also tried to make those characters complicated, citing the scene where a German sergeant refuses to give up intel to Raine, despite an attempt to intimidate him with Donowitz. . .who then, as threatened, stoves his head in. 'Under any criteria of bravery in the face of [the] enemy,' Tarantino said, the German sergeant 'passes the test'. You can't help but admire the guy, he insisted. 'And by the way, if he was a cringing coward when Donny the Bear-Jew comes out there, it would be a lot easier to have fun at his expense.'

Tarantino's playful disregard for the facts of history is

essentially a less literal symptom of his belief in the power of cinema than the use of nitrate film as a mass-murder weapon. Similar to how he could effectively bring Vincent Vega back to life through the 'magic' of editing in *Pulp Fiction*, here he could graphically stage the righteous execution of the Führer – whom Donowitz riddles with bullets twice, for good measure – rather than letting him escape justice, as he did in reality. For Tarantino, nurtured by cinema as a kid and defined by cinema as an adult, the movies were more dependable and satisfying than reality. Why let historical accuracy ruin that?

The audience seemed to agree. *Inglourious Basterds* was Tarantino's most commercially successful film to date, reaping over $321 million worldwide. It was widely regarded as his best work since *Pulp Fiction*.

In the film's final scene, Raine confronts Landa. Having made a deal with the Allied top brass that makes him complicit in the war-ending cinema massacre, Landa believes he's scot-free. He's secured amnesty, and a cosy repose on Nantucket Island. But Raine just can't let him walk away unscathed. He pins Landa to the ground and, in a signature move, carves a swastika into the screaming Standartenführer's forehead.

The film ends with a shot of Raine and B J Novak's Utivich from Landa's prone POV, as Pitt delivers the final line: 'You know something, Utivich? I think this just might be my masterpiece.'

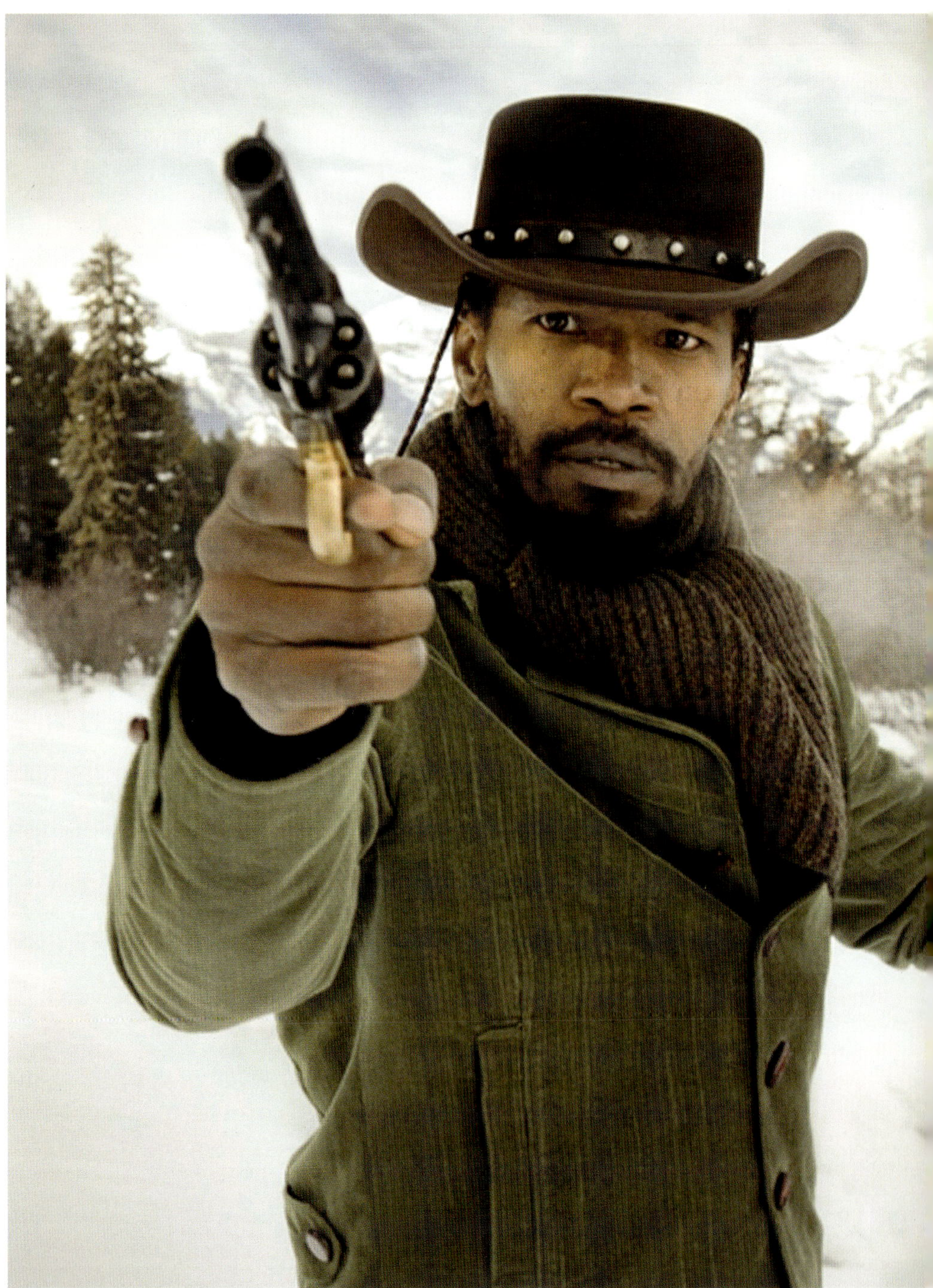

DJANGO UNCHAINED
2012

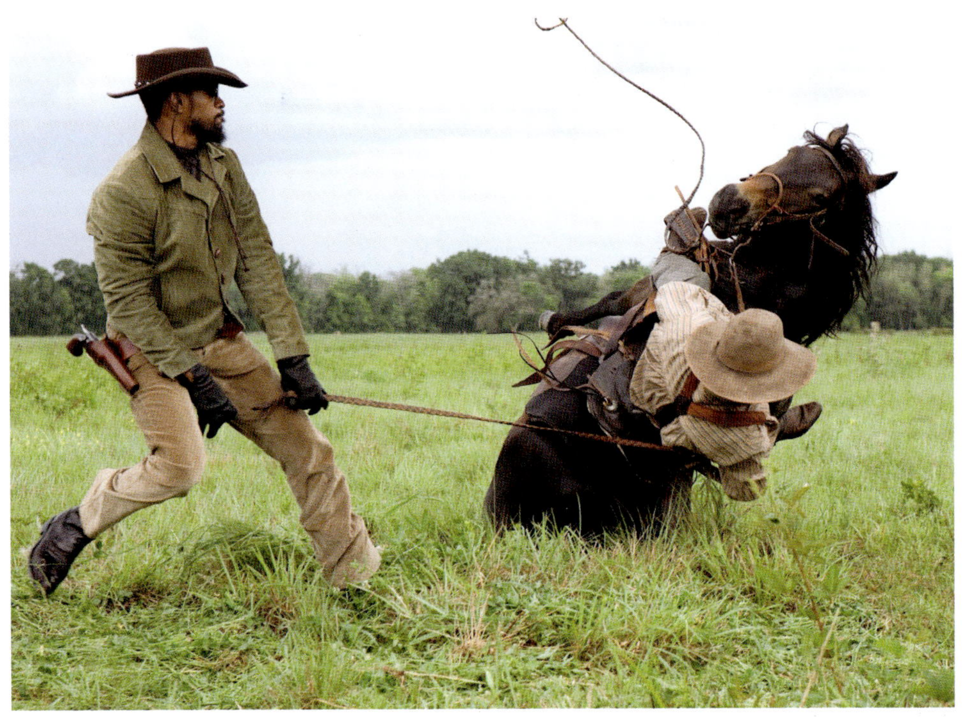

In late April 2011, after giving Samuel L Jackson the script for *Django Unchained*, Tarantino called the actor. There was something he needed to broach. Something awkward. Jackson had been expecting to play the title role of the gunslinging slave-turned-bounty hunter, but by the time the script was finished, Tarantino had decided the character needed to be 15 years younger. Rather than briefly telling Django's origin story and jumping forward in time to the post-Civil War West, as he'd initially intended, the film now focused on the origin story, and was firmly set in the antebellum South.

'As you can see, I kind of went a different way with the character,' Tarantino told Jackson over the phone.

'Yeah, I noticed that,' the former Jules and Ordell replied.

'So what do you think about Stephen?'

Stephen is the story's most problematic character. Though a slave himself, he is the spiteful head of the household in Candie Land, the Mississippi plantation lorded over by Southern gent Calvin Candie, who also owns Django's wife, Broomhilda. As an enforcer of the status quo, Stephen is complicit in the atrocities committed against his fellow slaves. In fact, it is thanks to his interference that Django's gambit to buy his wife's freedom goes so wrong.

'Do you have any problem playing him?' Tarantino asked.

'Do I have any problem playing the most despicable Black motherfucker in the history of the world?' Jackson responded. 'No, I ain't got no problem with that.'

Django Unchained was Tarantino's most controversial directorial work to date. It tackled one of the most painful, shameful aspects of US history, but did so within the framework of, well, a Tarantino movie. Like *Inglourious Basterds*, its deadly serious subject matter was handled with style, humour and hyper-real violence.

The seed was sown many years earlier, when Tarantino met filmmaker Reginald Hudlin (*House Party*, *Boomerang*) at an Oscar party in early 1998. They talked about Steven Spielberg's *Amistad*, which was nominated for a few awards, and Hudlin revealed he didn't like the movie. 'It was five minutes of slave revolt and 85 minutes of trial,' he explained, 'and I wanna see the reverse'.

Over the years, the idea of making the slavery-themed movie Hudlin would have preferred to see marinated in Tarantino's mind. Then, after completing *Inglourious Basterds*, he started writing an essay on Italian director Sergio Corbucci, including his 1966 film *Django*, a cult spaghetti Western so vicious it was banned in the United Kingdom until 1993.

OPPOSITE: Jamie Foxx's Django brings justice to the Old South, spaghetti Western-style.

The New Beverly Cinema

For most of his life, Tarantino loved going to the New Beverly Cinema on 7165 Beverly Blvd in Los Angeles. When it put on *Reservoir Dogs* every midnight for six months, he said it was 'better than getting an Oscar.' So, when the theatre was under threat of being shut down by developers after the death of its owner Sherman Torgan in 2007, Tarantino came to the rescue, buying the building and becoming the New Beverly's landlord. But his involvement didn't end there. In 2014, he became actively involved in programming alongside Sherman's son Mark, establishing Friday night midnight shows of his own movies, and providing prints from his personal collection.

'Corbucci had the most brutal, violent, slickest and surreal version of the West imaginable,' said Tarantino. Which, according to his analysis, was influenced by the director's experience of life under Mussolini. When Corbucci's bad guys took over a town it was like 'a Nazi occupation', Tarantino thought. He wondered what the American equivalent would be to this 'fascist-led bleak, barren, brutal, violent surreal West,' and decided it was 'being a slave in the antebellum South.' Now he saw he could tell his slave story in the style of Corbucci's *Django*. It could be something to 'give Black American males a Western hero that would actually be empowering and actually pay back blood for blood,' he thought. It wouldn't be treated as a 'big issue movie', but as a 'genre film', which would 'deal with everything that America has never dealt with because it's ashamed of it.'

Ever since *Reservoir Dogs*, Tarantino had been stealing from spaghetti Westerns, whether echoing their style and tropes, or lifting music from their scores. Now he could finally make an entire spaghetti Western. Except, being set in 1858 and mostly in Mississippi, *Django Unchained* pre-dates the Western era by seven years and is located far south of the frontier. In which case,

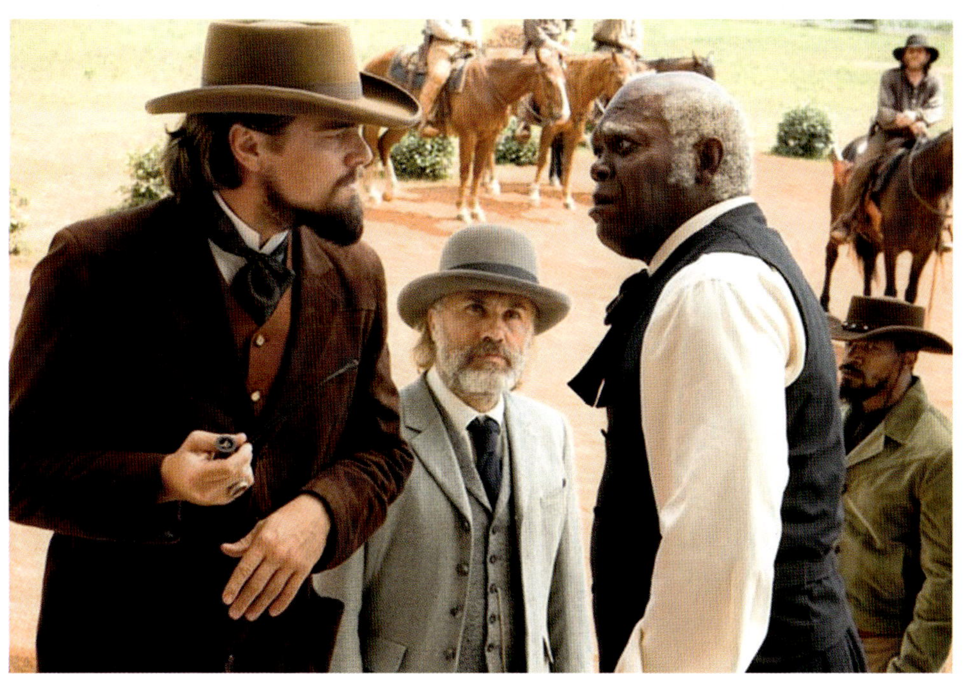

ABOVE: Leonardo DiCaprio and Samuel L Jackson make a great villainous double act, as Calvin Candie and his household head, Stephen.

Tarantino decided, it is a new genre: the 'Southern'. Not that that stopped him from taking the name of Corbucci's lead character and giving it to his own blood-spilling anti-hero.

Having necessarily ruled out Jackson for the now-younger lead role, Tarantino did not have a particular actor in mind. He approached Will Smith (who turned him down) and considered *The Wire*'s Michael K Williams, but in the end settled on Jamie Foxx: 'He just really understood what I was trying to do,' said Tarantino. 'He wanted to live in a world where *Django Unchained* already existed.' In contrast, the co-lead role of German bounty hunter Dr King Schultz was written with Christoph Waltz in mind.

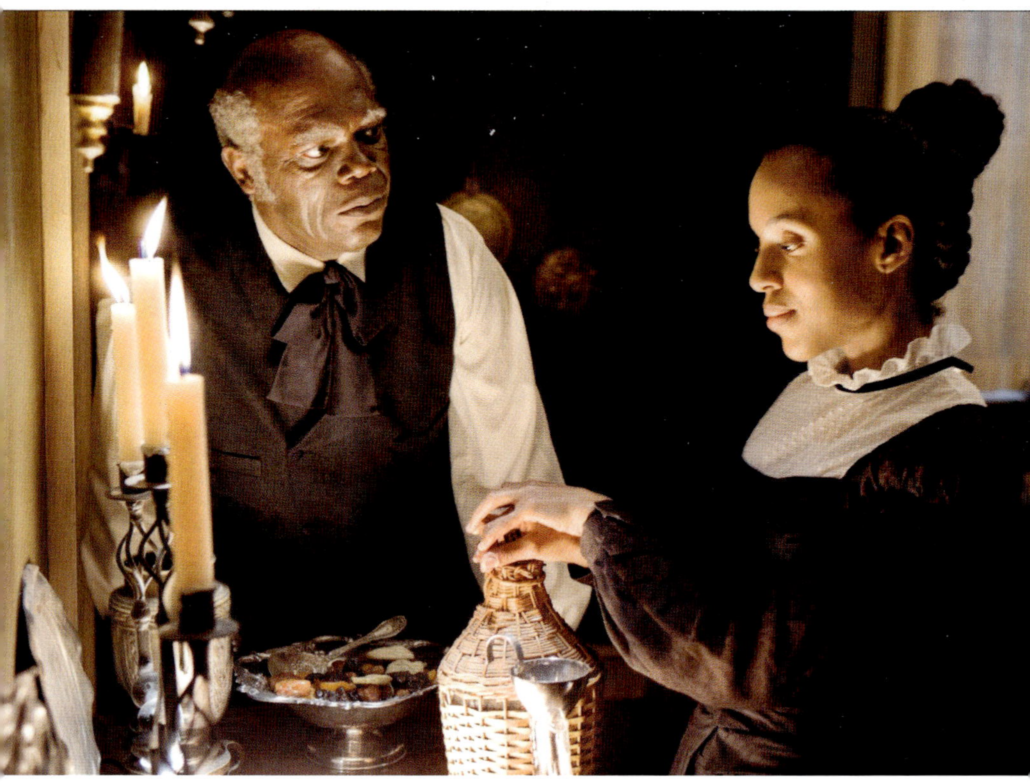

Having discovered him for *Inglourious Basterds* and realized Waltz 'sings' his dialogue better than anyone else, Tarantino felt like he had to have him in there somewhere. During the early part of the film, when Django is first freed and starts learning the bounty-hunting trade, he is effectively King's sidekick; something that Foxx pushed against in rehearsals until Tarantino took him aside. 'We don't have a story if Django is already this magnificent heroic figure who just happens to be in chains,' he said. 'You gotta grow into the jacket.'

One can hardly blame Foxx. Once again, Waltz makes a huge impact, this time in a heroic role that takes him from being a sure-footed, sharp-witted fast-talker to a man churned up and deeply

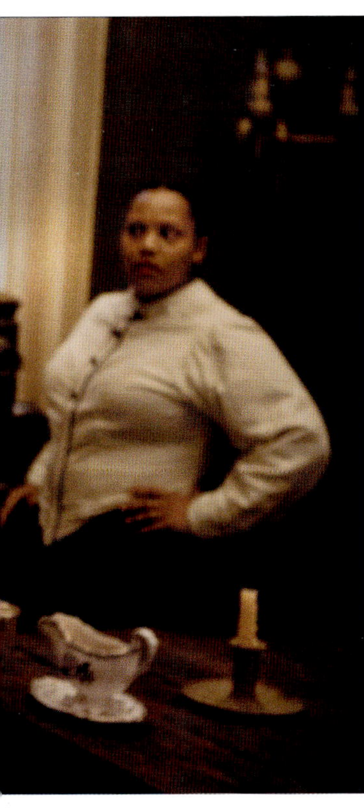

ABOVE: Stephen casts his suspicious eye on Broomhilda (Kerry Washington). In the script, Tarantino described Stephen as 'like the characters Basil Rathbone would play in swashbucklers'.

distressed by the moral repugnance of the antebellum South – to the degree that he'd rather die than shake a slave-owner's hand.

Kerry Washington is no less impressive as Broomhilda, the 'princess' who must be rescued from Candie's 'circle of hellfire', according to the German-legend parallel that Schultz lays out for Django. She must suffer the movie's most difficult and distressing scenes, such as when she is tortured in a hot box, and when she is whipped. Washington suffered nightmares about her scenes in the coffin-like box, during which she was bitten by spiders. 'I was concerned for my sanity,' she recalled. The whipping scene, meanwhile, was, 'very disturbing,' Tarantino said. Washington chose to forego a double and was hit for real with a nylon stunt whip. 'Kerry dug deep in herself to give a true human representation of what that must be like.'

Another actor who went above and beyond in their performance was Leonardo DiCaprio as Candie. Even though he'd once been in Tarantino's mind for Hans Landa, DiCaprio wasn't someone he'd imagined as Candie, being much younger than he'd written the character. But, having obtained the script, DiCaprio approached Tarantino and made a bid for the role. On reflection, Tarantino decided DiCaprio would work perfectly as a 'petulant boy emperor' version of the villain, like Caligula or King Louis XIV. Famously, during the filming of the dinner scene where Candie angrily discovers that Django and Schultz are not the Mandingo-buyers they claim to be, DiCaprio struck the table, accidentally cutting his hand open on a broken glass. Remarkably, he stayed in character as his blood dripped onto the dinnerware. Tarantino quietly kept rolling until the scene ended and the crew broke out in applause.

DiCaprio's wound and Washington's hardships were two of the most pronounced symptoms of a relentless and difficult shoot. As the first of Tarantino's films to be shot extensively on rural locations, *Django Unchained* brought with it the frustrating unpredictability of the weather. Having hoped to shoot in snow in Northern California, the unseasonably warm December weather meant that Tarantino's sets had to be shipped north to Wyoming. Even the usually upbeat Tarantino felt enervated at times. 'When you make an epic and you go through months and months with an army of people in extreme cold and heat, the hardest thing is remembering why you wanted to do it in the first place,' he said.

The production's core location was the Evergreen Plantation in Louisiana, a historic site on the west bank of the Mississippi River, where production designer J Michael Riva oversaw the construction of Candie Land's opulent 'Big House' in a back field. With the plantation's 22 slave cabins still intact, though unused in the film, the weight of its history bore down on the cast and crew.

Tarantino confessed to worrying about shooting in such an environment. 'I had a little trepidation about it and was actually trying to think of some way that maybe I could escape the pain of asking Americans to do that,' he said. He considered shooting

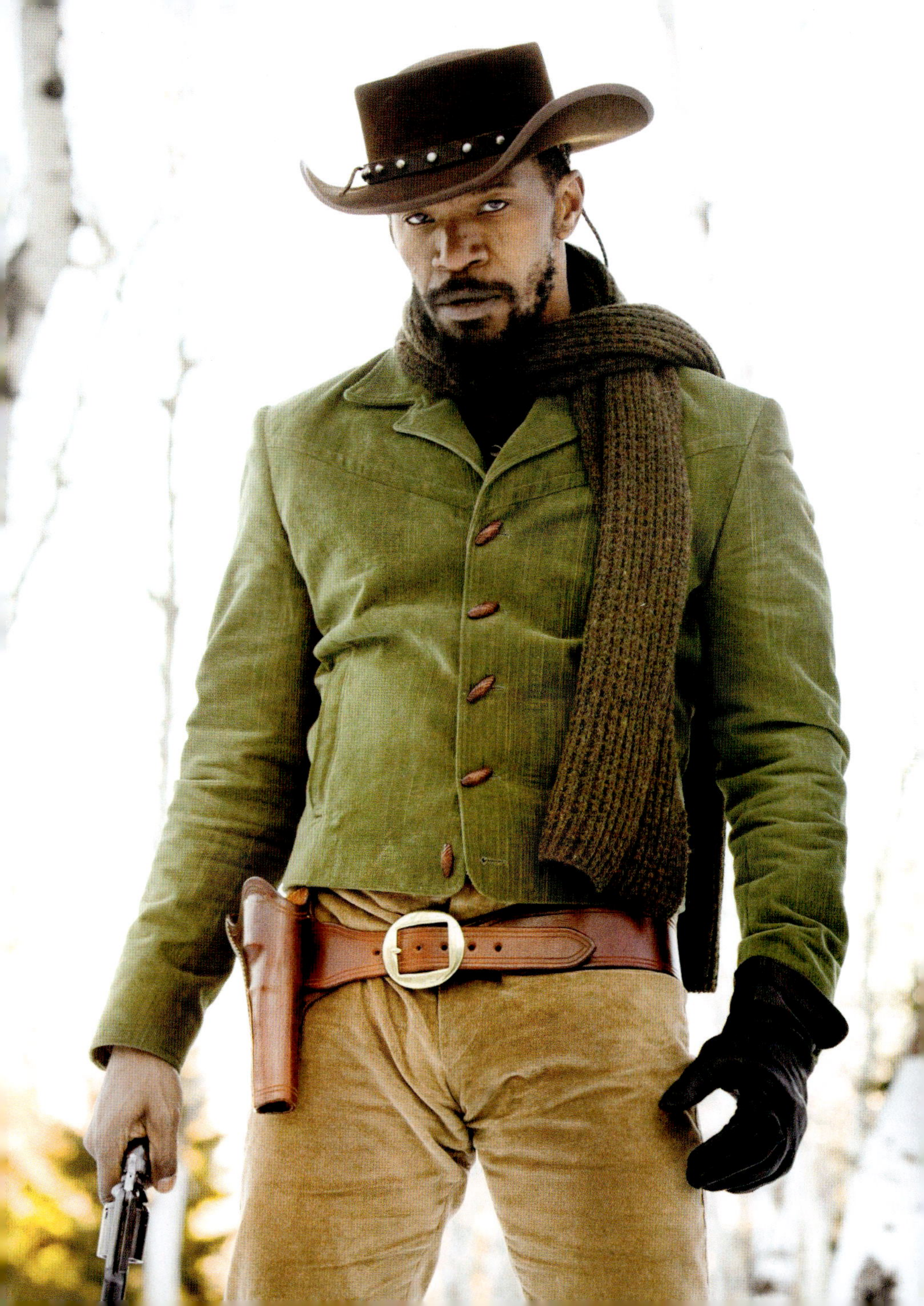

abroad, with actors who wouldn't have to relive the agonies of their own ancestors. But he was talked out of that by none other than Sidney Poitier. 'You're a little afraid of your own movie,' the veteran actor and civil rights activist told him over dinner, 'and you just need to get over that. Just treat everybody with the right kind of compassion and you have nothing to be worried about.'

According to Foxx and Washington, Tarantino kept his word. He cracked jokes and played gospel music between scenes to lighten the mood. He was also sure to check in with his actors. 'He went to every single person on that set,' Foxx said, 'whether they were extras or main characters, to make sure they were OK between each scene.' Washington described her director as 'respectful and compassionate' throughout the shoot. 'There's nothing easy about this character,' she said of Broomhilda. 'It's not easy to come to work and exist in a world where you're not considered fully human.' But she appreciated why Tarantino put her in this position. 'There are so many actors before us who have gone into this place and this time, but they went into it to portray *victims*. But we get to portray heroism and winning and liberation – to go into a difficult period and *kill* the bad guys!'

While depicting the violence in *Django Unchained*, Tarantino had to perform a tonal balancing act: between the righteous, cathartic, overblown and sometimes darkly humorous spaghetti retribution meted out by Django and Schultz, and the disturbing, traumatizing brutality of the Old South. In one moment, a gun will blast a woman unrealistically across a room for the sake of a comedic beat; in another, we'll witness an escaped slave being ripped apart by dogs. It is an uncomfortable mix. But deliberately so. When Schultz shows distress at seeing dogs set on someone, and Candie wonders why Django seems less bothered, the Black bounty hunter replies, 'I'm just a little more used to Americans than he is.'

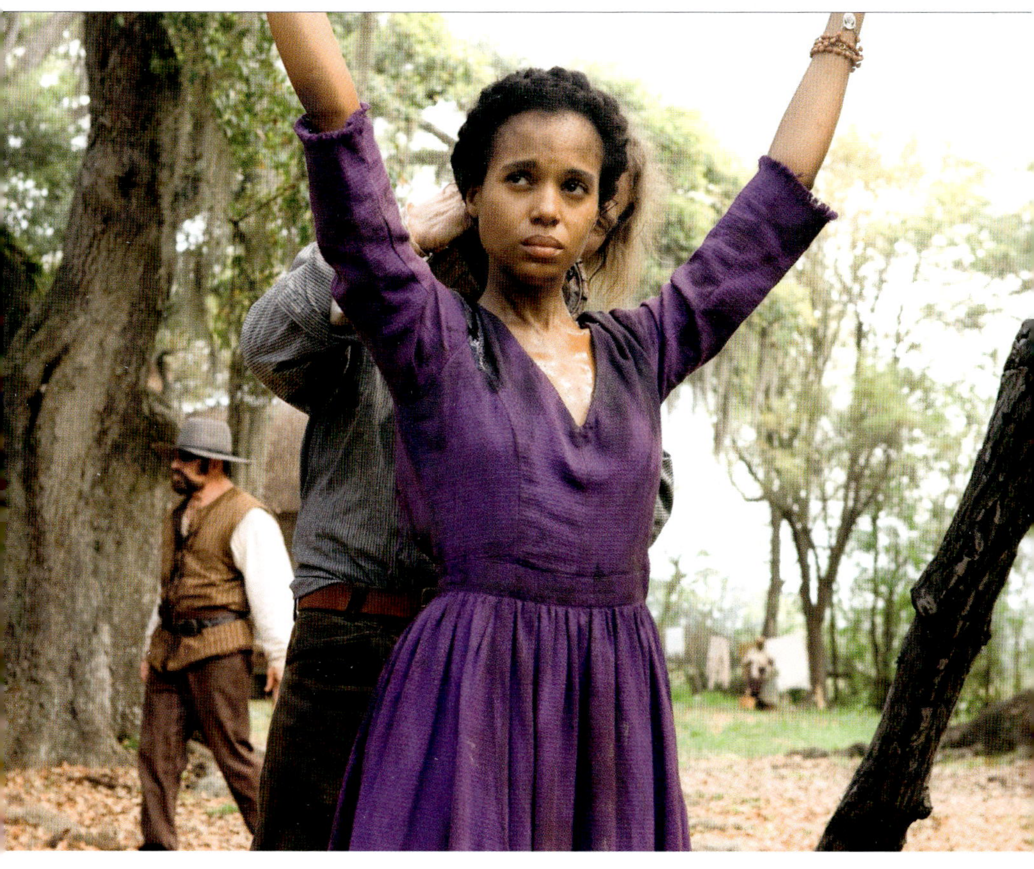

ABOVE: Kerry Washington as Broomhilda, just before her whipping scene – which caused Tarantino's camera eyepiece to fill up with tears, the director claimed.

Tarantino felt an obligation, he said, 'to take 21st-century viewers and physically transport them back to the antebellum South in 1858 and have them look at America for what it was back then. I wanted it to be shocking.' But as well as shocking his audience, he wanted them to be 'cheering in triumph at the end,' when Django kills every white member of the Candie household, plus Stephen, and blows up the Big House. When he screened the

The further adventures of Django

A sequel to *Django Unchained* appeared in 2015, though it took the form of a comic book that Tarantino co-wrote with Matt Wagner (*Mage, Grendel*), which enticingly teamed the bounty hunter with author Johnston McCulley's masked swordsman Zorro. Set years after the movie, *Django/Zorro* involves Django encountering the now silver-haired Diego de la Vega and teaming with him to foil the schemes of the cruel 'Archduke of Arizona' Gurko Langdon, who's enslaved the local Yaqui tribes to build a railway.

In 2019, this pulpy crossover looked like it might become a cinematic sequel, with comedian Jerrod Carmichael tapped up by Tarantino to co-write the script, and Antonio Banderas – who portrayed Zorro in Sony movies *The Mask of Zorro* (1998) and *The Legend of Zorro* (2005) – confirming that Tarantino had asked him to return to the role. However, while Banderas loved the idea, it has yet to crystallize as a reality and looks unlikely ever to.

movie for a Black audience, he said, 'You would've thought it was 1973 and they were watching the end of *Coffy*.'

It seemed he had succeeded in making the kind of film that Reginald Hudlin wanted to see in 1998 – as the film's producer, Hudlin certainly thought so. And Tarantino's approach was vindicated by the movie's commercial success. Taking $426 million worldwide, it is Tarantino's biggest hit, with *The Hollywood Reporter* stating that 42 per cent of its US opening weekend audience in the US was Black. It also earned both he and Waltz their second Oscars, for Best Original Screenplay and Best Supporting Actor, respectively. But with greater attention came greater criticism.

OPPOSITE: DiCaprio cut his hand for real during one of the film's most excruciatingly tense scenes.

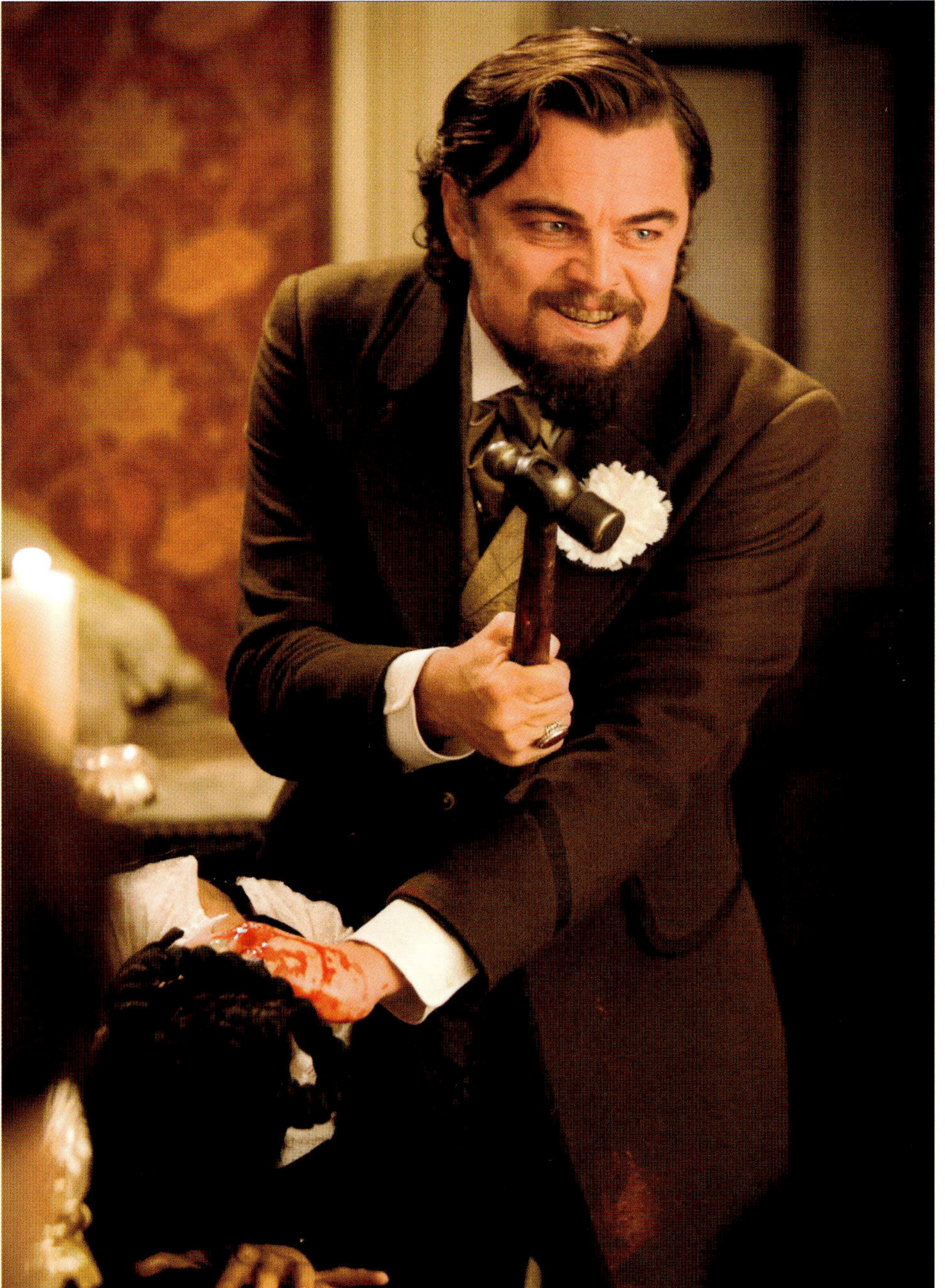

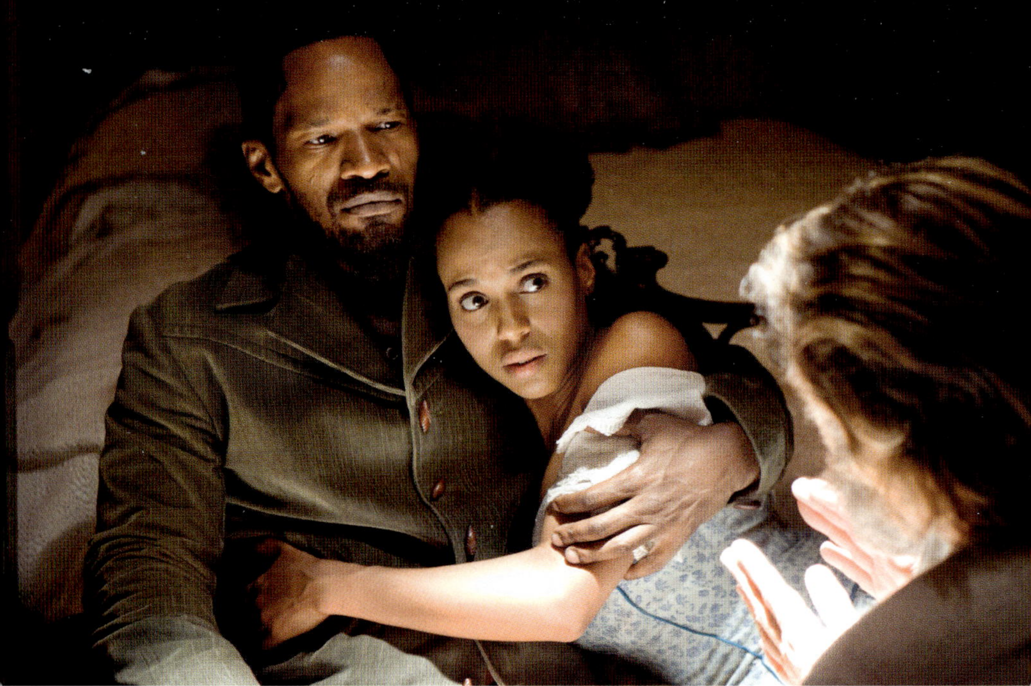

ABOVE: Django and Broomhilda reunited, shortly before Stephen ruins the former's rescue plan.

In a flashback to *Jackie Brown*, the movie's extensive use of the n-word brought much opprobrium, with Tarantino's old adversary Spike Lee slamming it on Twitter. 'American Slavery Was Not A Sergio Leone Spaghetti Western,' he posted. 'It Was A Holocaust. My Ancestors Are Slaves. Stolen From Africa. I Will Honor Them.'

To Tarantino, the criticism was ridiculous. 'It would be one thing if people are out there saying, 'You use it much more excessively in this movie than it was used in 1858 in Mississippi,' he said. 'And if you're not saying that, you're simply saying I should be lying. I should be watering it down. I should be making it more easy to digest. No, I don't want it to be easy to digest. I want it to be a big, gigantic boulder, a jagged pill and you have no water.'

Tarantino's use of violence – whether spaghettified or serious – also once again came under scrutiny by the media, with the

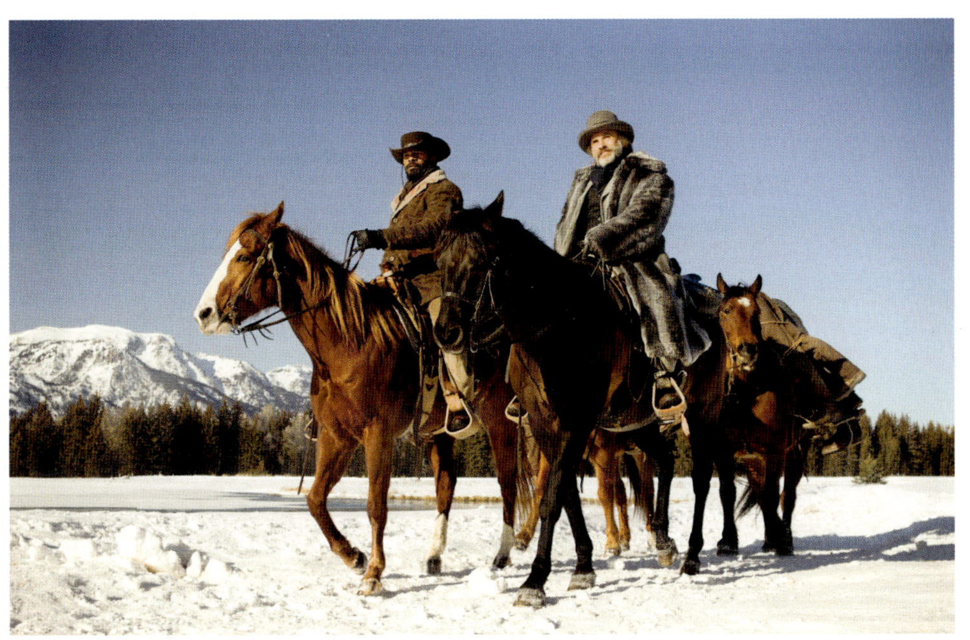

ABOVE: Django with his German bounty-hunting mentor King Schultz, a role written for Christoph Waltz.

issue freshly stoked by the Sandy Hook Elementary shooting in Newtown, Connecticut, when 26 people, 20 of them children, were killed by a 20-year-old gunman just two weeks before the film's Christmas release. But the director had no patience with interviewers who brought it up. As far as he was concerned, there was nothing new to say about the subject. In 20 years, he insisted, 'I haven't changed my opinion one iota.'

This was true. Tarantino never wavered from his assertion that it's impossible to correlate film violence with real violence. 'I'm not going to be handcuffed by what some crazy fuck might do who sees my movie,' he said in 1992. 'The minute you put handcuffs on artists because of stuff like that, it's not an art form anymore.' And he was far from done with violence – or, indeed, its integrality to his nation's history.

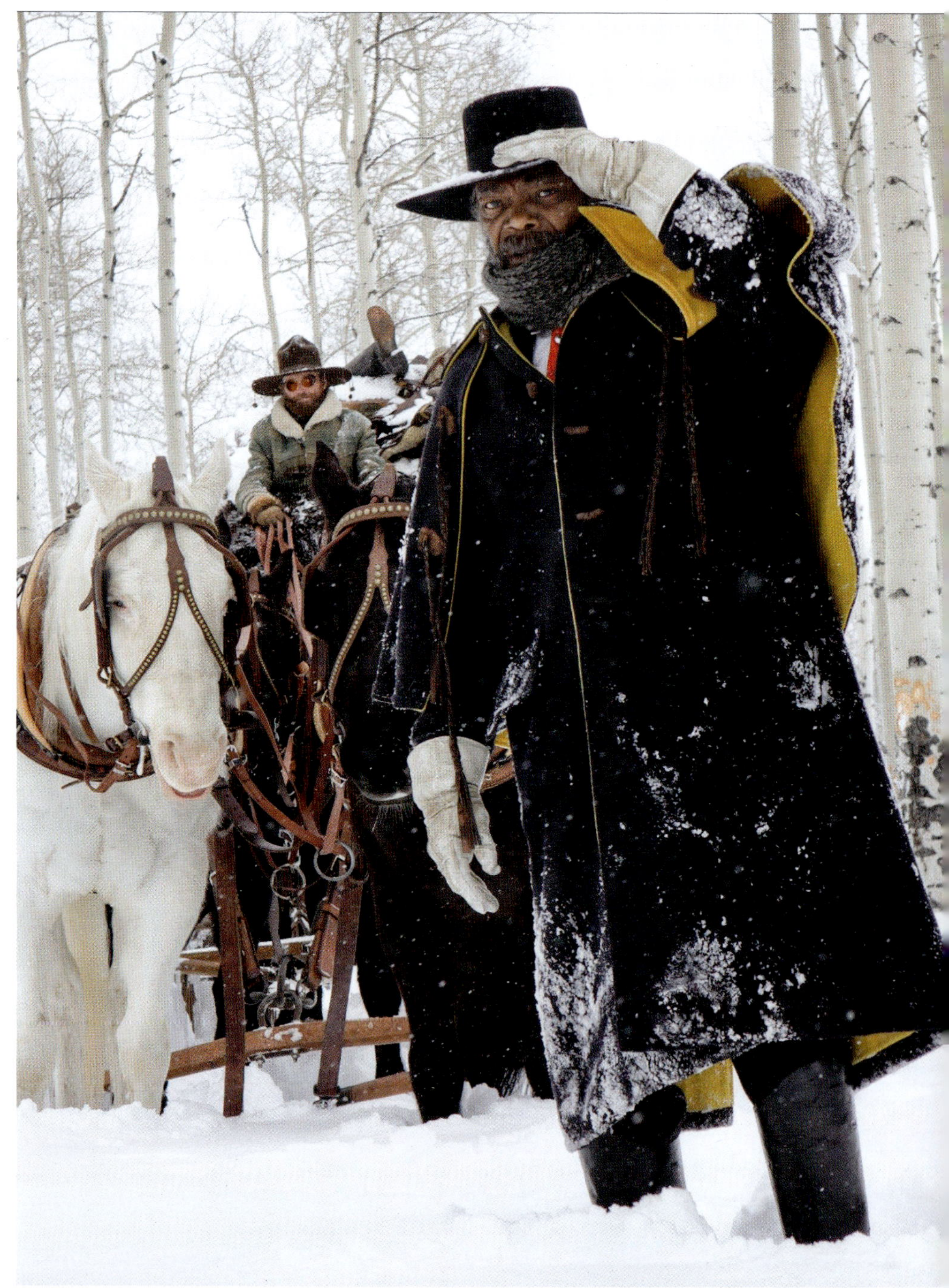

'Move a little sudden, a little strange,
you're gonna get a bullet'

THE
HATEFUL
EIGHT
2015

The Western had always captivated Tarantino. He was by no means the first to realize how potent the genre was for mirroring contemporary American society, but he loved to expound upon it. 'The Westerns of the Fifties reflected Eisenhower America better than any other films of the day,' he pointed out; those of the Sixties were 'the hippie Westerns and the anti-Westerns'; and Seventies Westerns were 'Watergate Westerns' that said: 'now we're gonna rip down everything we believed about [Western] heroes.'

The Hateful Eight, his second Western in three years, was no different. 'It reflects that whole Blue State/Red State divide that exists in America at this time,' he said during the shoot. 'Everyone nowadays just keeps saying, "Well, the country's never been as

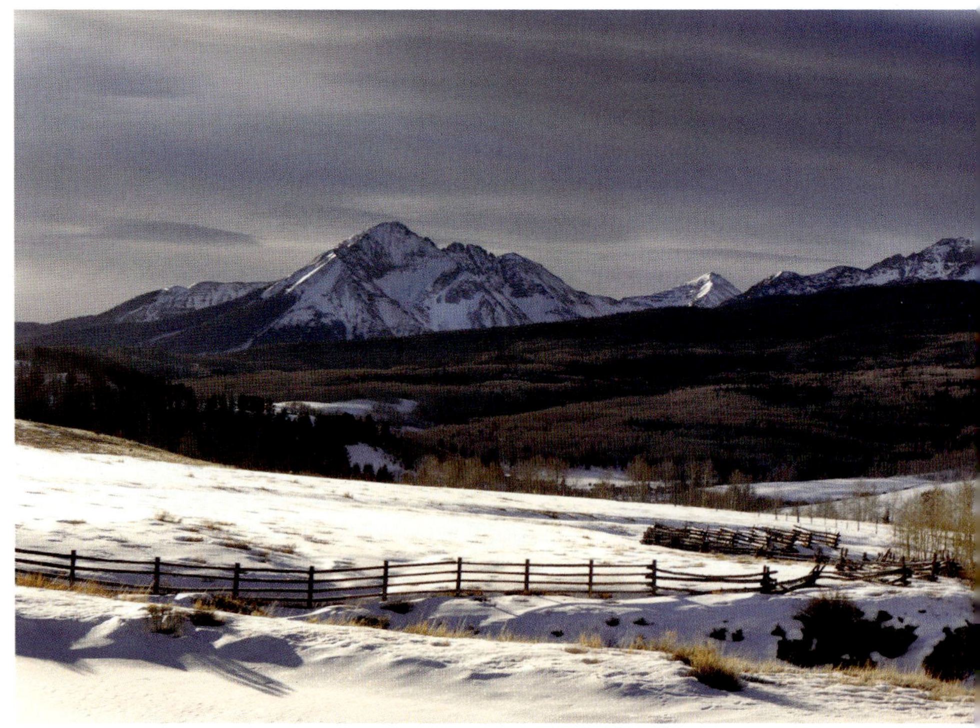

divided as this since after the Civil War." Alright, well that's when this movie takes place.'

After the furore over *Django Unchained*, Tarantino could have been forgiven for shying away from again using the Western to tackle racial politics and violence in the United States. But with *The Hateful Eight*, he went further. '*Django* was definitely the beginning of my political side,' he said, 'and I think *The Hateful Eight* is the logical extension and conclusion of that. It's like *Django* was the question and *Hateful Eight* is the answer.'

That 'answer' started life, appropriately enough, as a *Django Unchained* sequel titled *Django in White Hell*, which Tarantino originally intended to publish as a novel. His main inspiration came from Sixties Western TV shows like *Bonanza* and *The High*

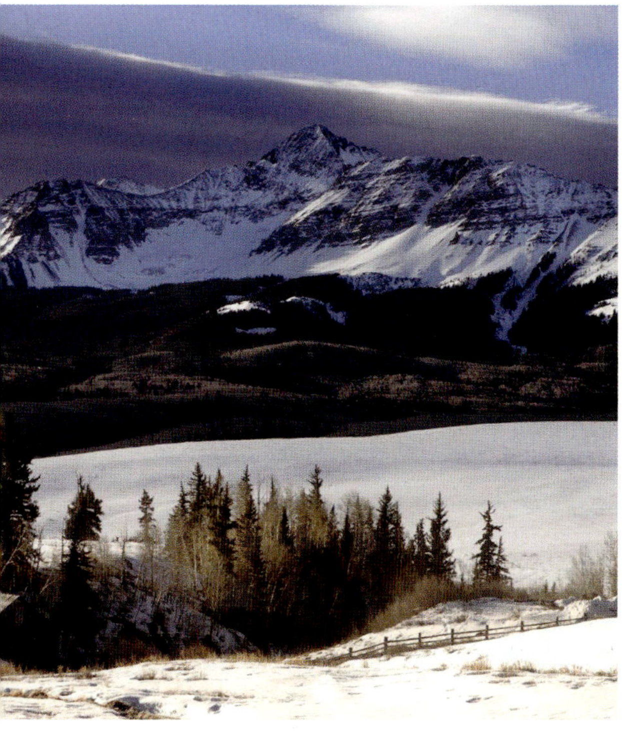

LEFT: Foregoing the relative comfort of a soundstage, Tarantino shot the entirety of *The Hateful Eight* in Telluride, Colorado.

Chaparral, where his favourite episodes would feature a guest star, such as Charles Bronson or David Carradine, playing a mysterious antagonist whose true motives aren't revealed until the end. The idea was, he said, to take a group of these 'sketchy guest-star characters, have them be played by the same kind of cool, groovy actors, then trap them in a room and have them hash it out.' The problem with putting Django in the mix was that the audience – for, by now, he'd decided it should be a film – would automatically accept him as the good guy. There should be 'no heroes,' Tarantino decided. 'Just a bunch of nefarious guys in a room, all telling backstories that may or may not be true.'

So, Django was replaced by a different African American bounty hunter, a one-time Yankee cavalryman named Major Marquis Warren, played by Samuel L Jackson. During a fierce winter blizzard in post-Civil War Wyoming, the sly, perceptive Warren holes up in stagecoach-stop Minnie's Haberdashery with fellow 'sketchy' folk. These include another bounty hunter named John 'The Hangman' Ruth (Kurt Russell), a stomping, no-nonsense alpha who is manacled to 'Crazy' Daisy Domergue (Jennifer Jason Leigh), a wanted criminal already bearing the bruises of Ruth's frontier justice. Then there's former Confederate fighter Chris Mannix (Walton Goggins) who claims to be the new sheriff; Señor Bob (Demián Bechir), the supposed caretaker of Minnie's, who is looking after the place while Minnie visits her mother; an Englishman named Oswaldo Mobray (Tim Roth), who introduces himself as the local hangman; a laconic cowboy named Joe Gage (Michael Madsen); and an old, bitter, deeply racist Confederate general (Bruce Dern). However, more than one of this motley gathering is not who they claim to be.

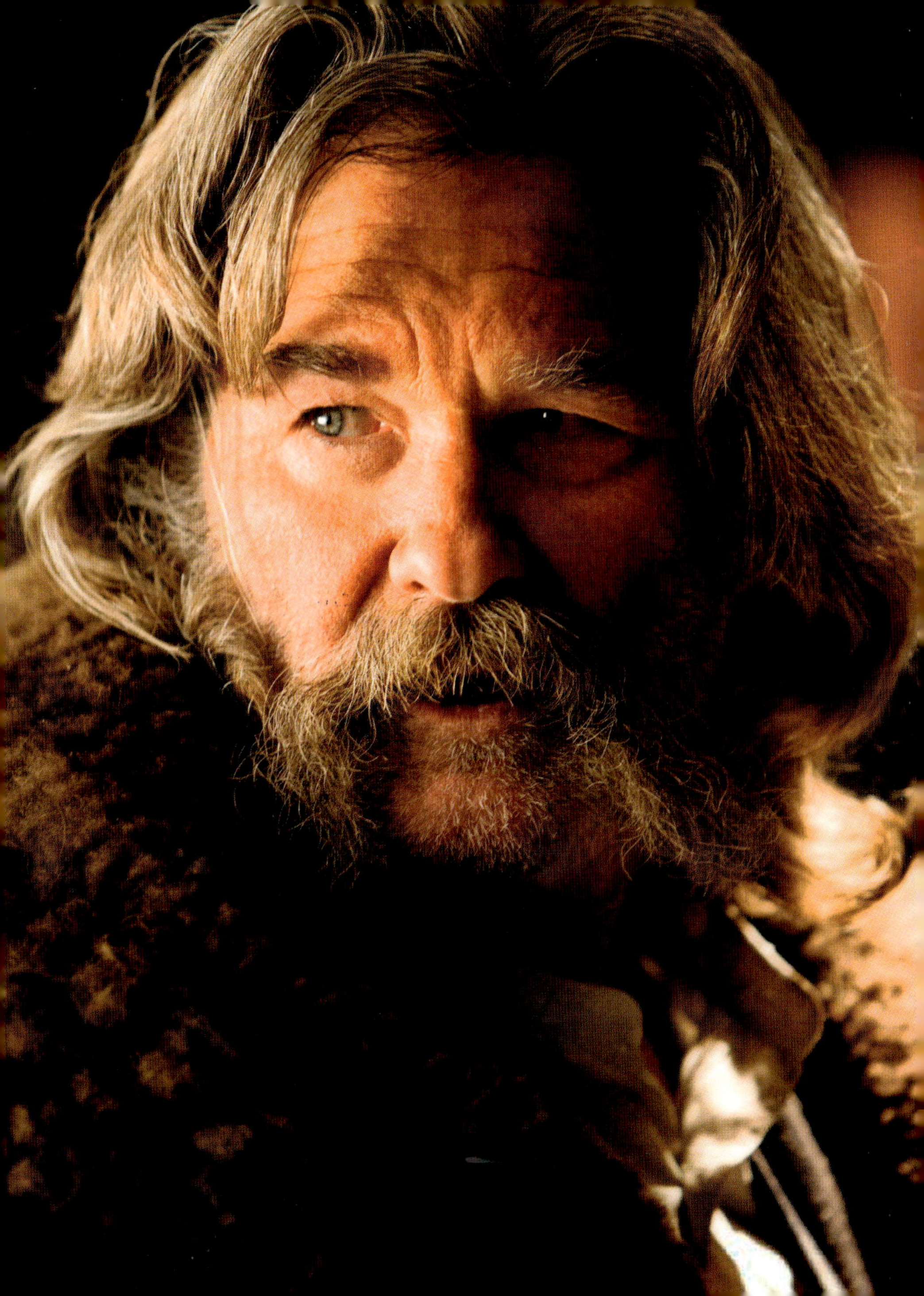

While opening with, and flashing back to, scenes mounted amid the snowy grandeur of southwest Colorado, most of *The Hateful Eight*'s duplicitous drama plays out in the single location of Minnie's Haberdashery. It's an odd choice for a Western, a genre built on vast, sweeping landscapes. But when did Tarantino ever tackle a genre without giving it a twist? The director compared Minnie's with the warehouse in *Reservoir Dogs* and the La Louisiane bar in *Inglourious Basterds*. Except this time the tension would be building for three hours, rather than just 25 minutes.

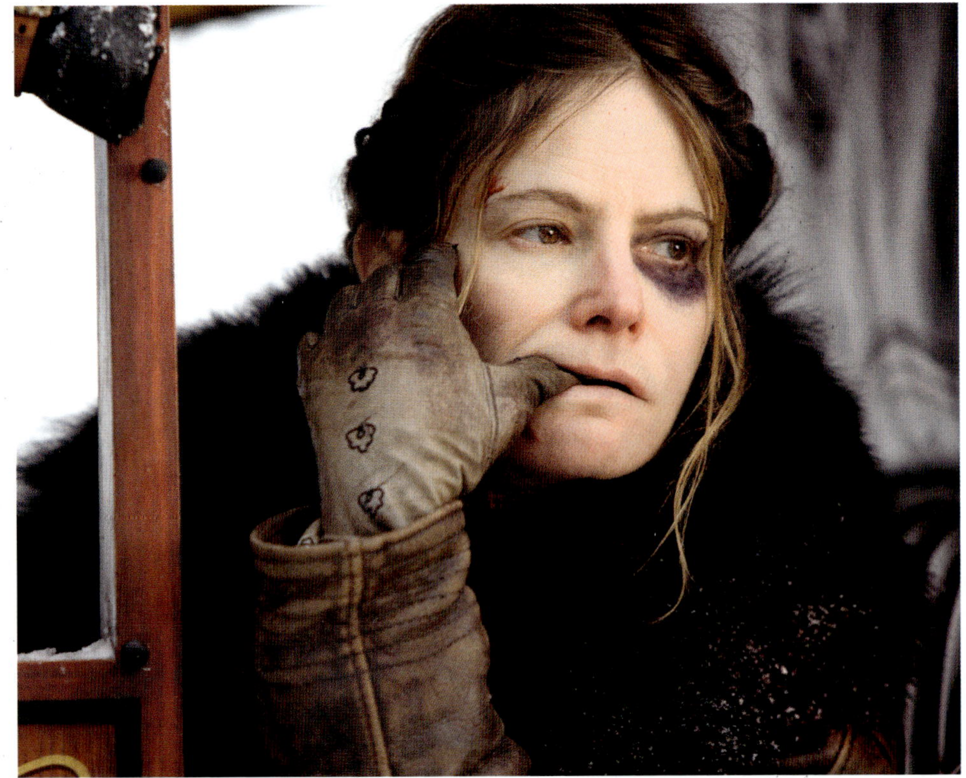

BELOW: Jennifer Jason Leigh as the only female 'Hater', the perpetually abused prisoner Daisy Domergue.

Tarantino carefully constructed the film as a mystery thriller, which even brings in a whodunit element halfway through when someone poisons the coffee, taking out John Ruth in a geyser of vomited blood. He wanted to keep his audience guessing throughout. Even before Ruth is poisoned, there is the question of Minnie's mysterious absence and Bob's surprise presence, which Bob unsatisfactorily explains to Warren. Then there is the question of which of the Eight might be secretly in league with Daisy – a conundrum that eventually results in the appearance of a surprise

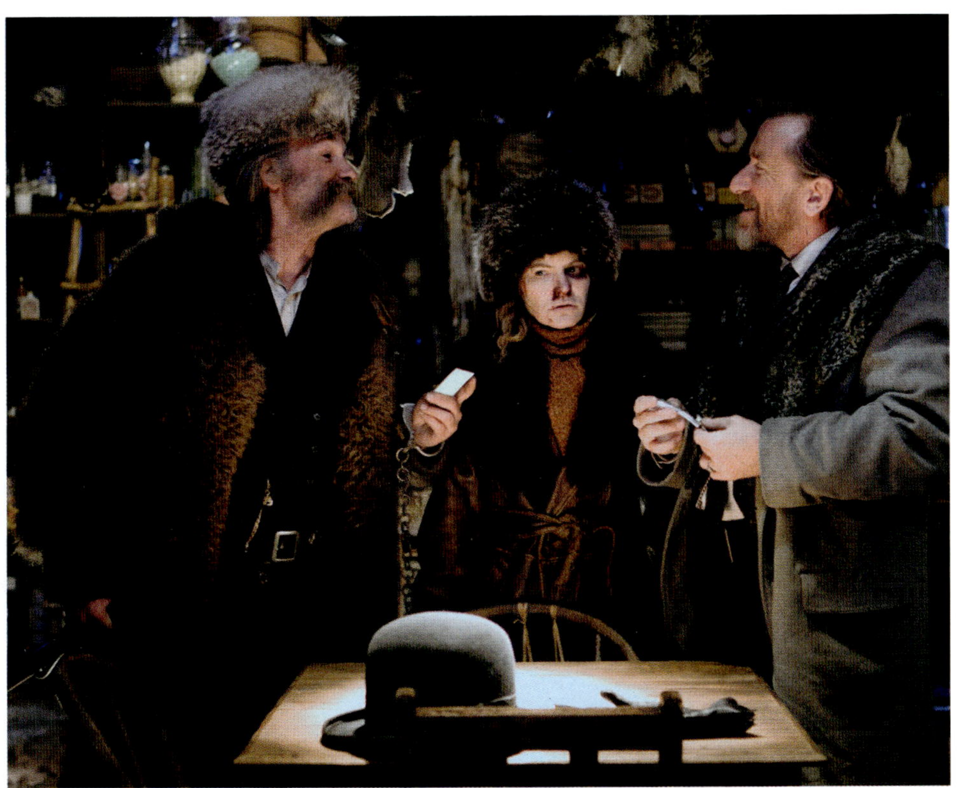

BELOW: Tim Roth (right) returned for his fourth collaboration with Tarantino, as hangman Oswaldo Mobray.

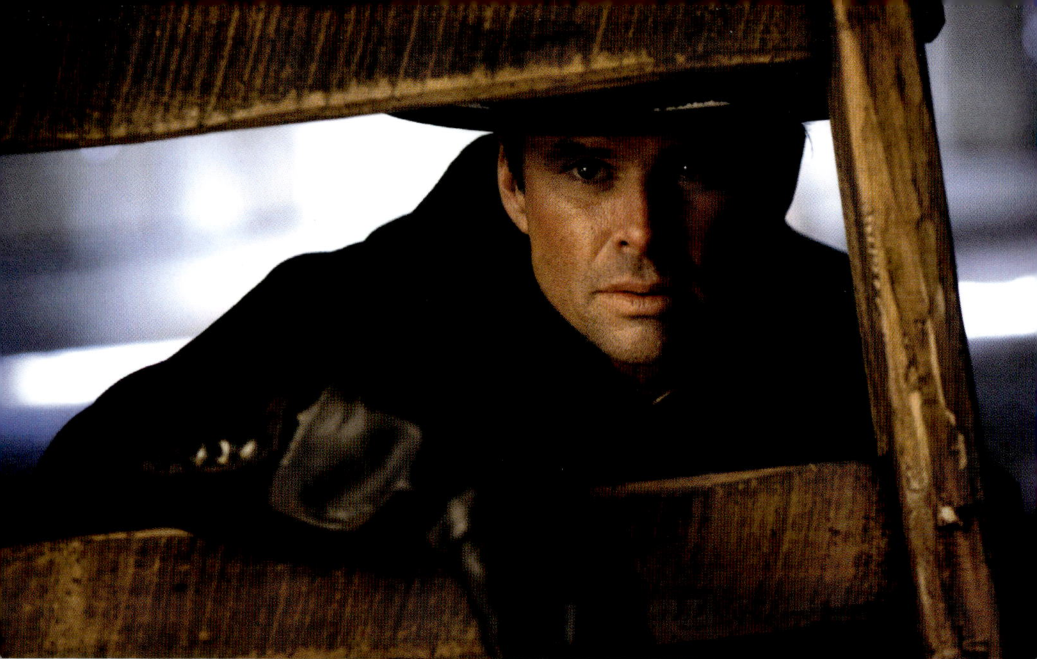

ninth character: Channing Tatum as Daisy's murderous brother, who's been hiding in the cellar all this time. Though Tarantino included a mystery element in *Reservoir Dogs* (the identity of the undercover cop), this was the first time he'd built an entire film around one.

It was also the first time he shot a film in Ultra Panavision 70. In fact, it was the first time any filmmaker had used the luxurious format in 49 years, with only 10 features having used it previously, including *Ben-Hur*. Yielding an aspect ratio of 2.76:1, it was the widest format ever created. But Tarantino wanted it for a film that was character-based and mostly set in a single room.

This wasn't just a film-nerd gimmick. It was essential, he insisted, to remind audiences, 'why this is something you can't see on television, and how this is an experience you can't have when you watch movies in your apartment, your man cave, or on your iPhone or iPad.' To underline this, he would convince The Weinstein Company to fund a limited 'roadshow' release of the movie in the United States in addition to its regular release, where a longer cut was projected in 70mm – complete with an overture, a 12-minute intermission and a souvenir programme – as had happened with certain prestige pictures during the late Fifties and Sixties. 'When you see the grain of 70, you see the colour of 70 – like the wide shot inside the bar and the close-ups of the faces – it's beautiful,' enthused cinematographer Robert Richardson.

The format served a storytelling purpose, too, enabling Tarantino to keep as many different shifty players in frame as possible. Comparing his characters with the pieces on the chessboard that sits at the centre of the haberdashery, the director carefully staged each scene so it not only presented the 'foreground play' of the actors closer to the camera, but also the 'background play' of those further away. 'Unless I don't want you to know where the other characters are, the point of this story is that you always know where the other characters are in the room in relation to everybody else,' he said.

In order to pull this off, he and Richardson sought permission from Panavision to refurbish a set of lenses that hadn't been used since 1966 historical epic *Khartoum*. It was a risky move. 'We knew they worked,' said Tarantino. 'We wouldn't be mounting this entire production with one foot on a banana peel and the other on a roller skate. But the fact that we would be in the freezing cold was an issue.'

Tarantino wanted his entire 10-week shoot to take place in the frosty environs of Telluride, where the temperatures could drop to minus 30 degrees Celsius and he'd be able to see his actors' breath for real. As it turned out, the precious lenses bore up well considering the harsh conditions. But it wasn't easy manoeuvring six-horse stagecoaches in heavy snow, or constantly brushing over the vehicle tracks between takes, and the shoot was consequently slow and laborious. It was tough on the actors, too. 'There were one or two days where you were like, "I can't feel my feet",' said Leigh. 'It was cold, but it all worked for the character.'

Tarantino's quest for authenticity extended to the props. The chain that shackled Daisy was made of metal rather than rubber, and the guitar on which she played an Australian ballad was an 1870s Martin, on loan from the Martin Guitar Museum. (Just a year earlier, a similar guitar had sold at auction for $335,000.) In one scene, irked by Daisy's lyrical jibing, Ruth snatches the guitar from her and smashes it to pieces. As Russell slams the antique instrument into a pillar, Leigh gives a horrified shriek that is all too real: she knew he was accidentally destroying the genuine article, as opposed to its worthless stunt double. It has never been revealed whether or not Tarantino was aware of Russell's error, but it can't be denied that Leigh's reaction gives the moment some extra oomph.

Leigh's ability to shriek was a major factor in Tarantino casting her as Daisy, the only woman in the eponymous ensemble. Most of the Haters (the name the actors gave themselves) were drawn from his unofficial company, or 'The Gang'; only Bechir hadn't worked with him before, and he came recommended by Robert Rodriguez, who had cast him in *Machete Kills*. So, Tarantino approached Daisy with an open mind, speaking to different actors, including Jennifer Lawrence who'd impressed him in her movies with David O Russell. But Lawrence wasn't available, and Tarantino felt that Daisy might work better as an older person. Given the movie's similarity to *Reservoir Dogs*, he saw it as 'kind of a throwback to the Nineties,' so figured 'the actress should be an actress from the Nineties.'

Quentin and Ennio

The Hateful Eight is the only Tarantino film to have a complete original score. Previously, the director had preferred to select his own needle drops, but his snowbound Western felt different. As several of his films featured cues from Ennio Morricone scores, it made sense that he'd want the octogenarian maestro himself for the job. But there was a hitch. In March 2013, it was reported that Morricone had criticized Tarantino for placing his 'music in his films without coherence,' and claimed, 'I wouldn't like to work with him again, on anything.' However, Tarantino was happy to forgive the maestro, and confirmed that Morricone had since apologized. Morricone ended up providing 35 minutes of music, all without even seeing the film, and agreed to give Tarantino some unused orchestral pieces that had been written for John Carpenter's *The Thing* back in 1980. In 2016, Morricone won an Oscar for his efforts – astonishingly his first for Best Original Score.

He considered Leigh to be 'a female Sean Penn. That's what I needed for Daisy: I needed a female Sean Penn to throw her weight around.' During her audition, he said, 'she went for a couple of things that other people just kind of play-acted. She had to act like she got shot, and she just screamed bloody murder. I kept remembering Jennifer's bloodcurdling scream. If it had happened in a house, somebody would have called the cops.'

The incredibly rough treatment of Daisy makes for some of *The Hateful Eight*'s most uncomfortable moments and became a critical flashpoint in the reception to the film which, like almost every Tarantino movie, attracted controversy on its release over Christmas 2015. Daisy is elbowed in the face, pistol whipped, drenched in Ruth's scarlet puke, shot in the foot and, after most of the other characters are blasted to bloody pieces, ultimately

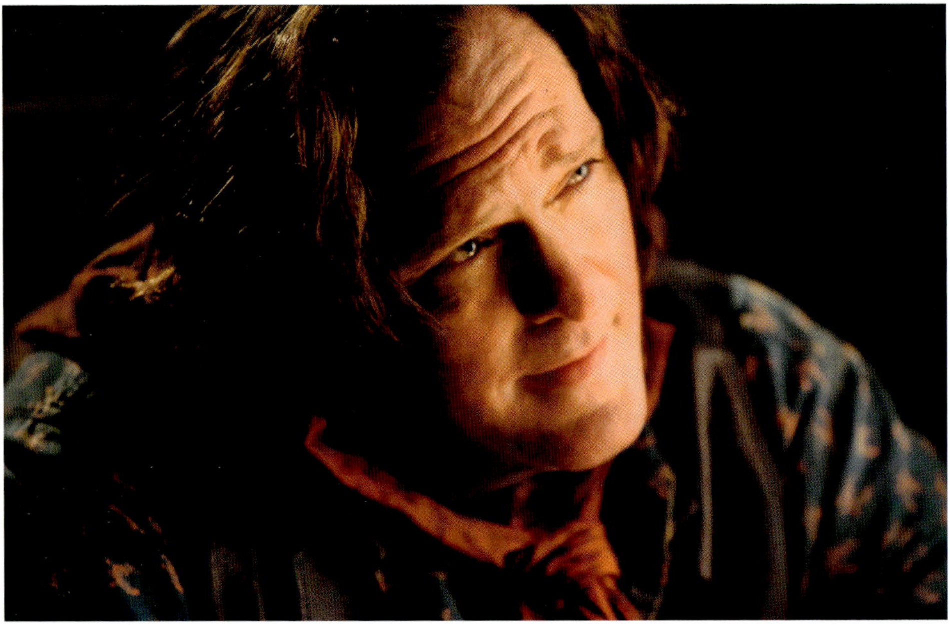

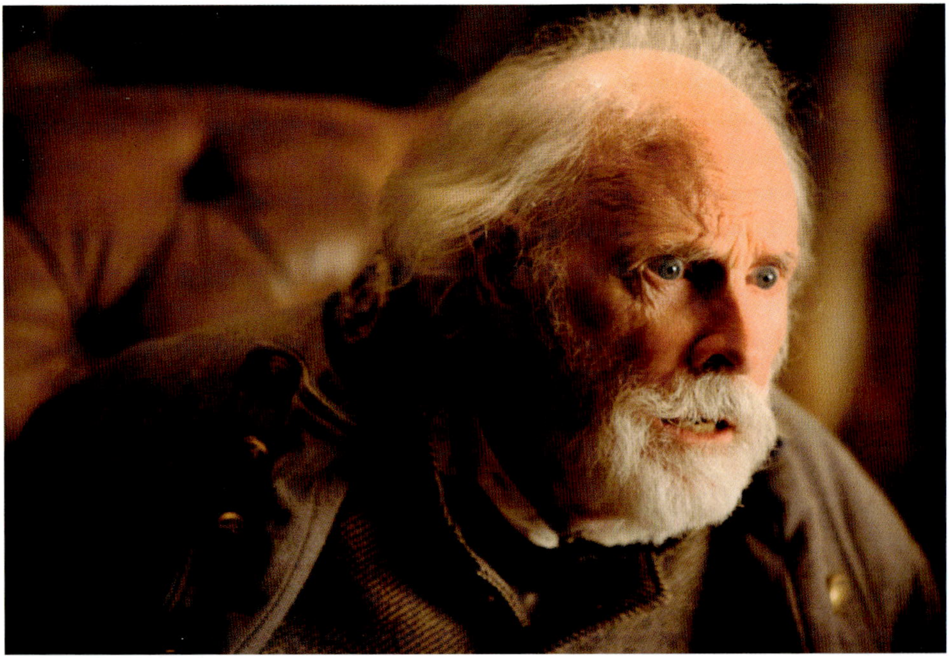

hanged by Mannix and Warren (both of whom are bleeding out themselves) in a horribly graphic indoor lynching. *The New York Times'* A O Scott described the film as 'an orgy of elaborately justified misogyny,' just one of several reviews that levelled the accusation at Tarantino.

Leigh, who would receive her first Oscar nomination for her performance, was quick to defend the director. 'I didn't think it was misogynistic for a second,' she said, describing Daisy as 'a leader. . .she's tough. And she's hateful and she's a survivor.' Tarantino, she added, 'doesn't have an ounce of misogyny in him'. The director himself argued that he was just being an equal opportunities abuser, narratively speaking. 'Violence is hanging over every one of those characters like a cloak of night. So, I'm not going to go, "OK that's the case for seven of the characters, but because one is a woman, I have to treat her differently."'

Tarantino's social commentary, meanwhile, was picked up by many reviewers. Whether they appreciated it or not, they caught the resonance of the dialogue, such as Warren's statement to Ruth that 'You got no idea what it's like being a Black man facing down America,' while justifying why he carries a fake letter from Abraham Lincoln. 'Black folks' are only safe, he says, 'when white folks is disarmed.'

Despite insisting that his script's 'social relevancy' emerged through narrative instinct rather than intention, Tarantino said that 'dealing with race in America is one of the things I have to offer to cinema. That is one part of my interest in American

OPPOSITE (TOP): Quiet cowpoke Joe Gage was Michael Madsen's third role for Tarantino, following *Reservoir Dogs* and *Kill Bill*.

OPPOSITE: Bruce Dern as former Confederate general Sanford Smithers, who has history with Samuel L Jackson's Major Marquis Warren.

society, and so the fact that it bleeds into my work makes perfect sense.' While *Django Unchained* talked about 'America's culpability in [its] past,' *The Hateful Eight* taps into 'the white supremacy that has existed since and that is rearing its ugly head again, to such a degree that it's being dealt with by the Black Lives Matter movement.'

As if to underline this message, on 24 October 2015, two months before *The Hateful Eight*'s release, Tarantino attended and briefly spoke at Rise Up October's anti-police brutality protest in New York in October 2015. 'I have to call a murder a murder, and I have to call the murderers the murderers,' he said. In response, the Patrolmen's Benevolent Association (New York City's biggest police union) called for a boycott of the film.

It did not have much effect. True, *The Hateful Eight* yielded Tarantino's smallest box office since *Death Proof* (taking $156 million worldwide), but this was more the result of its long running time and the absence of big-name stars, such as *Inglourious Basterd*'s Brad Pitt or *Django Unchained*'s Leonardo DiCaprio. This latter aspect was a very deliberate choice. Just as he'd ejected Django from the story in the early stages of writing, Tarantino didn't want any cast members drawing too much audience attention. Everyone in the ensemble needed to be on the same level. Besides, his next movie would make up for it by being his starriest yet.

OPPOSITE: Channing Tatum, arguably the biggest name on the cast list after Samuel L Jackson, made a surprise appearance as Daisy's brother Jody.

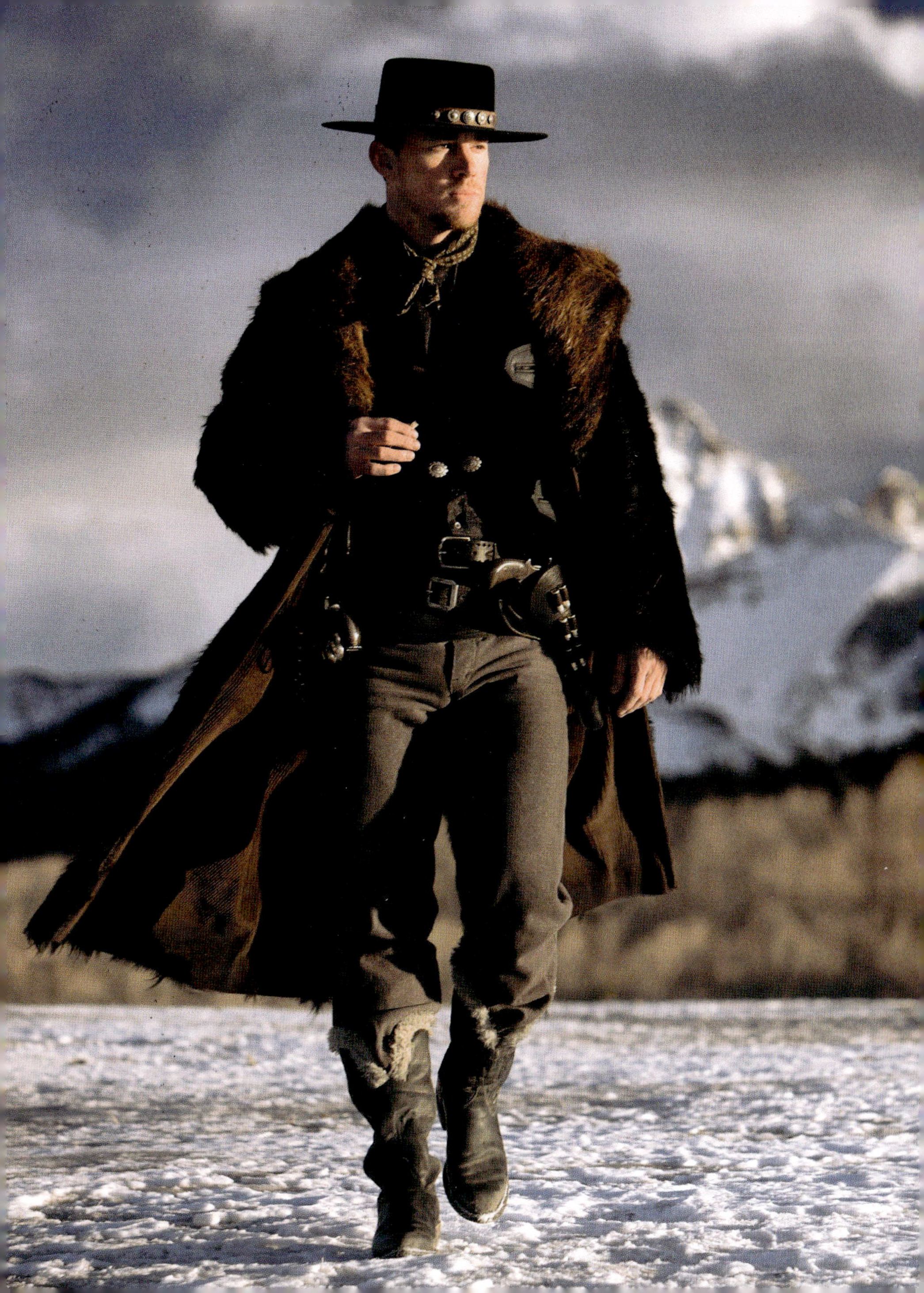

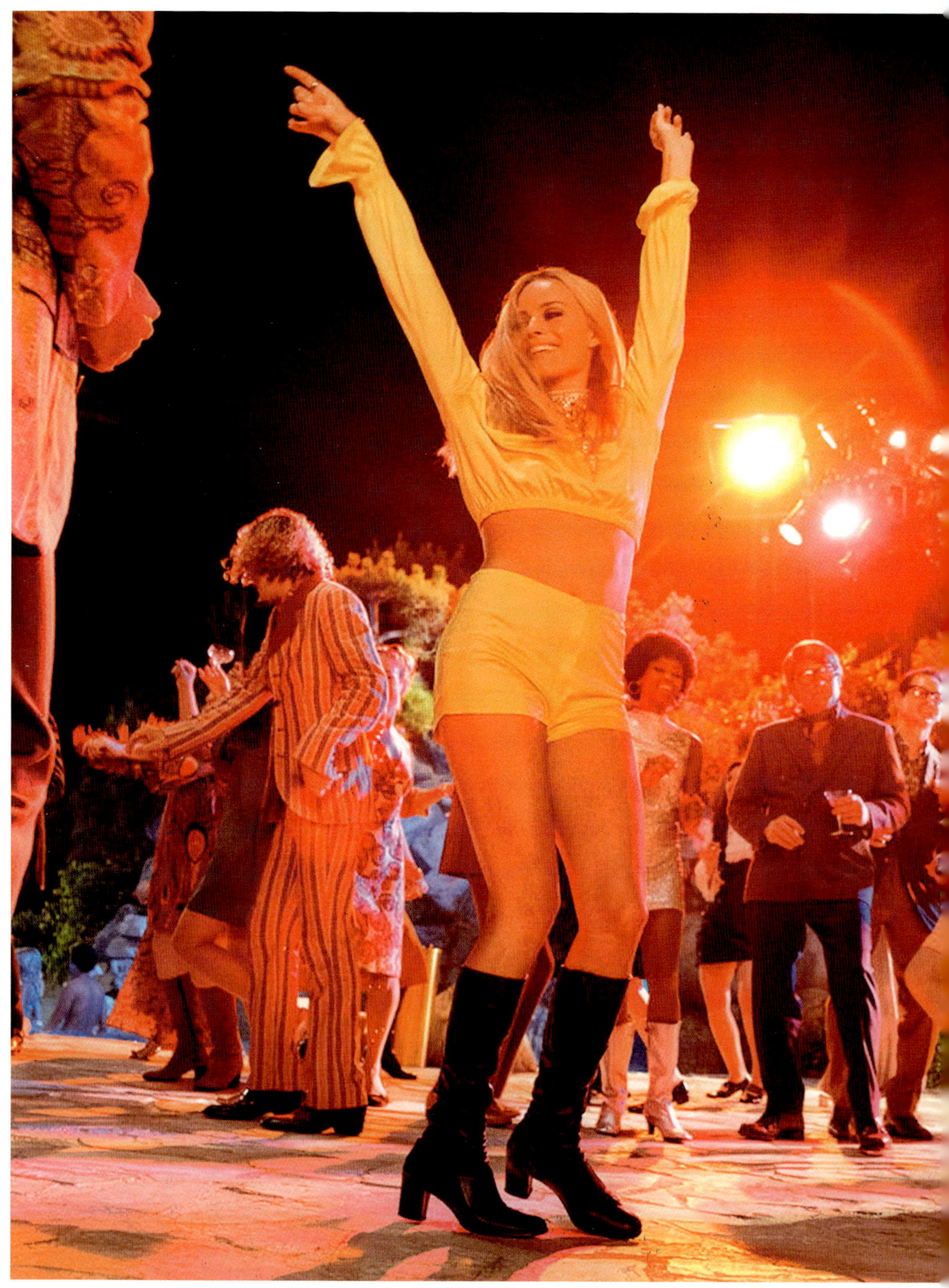

ONCE UPON A TIME. . .IN HOLLYWOOD

2019

One of Tarantino's strongest memories of Los Angeles in 1969 is sitting in his stepfather's Karmann Ghia as a six-year-old boy, listening to The Real Don Steele on the radio, and watching the world go by in all its heightened colour. They'd pass an Earl Scheib Auto-Painting sign, the Hollywood Wax Museum sporting a huge image of Clark Gable, bus stops advertising re-runs on local TV stations, and billboards pushing such tasty beverages as Diet Rite and RC Cola.

It is a memory he recreated for his ninth movie, *Once Upon A Time. . .In Hollywood*. In one shot, ruggedly handsome stuntman Cliff Booth (Brad Pitt) drives past those signs in February 1969, at the wheel of his own Karmann Ghia. The audience's perspective of Booth is angled to match six-year-old Quentin's view, looking up at his stepdad Curt. We are, in this moment, seeing LA through Tarantino's childhood eyes.

Another memory was significantly darker. During the late summer of 1969, little Quentin got wind of a series of murders that shocked the world and, to paraphrase writer Joan Didion, abruptly ended an era. The young members of a local cult in the thrall of Charles Manson were breaking into Los Angeles homes and murdering their residents. Among the nine confirmed victims was ascendant actor Sharon Tate, at the time married to director Roman Polanski and eight-and-a-half months pregnant. 'Who is this Manson guy?' the boy asked Curt, referring to the cult's leader. 'Oh Quentin, you don't want to hear about it,' his stepfather replied. And he left it there.

While *Inglourious Basterds* enabled Tarantino to rewrite the history of World War II and *Django Unchained* gave him the opportunity to avenge slavery, *Once Upon A Time. . .In Hollywood* saw Tarantino go back to his own childhood. In his most personal movie yet, he would use his distinct brand of cinema to once again right a terrible wrong.

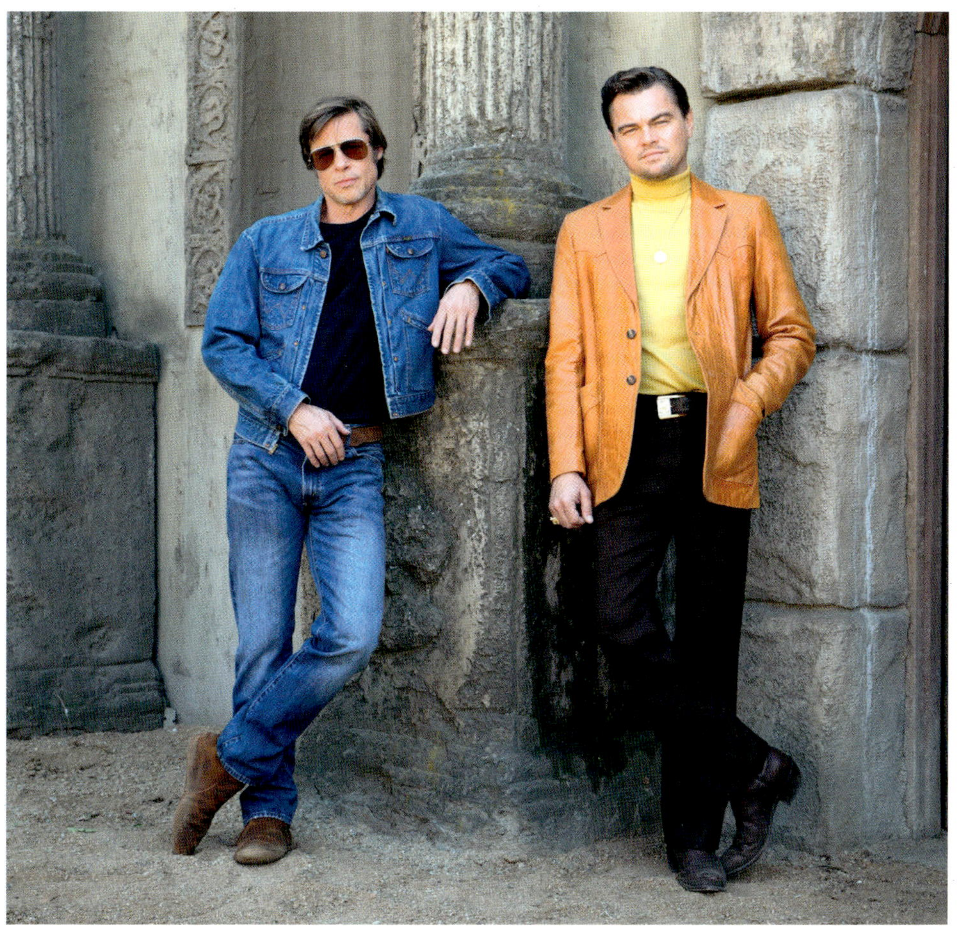

ABOVE: Brad Pitt and Leonardo DiCaprio as Cliff Booth and
Rick Dalton – the old guard in a New Hollywood.

The script Tarantino originally titled 'MAGNUM OPUS' did not start
with the Manson Family murders, but with the character of Cliff
Booth. During one of his shoots, an actor (he won't say who) asked
if Tarantino could give a little work to his long-time stunt double.
The director agreed, and observed the pair. It was clear they'd been
working together for a long time, 'but you could tell, OK, this is the

end. Because everyone's gotten older.' It was, he said, 'an interesting dynamic.' Cliff came from combining that dynamic with the stories Tarantino had heard in the stunt community about a notorious guy who apparently 'could not be hurt,' who 'scared everybody' and who 'killed his wife on a boat and got away with it.' Tempering the scariness with a Zen-like charm, he had a character he felt it would be interesting for an audience to hang out with.

Soon after came the fictional actor Cliff doubled for: has-been Rick Dalton, loosely modelled on the likes of George Maharis, Ty Hardin and Edd Byrnes, whose brief success on TV has failed to yield a movie career beyond second- or third-billed roles in a bigger star's picture. Together, Rick and Cliff are starting to feel outmoded in a Hollywood that's embraced the counterculture and a new kind of leading man: groovy, long-haired, less overtly masculine.

While writing, Tarantino did not envision pairing two of 21st-century Hollywood's biggest names in the roles, namely Brad Pitt and Leonardo DiCaprio. 'I would have been an idiot to write it with Brad and Leo in mind,' he said, 'because I didn't know I could get them.' But he knew his two actors would have to portray a convincingly 'symbiotic connection', and, while he did consider other actors, he admitted they were his dream cast.

There's a genuine affection between the world-weary Cliff and the sensitive, self-sabotaging Rick. This is most pronounced towards the close of the movie when Rick, by now a big name in Europe and married to an Italian wife, says he needs to let Cliff go. There is no drama or recrimination in this moment, just the gentle melancholy throb of a friendship – and a way of life – ebbing.

The third component to fall in place was Sharon Tate, whom Tarantino made Rick's new next-door neighbour on Cielo Drive, where the real Tate lived and was killed. With her as a character, Tarantino would be able to show 'the three social strata of

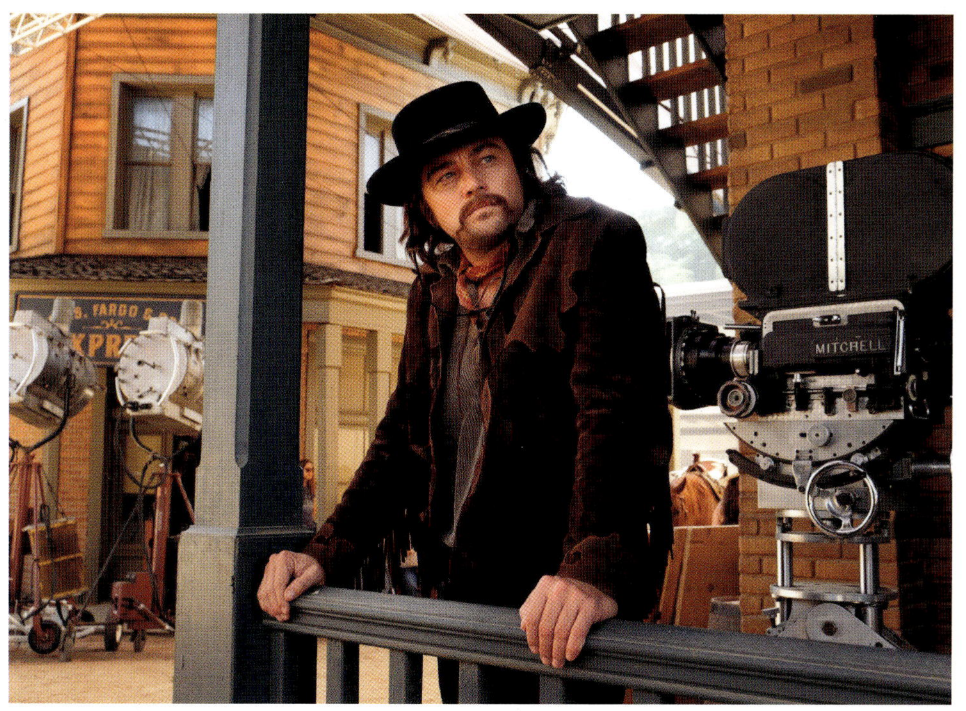

ABOVE: Rick Dalton, forced into a counterculture-friendly long-haired wig and moustache for his guest role as 'the heavy' in TV Western *Lancer*.

[Hollywood]'. Cliff is at the bottom, working hard but with nothing to show for it, living alone in a trailer behind a drive-in with only his pit bull Candy for company. Rick is in the middle, getting by but feeling under-appreciated. And Sharon is at the top, 'truly living the Hollywood life'.

The problem was, Tarantino knew he'd have to incorporate Charles Manson, the Manson Family, and Sharon's murder, together with the killing of Hollywood hairdresser Jay Sebring and three of their friends. He recognized that dealing with Tate's death and the Manson Family was risky. 'Maybe it falls into bad taste, it seems ugly, opportunistic. I was aware of all those things. But that doesn't mean

I didn't want to try. I knew that if I was going to do this, I had to earn the right to do it at some point in the material. So I risked going for it.'

The key, he saw, was not to make *Once Upon A Time. . .In Hollywood* a genre piece, hooked on some 'melodramatic plot'. Instead, it would be 'a day in the life' of these characters (though it is actually two-and-a-half days, with a six month jump before the final half-day). So we follow Rick's first two days playing a 'heavy' for the pilot to TV Western *Lancer*; Cliff running errands and encountering the Manson Family on the Spahn Movie Ranch in another Tarantino-trademark tension-wringing sequence; and Sharon just partying, shopping and watching herself at a public screening of Dean Martin spy comedy *The Wrecking Crew*.

The Sharon scenes are performed luminously by Margot Robbie. It is deeply touching to watch her as Sharon watching herself in the cinema, wearing huge spectacles and with her filthy-soled feet up on the seat in front. When Tate performs a pratfall on screen and the audience laughs, Robbie's face turns from relief to sheer joy, as Sharon realizes that she herself has brought joy, even if it's just in a silly Dean Martin comedy. Wisely, Tarantino doesn't recreate Tate's *Wrecking Crew* scenes; he uses the real footage, so Robbie is actually watching the real Tate. The moment celebrates her talent, rather than mourns her loss.

'I tried not to turn Sharon into a Quentin Tarantino character,' the filmmaker explained. 'I wanted her to be the person that she is now. All the bright and the light stuff. . .that really seems to be who she is. She was almost supposed to represent normalcy [in the film]. She doesn't have any plot to do. We're just watching her live her life because that's what was robbed from her: living

OPPOSITE: Margot Robbie as Sharon Tate, just living her life in 1969. Tarantino said he hoped the movie would 'save her from her tombstone'.

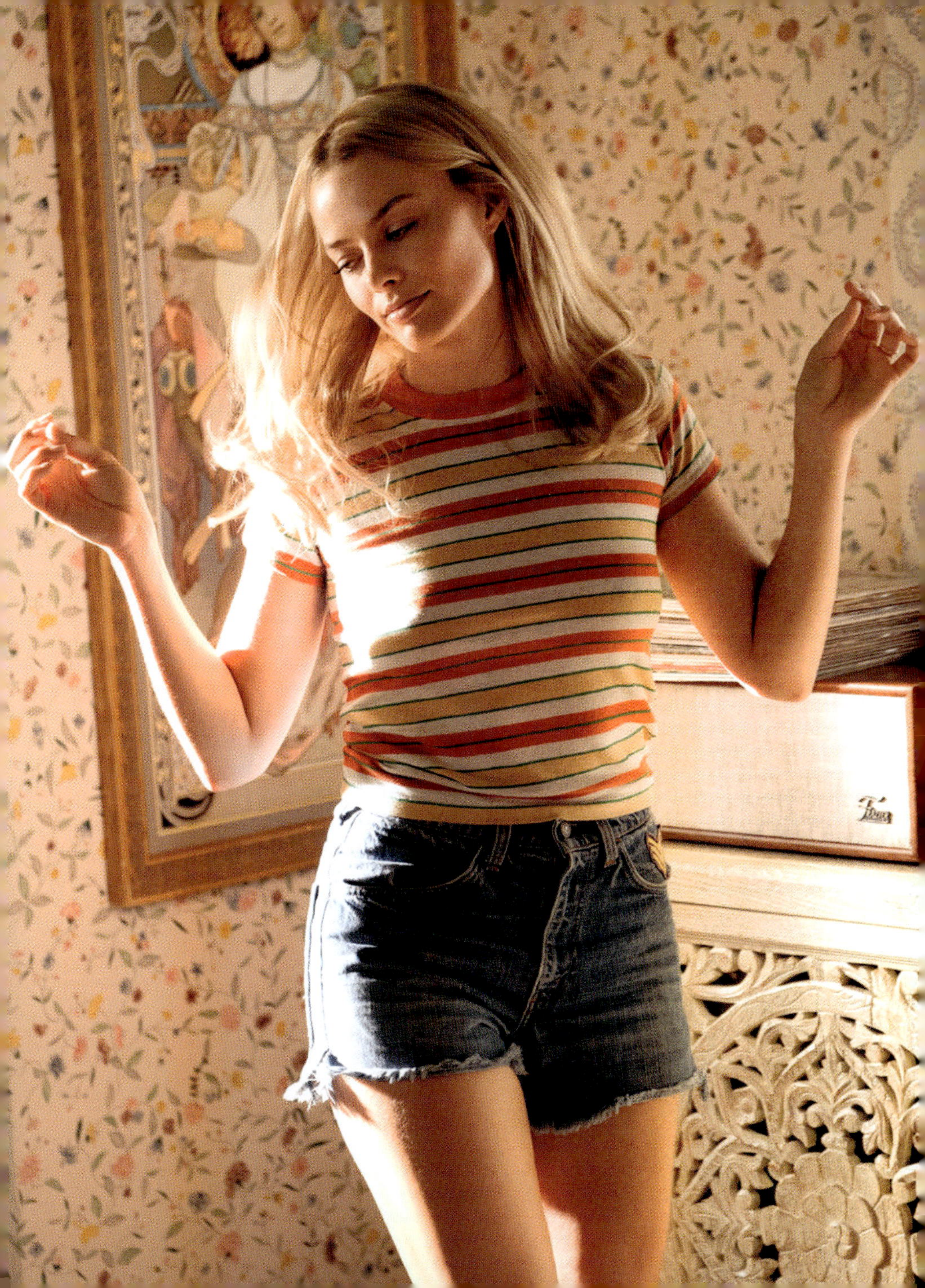

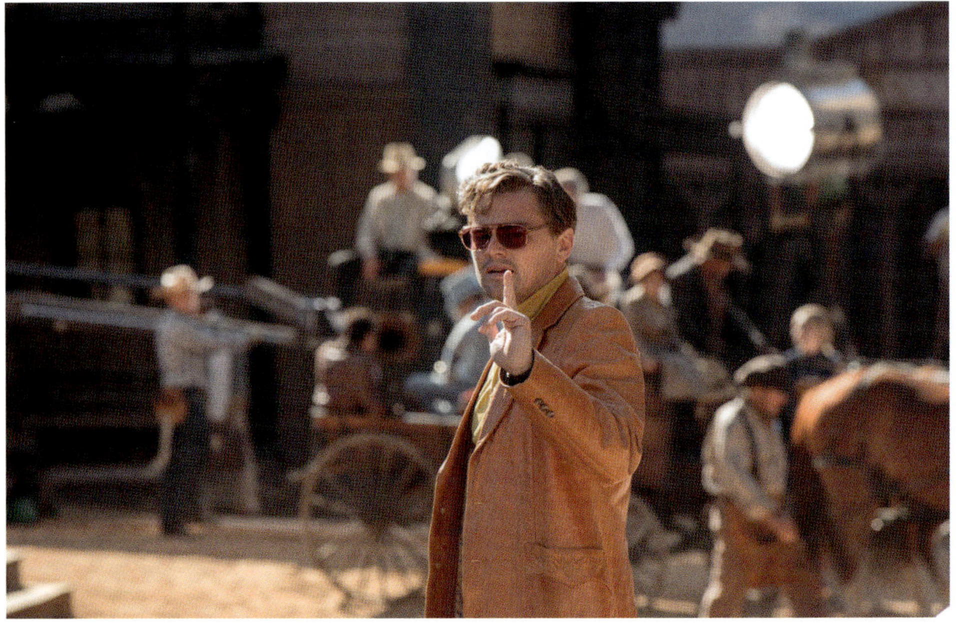

ABOVE: DiCaprio as Dalton on the set of *Lancer* – a show
that really aired between 1968 and 1970.

her life.' Tarantino wanted Tate to be defined by how she lived, he
said, rather than how she tragically died.

To allow his three main characters to live their two-and-a-half
days of life convincingly, Tarantino and his crew had to recreate
the Los Angeles of 1969 as vividly and accurately as possible in the
Los Angeles of 2019. To achieve this, the director recruited
production designer Barbara Ling on the strength of her work in
Oliver Stone's Sixties-set *The Doors*, as well as the fact that she,
like he, grew up in the city. (Ling would earn an Oscar for her work.)

One of her biggest challenges was shutting down four straight
blocks of the always bustling Hollywood Boulevard to re-dress it
with facades replicating the area at the end of the Sixties.
Fortunately, while all of its cinemas were shut down and converted,

their marquees had been retained for their historical significance. 'So we could spruce them up and replace the neon of all those signs that are important,' said Tarantino. 'It was exciting to let the lights blink again in Hollywood Boulevard.'

Tarantino and Ling were able to use the real Playboy Mansion for the party scene, where Sharon, Jay (Emile Hirsch) and Polanski (Rafal Zawierucha) join Mama Cass (Rachel Redleaf) and Steve McQueen (Damian Lewis). Meanwhile, the *Lancer* recreation scenes used Universal Studio's Western Street. It is here that Rick's soul is laid bare in a scene that Tarantino added very late in the process, where the actor encounters a precocious eight-year-old starlet named Trudi Fraser (Julia Butters). While explaining to her the plot of the pulp Western novel he's reading – about a bronco buster who's seen better days – its relevance to his own situation suddenly hits Rick and he breaks down into tears. We've seen Rick weeping previously, but this is a moment of self-revelation, beautifully handled by DiCaprio, who followed it up with an improvised meltdown tantrum in Rick's trailer that didn't appear in the original script.

The shoot's key location, however, was Spahn Movie Ranch, where the Family resides with its elderly, blind owner George Spahn (Bruce Dern). It was built from scratch in a park close to its original location in Chatsworth. The sequence where Cliff arrives at the dusty, rundown former Western set – having given Family member Pussycat (Margaret Qualley) a lift home and keen to check in on his old colleague George – is the movie's nail-biting centrepiece. Manson's callow, barefoot faithful (played by Austin Butler, Dakota Fanning, Lena Dunham, Sydney Sweeney and Victoria Pedretti, among others) lurk ominously in the background, as excited dogs scamper around them.

For all his physical prowess, the jeopardy Cliff unwittingly faces is intense. He is alone and surrounded by cult members who, we

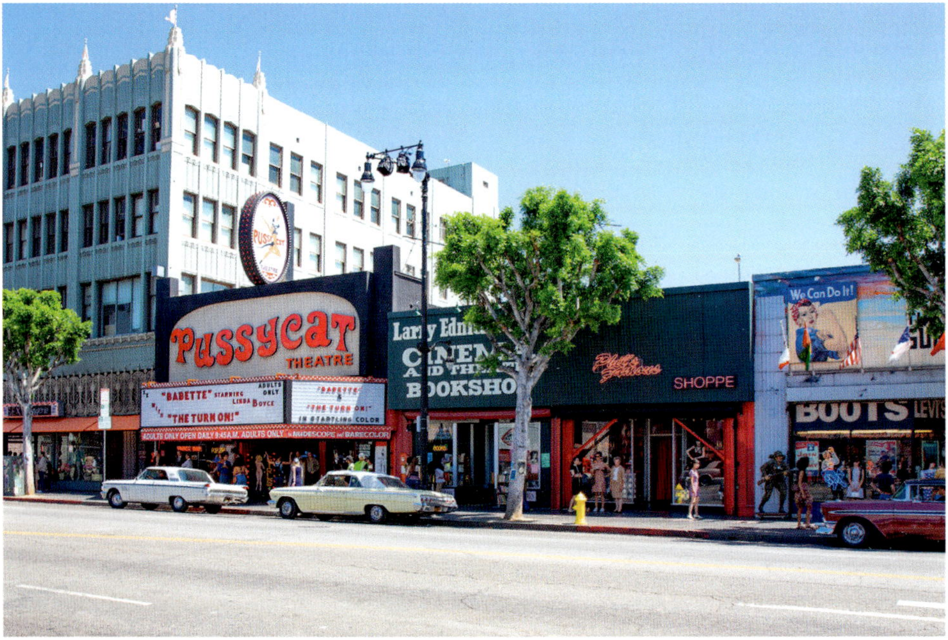

Pussycat THEATRE
"BABETTE" STARRING LINDA BOYCE
"THE TURN ON!"
ADULTS ONLY
IN STARTLING COLOR
ADULTS ONLY OPEN DAILY 9:45 A.M. ADULTS ONLY
Larry Edmunds
CINEMA AND THEATRE BOOKSHOP
SHOPPE
We Can Do It!
BOOTS
LEVIS

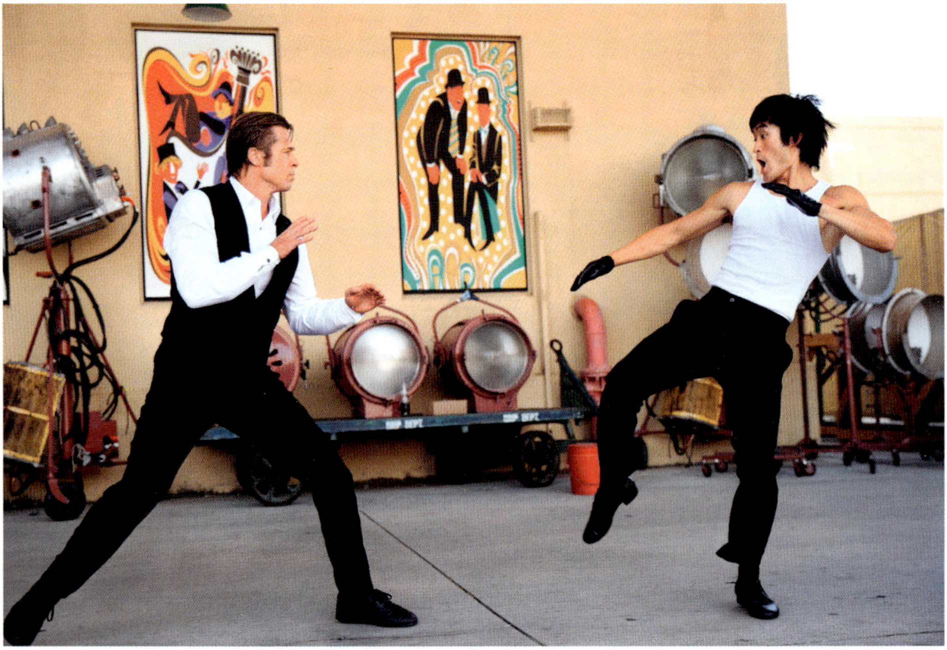

know, are capable of murder. And being played by a star of Pitt's magnitude does not make him safe in a Tarantino story. Ultimately, however, the encounter results in little more than a confused conversation with the blind old man and Cliff realizing that, as fishy as this hippie-commune situation seems, there's nothing he can do.

Originally, Tarantino cast Burt Reynolds, an icon of his childhood, in the role of Spahn. Sadly, after attending rehearsals, he died of a heart attack at the age of 82. But not before he told Tarantino he thought Pitt was 'too pretty' to be a stuntman – words the filmmaker put into the mouth of Bruce Lee (Mike Moh), with whom, in flashback, Cliff has an altercation on the set of *The Green Hornet*. Lee's appearance in the film did not go down well with his family. The martial arts legend is presented as a court-holding blowhard, and when his claims he could beat Muhammad Ali are met with derision by Cliff, he challenges the stuntman to a 'best of three' duel. First, he knocks Cliff to the ground with a kick. Then Cliff effortlessly counters his second kick by swinging him into the door of a nearby car. A brief and furious exchange of blows is cut short by the arrival of the stunt gaffer's wife (Zoë Bell), who despises Cliff and has him thrown off the set by her husband (Kurt Russell).

Tarantino claimed the portrayal of Lee, while fictionalized, was accurate. 'The stuntmen hated Bruce on *The Green Hornet*,' he said. 'It's in [Lee biographer] Matthew Polly's book.' Lee's daughter Shannon was not impressed. While she recognized that the scene helped establish how much of a badass Cliff is, she saw it as 'an uninteresting tear-down of Bruce Lee when it didn't need to be'.

OPPOSITE (TOP): Hollywood Boulevard with its Tarantino '69 makeover – including the Pussycat Theatre, where he ushered as a teenager.

OPPOSITE: Cliff proves his physical ability by besting Bruce Lee (Mike Moh) in a scene that upset Lee's fans and family.

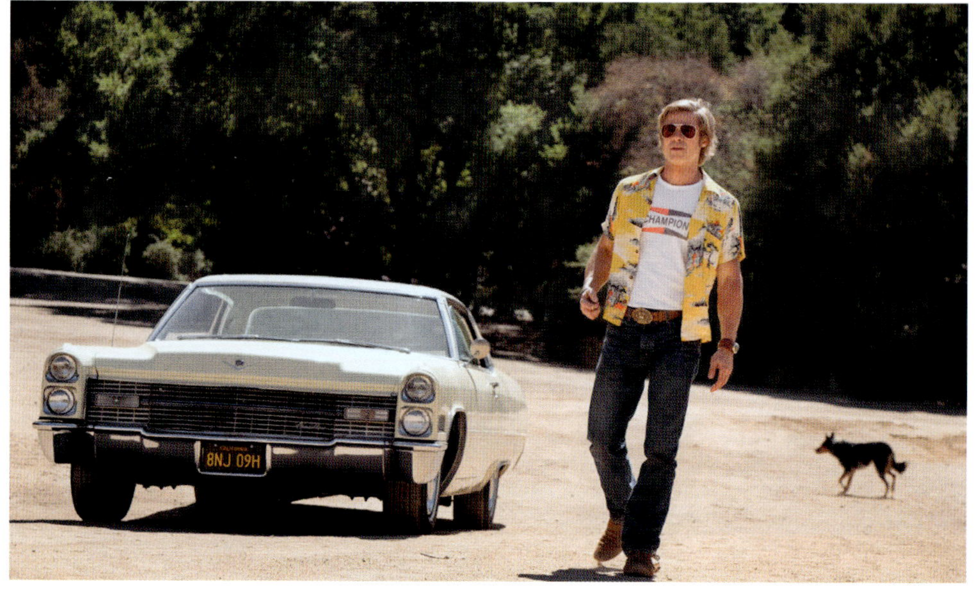

ABOVE: Cliff arrives at Spahn Movie Ranch, where he'll have a close encounter with the Manson Family.

The way Tarantino chose to conclude *Once Upon a Time. . .In Hollywood* was similarly divisive. Throughout writing his opus, 'the thing that really led me along the way was that ending shot,' he said. For the first time in his career, he had the ending of his movie before he'd written the majority of the rest of it. 'Everything else was working backwards.'

In the early hours of 9 August (by which time Tate and her friends had in reality been murdered), Tarantino depicts Rick being welcomed into the Polanski home and, seen from a distance, hugged by a very much still-living Sharon. It is a quiet and poignant denouement. Tarantino, who has revelled in Sharon doing little more than living her life, allows her to continue doing so. But this gentle finale belies what's just happened previously.

Like *Inglourious Basterds* and *Django Unchained*, *Once Upon a Time. . .In Hollywood* is another audacious spin on reality, executed

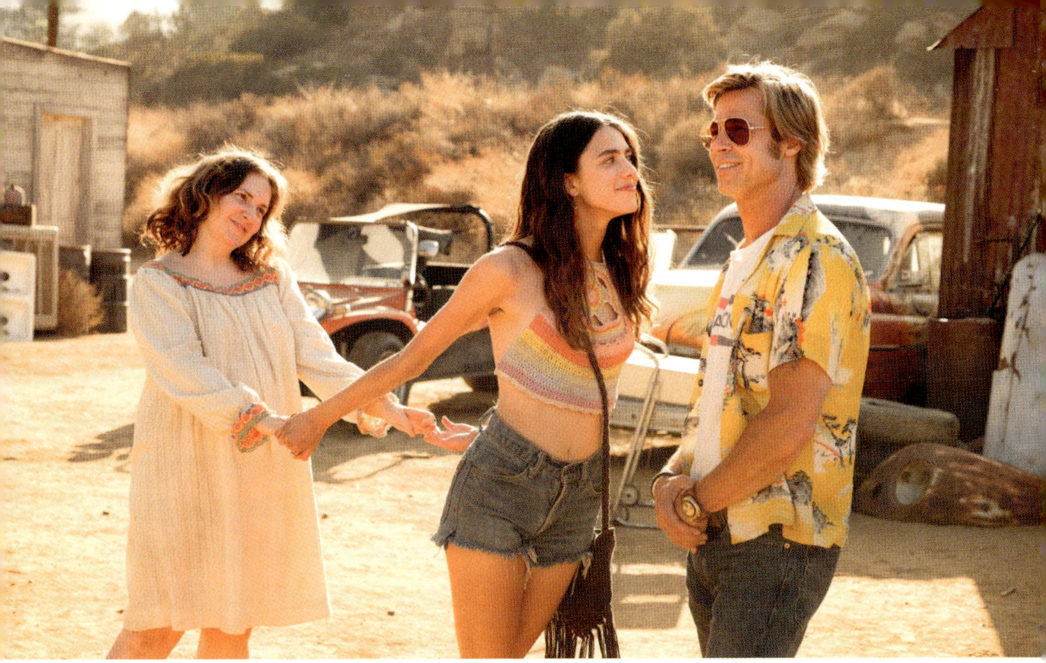

via an outburst of hyper-violence no less impactful than those which forged his other alt-histories.

When a drunk Rick spots four Family members (Butler, Madisen Beaty, Mikey Madison and Maya Hawke) lurking in a car in Cielo Drive's cul-de-sac, he angrily shoos this 'buncha goddamn fuckin' hippies' away. So, they recalibrate their kill-mission to take out Rick, too. With a meta-level irony that isn't hard to miss given Tarantino's own cultural reputation, Sadie (Madison) points out that Rick starred in shows that brought violence into US households. 'My idea,' she says, 'is we kill the people that taught us to kill!'

After Hawke's character gets cold feet and hightails it, the remaining three enter the Dalton residence, where Cliff is coming up on acid, having chosen that night of all nights to smoke an LSD-dipped cigarette. But these 'fuckin' hippies' have broken into the wrong house in more ways than one. Cliff's attack-dog Candy

Unmade Tarantino: *Bounty Law*

Alongside his loving recreations of *Lancer*, Tarantino includes snippets of an entirely fictional black-and-white Western serial show, *Bounty Law*, starring Rick Dalton as bounty hunter Jake Cahill. In one scene, we see him encounter a shifty sheriff played by none other than Michael Madsen. While researching Western shows for *Once Upon a Time. . .In Hollywood*, Tarantino wrote five episodes of *Bounty Law*, as a means of providing more detail on Rick's character. In early 2020, his intention was to write another three and direct all eight episodes, even if DiCaprio wouldn't do it; 'This is not about Rick Dalton playing Jake Cahill. It's about Jake Cahill.' However, during the pandemic, Tarantino focused instead on his *Once Upon a Time* novel and his film criticism book/memoir *Cinema Speculation*. Since then, his 10th film has become the priority. But, he teased, *Bounty Law* may still happen, with Sony head Tom Rothman apparently telling him, 'We'll make that show if you want to do it.'

mauls both Sadie and Tex (Butler), before Cliff blearily beats Tex, then Katie, to death. The latter's demise is the most explicit, played almost for sickening laughs, grindhouse style, as Cliff slams her mushily disintegrating head into a variety of hard household surfaces. Finally, a banshee-screaming Sadie is burned to death in the swimming pool when Rick, rather improbably, retrieves a still-functioning flamethrower from his World War II men-on-a-mission movie *The 14 Fists of McClusky*, and uses it to torch her.

As cathartic releases go, it could hardly be more extreme. The body count is lower than *Inglourious Basterds* and *Django Unchained*, but this table-turn slaughter is heightened in relief to the meandering, melancholy nostalgia that's gone before. Rick and Cliff, relics of old Hollywood, become Tarantino's instruments of retrospective wrath against the monsters that robbed his silver-screen-illuminated childhood world of Sharon Tate.

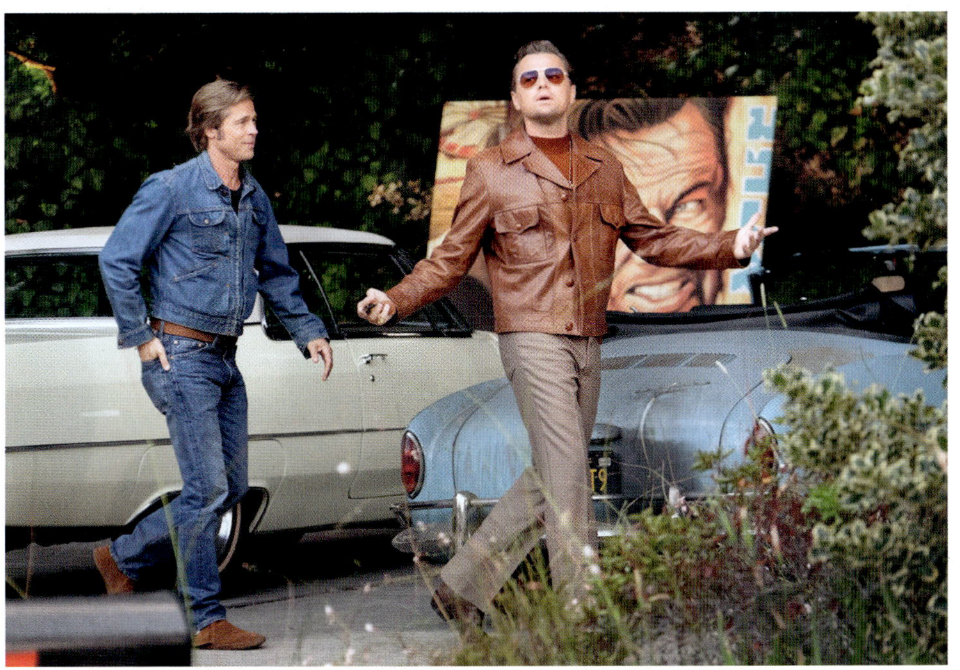

ABOVE: Cliff and Rick, arriving at Rick's home on Cielo Drive, where they will battle the Manson family and change Hollywood history.

For some critics, this climactic blowout wasn't just retrospective, it was retrograde. 'The heroism of his Hollywood characters is an idea that Tarantino works out gradually until it bursts forth, in a final-act twist, with a shocking clarity,' wrote *The New Yorker*'s Richard Brody, who also called out Tarantino's depiction of Lee and his treatment of Mexicans. '*Once Upon a Time. . .In Hollywood* has been called Tarantino's most personal film and that may well be true – it's far more revealing about Tarantino than about Hollywood itself, and his vision of the times in question turns out to be obscenely regressive.' The thesis being, Tarantino believed everything would have been just wonderful if those damn hippies hadn't ruined it all.

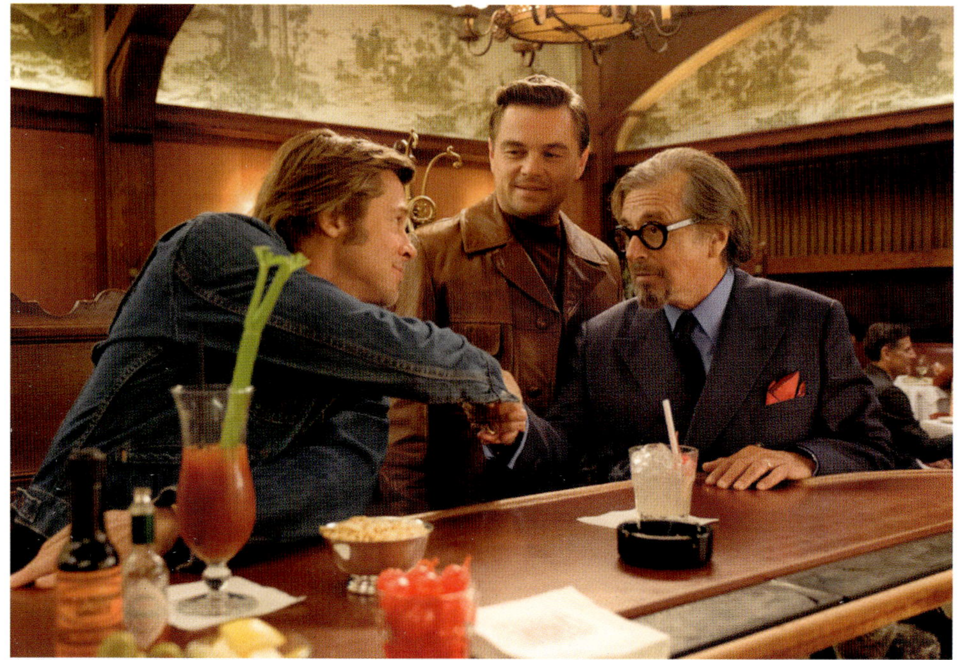

ABOVE: Al Pacino makes a brief appearance as the agent throwing Rick a lifeline with an offer of work in Sergio Corbucci spaghetti Westerns.

But we shouldn't mistake Rick's hatred of hippies for Tarantino's; Rick can't stand them because to him they represent the kind of leading men (Jack Nicholson, Peter Fonda, Warren Beatty, et al) who are replacing him. Besides, the counterculture is warmly embraced by Sharon, who has our sympathies entirely. And the brutal treatment of the house-invading Mansons feels more like a specific retribution against these killers than a symbolic evisceration of an entire movement; one that facilitated the New Hollywood that meant so much to Tarantino.

To prominent theologian David Bentley Hart, who was not previously a Tarantino fan, the film's climax gives 'glorious expression to a perfectly righteous rage,' which made him glad 'to slip briefly into some other order of reality, if only an imaginary one, where ethereal sweetness had survived and horror had perished.' To Hart, *Once Upon a Time. . .In Hollywood* is a deeply moral movie in which 'cosmic justice' is served. 'Who would be so callous or morally confused,' he asked, 'as not to want to go back and prevent the evils of the past?'

The First Novel by Quentin Tarantino

For a time, Tarantino considered releasing a longer, four-hour version of *Once Upon a Time. . .In Hollywood*, but when Covid-19 hit, he instead decided to put it all down on paper, publishing 'The First Novel by Quentin Tarantino' in June 2021. Except, rather than being a longer, deeper version of the movie, the author created a 400-page alternative take.

As well as revealing such details as how Cliff obtained his dog Candy and what really happened on the boat with his wife, the novel spends a lot of time in the world of *Lancer*, exploring long, winding avenues of Hollywood history, and detailing why Rick hates the story about him nearly being cast in the Steve McQueen role in *The Great Escape*. Most remarkably, the movie's bloody climax is described only briefly, in passing, in a flash-forward that happens less than halfway through, and ends instead with a phone call between Rick and Trudi – a scene that was cut from the movie, despite being one of Tarantino's favourites. It was 'a complete rethinking of the entire story,' he said. 'You know how you take an unwieldy novel and try to turn it into a movie? Well, to me, the movie is that. This is the unwieldy version of the movie.'

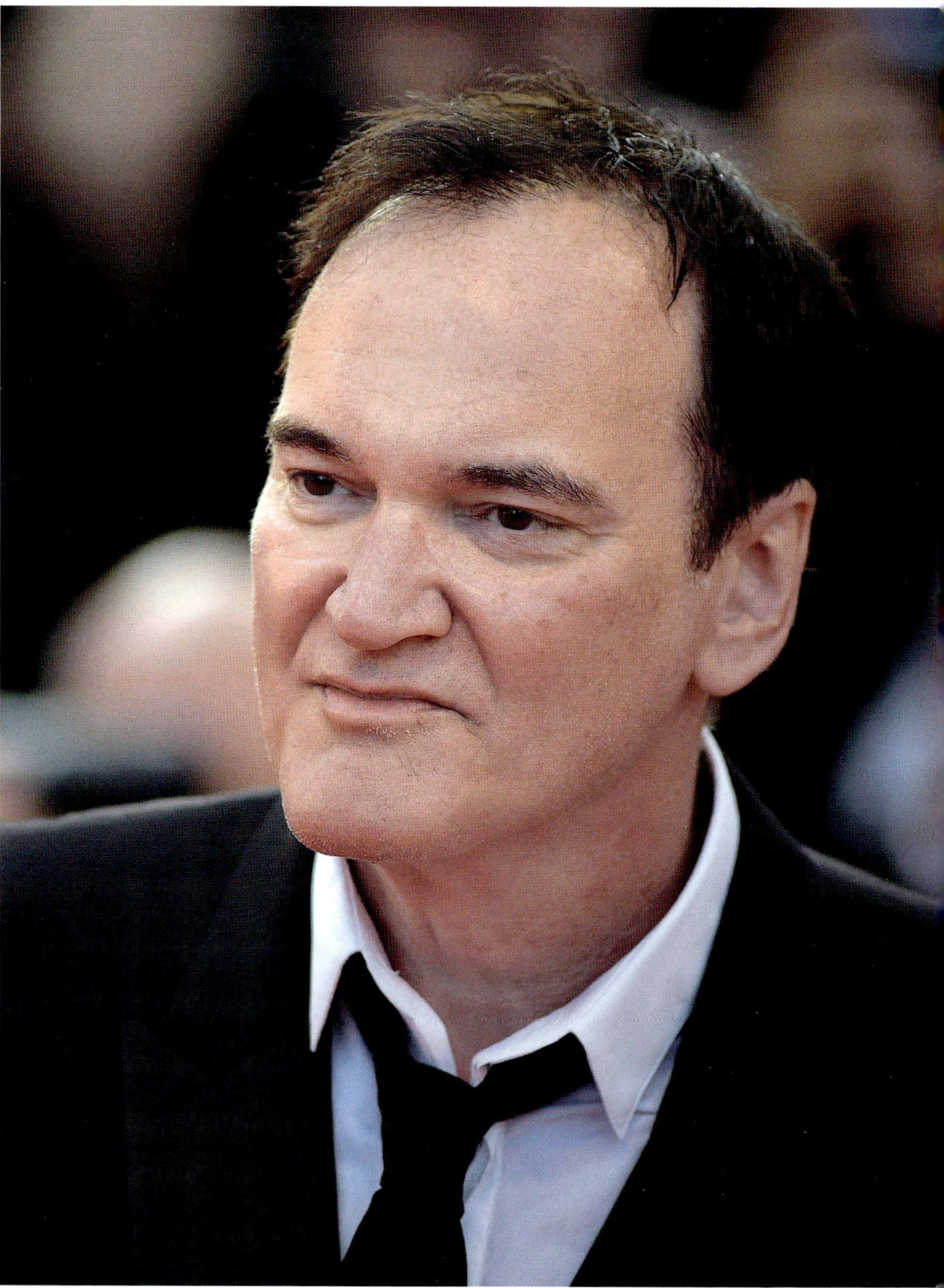

'I would rather choose my own ending'

THE FINAL FILM BY QUENTIN TARANTINO

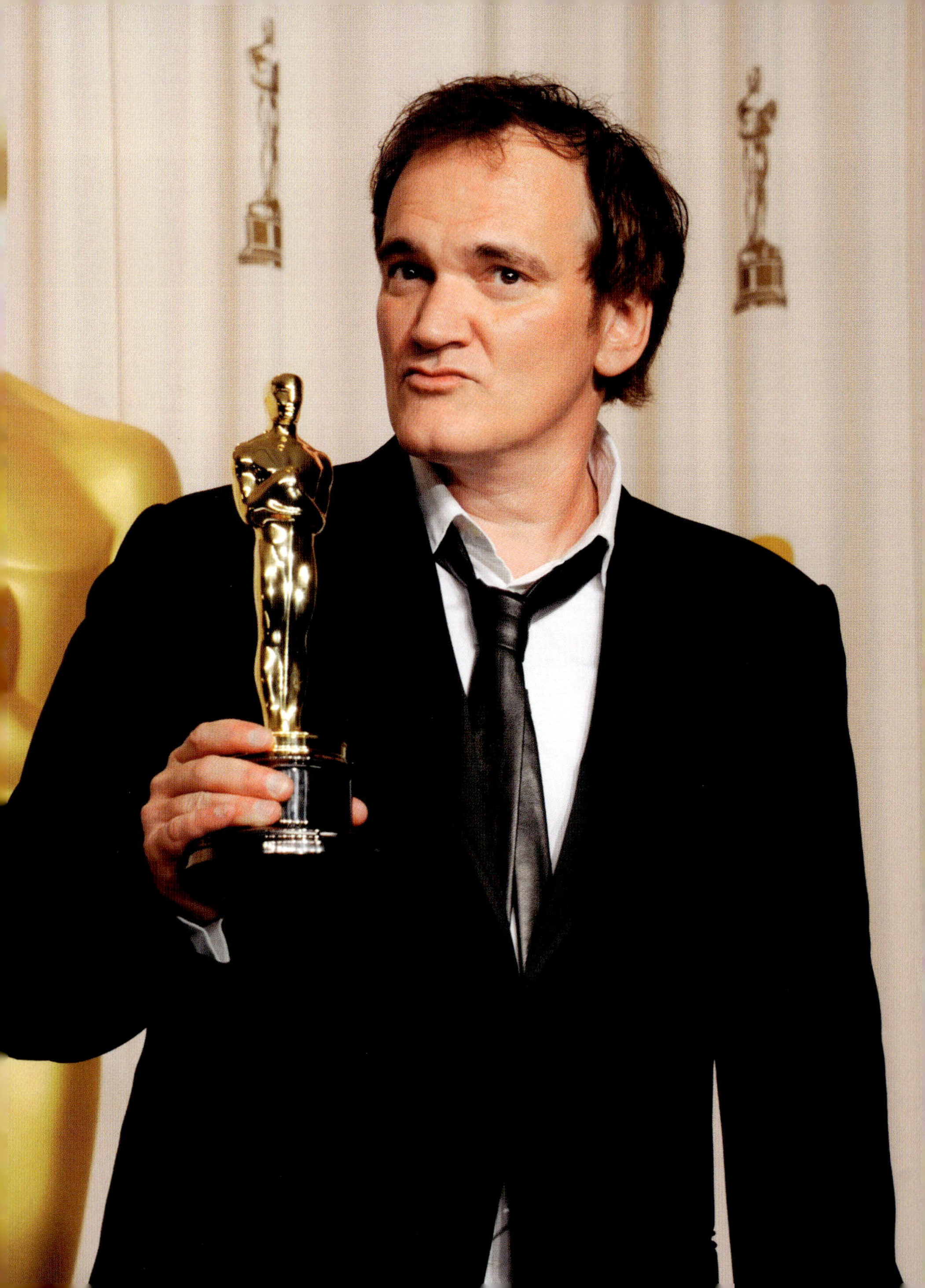

For a long time now, Tarantino has insisted he'll retire from film directing after he's completed his tenth movie. 'Directors are not famous for knowing when to leave the party,' he said as far back as 2010. 'I don't want to make old geriatric colostomy-bag movies. I want to make hard-dick movies and I want them all to come from the same place as *Reservoir Dogs*; from the same artist, from the same man.'

The idea, quite simply, is to quit while he's ahead, before his legacy becomes tainted by his autumn years. 'I don't wanna fuck up my filmography,' he said. 'I wish so many directors would've stopped when they were good. One bad movie fucks up your filmography – your grade-point average is gone, it is officially fucked up. And then they keep on making movies, keep fucking their average down even further and even further. I don't want that. I'm all about my filmography. That is the most important thing. I want to go out with 100 out of 100. At the very least 95.'

Tarantino recognizes that he's been very fortunate to be able to make movies 'at a high level of opportunity,' where he can put everything into each project and push for it to be a masterpiece. Even after he severed ties with The Weinstein Company, he's remained free to make movies exactly how he wants. 'I've built my whole life to do that,' he said, noting that he never got married and never had kids. At least, until November 2018, when he wed Israeli actor and singer Daniella Pick, whom he met while promoting *Inglourious Basterds*. (They now have two children, and live in Tel Aviv.) He also accepts there are exceptions to his 'old directors make worse movies' rule, including George Miller (*Mad Max: Fury Road*) and Stanley Kubrick. But most directors' third acts, he's

OPPOSITE: Tarantino with his second Academy Award for Best Original Screenplay, which he won for *Django Unchained* in 2013.

observed, downgrade from a commitment to 'make each movie the masterpiece of all time,' and become more about 'it'll be fun to work with so-and-so,' or 'this is a good book, that would make a good movie, so I'll do that.' That is not for Tarantino. 'I would rather choose my own ending,' he said.

However, he has evidently found it difficult to make that choice. Since March 2023, it had appeared his final film would be *The Movie Critic*. It was not the most exciting title, but an intriguing one, promising a similarly personal, cinema-celebrating film to *Once Upon a Time. . .In Hollywood*. Following early speculation that it would be set in the late Seventies and focus on game-changing critic Pauline Kael (cited by Tarantino as his favourite writer), he confirmed that the film was instead 'based on a guy who really lived, but was never famous, and used to write movie reviews for a porno rag.' The writer, whom Tarantino hasn't named, was 'as cynical as hell,' and died in his late thirties, he explained, from complications due to alcoholism. Meaning all the filmmaker's regular gang of actors were already too old for the role; 'It'll definitely be a new leading man for me.'

This was seemingly proven untrue in February 2024, when the casting of Brad Pitt was announced. Enthused by his own

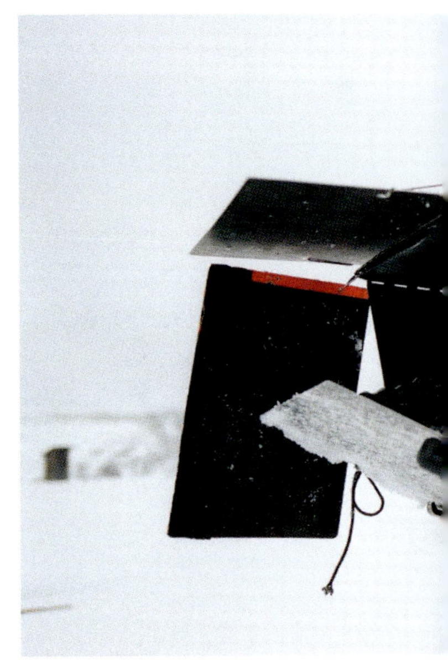

ABOVE: Tarantino, undeterred by the snows of Colorado on the set of *The Hateful Eight* in 2015.

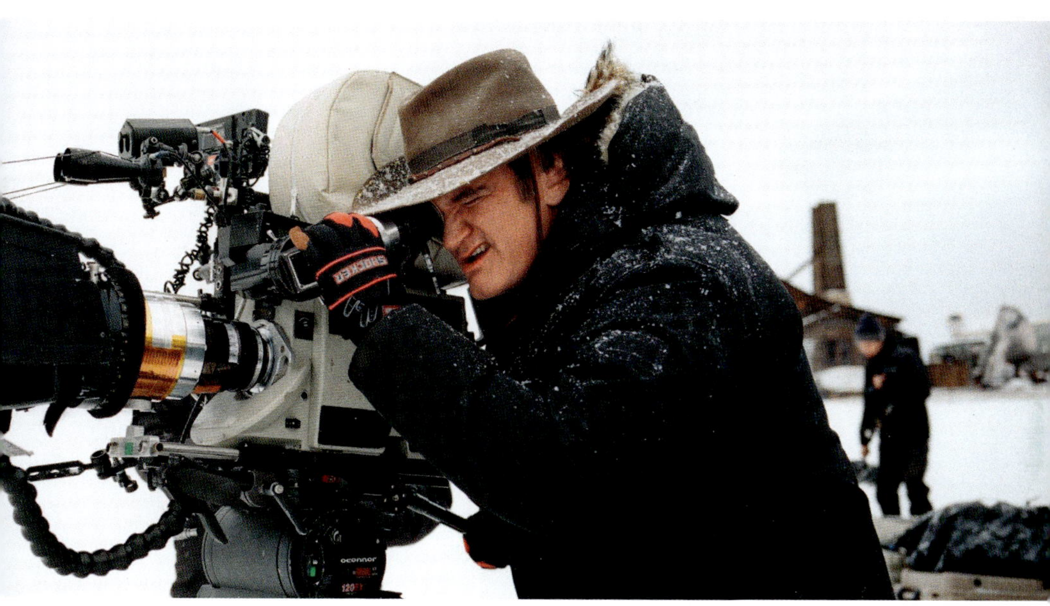

expansion of Cliff Booth's story in the *Once Upon A Time. . .In Hollywood* novel, Tarantino apparently decided to bring Pitt's character back, with the project possibly even pivoting away from the movie-critic concept and towards something closer to a *Once Upon A Time. . .* sequel. Although, according to *The Hollywood Reporter* in April 2024, it may have been even more ambitious than that, folding in movie-within-a-movie moments featuring other stars from his films – including John Travolta, Jamie Foxx and Margot Robbie – as fictional versions of themselves. Tom Cruise was also mentioned as being in the mix, while rumour had it that a teenage version of Tarantino himself would appear as a character.

But then, suddenly, it all collapsed. On 17 April 2024, *The Hollywood Reporter* revealed that *The Movie Critic* was no more, and that Tarantino was 'going back to the drawing board'. The pressure to ensure his swansong hit exactly the right notes proved too much for the concept to bear. The filmmaker's perfection has proven the enemy of progress, to paraphrase Winston Churchill. At the time of writing, The Tenth Film By Quentin Tarantino has returned, once more, to the realm of pure conjecture.

Even when it is finally made, will it really be his last? Given the intensity of his insistence, it's hard not to take Tarantino at his word. But as his activities between movies suggest, he's unlikely to ever recede from culture. He'll probably write more novels, perhaps even adaptations of his earlier films. 'Reservoir Dogs just seems like it would work really good as a little paperback,' he noted, while he's also considered novelizing True Romance. 'There's a lot more there between the characters, I think, that could be said.'

He's also expressed a desire to write and direct for theatre, again adapting his previous work. 'The next thing I'd like to do is a theatrical adaptation of Hateful Eight,' he revealed in 2015, 'because I like the idea of other actors having a chance to play my characters.' He may also one day deliver on his promise to make Bounty Law, or perhaps settle on another TV series idea. And he has already ventured into revival-cinema programming and patronage with his New Beverly project, as well as presenting the Video Archives podcast with Roger Avary. But more than anything, as both the publication of his book Cinema Speculation and the working title of his once-mooted swan song suggest, he loves the idea of becoming a critic himself. 'That will be a lovely thing to do as an older man. It's a reward I intend to give myself for dedicating so much of myself to the thing I'm doing now.'

If we are indeed at the final chapter of his directing career, and there is truly no Film By Quentin Tarantino beyond his tenth, we will surely still be hearing from him for many years to come. His vocal, sometimes belligerent cineastic passion shows no sign of waning. And even if he doesn't ever get to ten, then the nine films he has directed – plus the trio he only wrote – will speak for themselves more loudly than virtually any other body of work in this era. Slurs, curses and all.

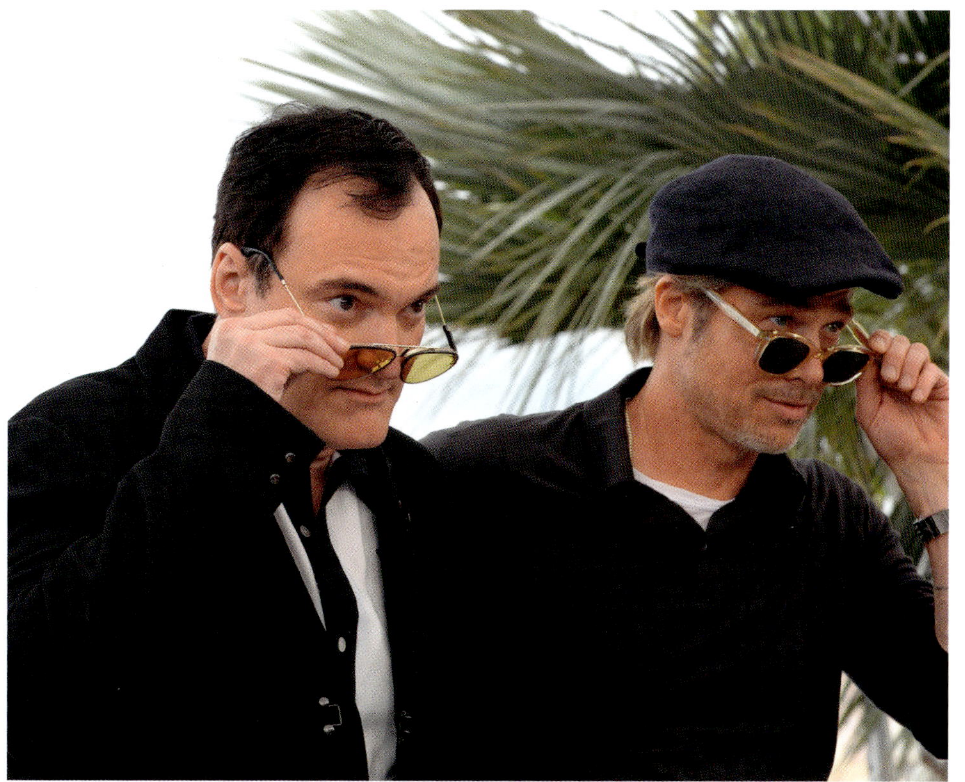

BELOW: Tarantino and Brad Pitt, at the Cannes Film Festival in May 2019, with *Once Upon A Time...In Hollywood*.

Resources

Introduction

Biskind, Peter, 'The Return of Quentin Tarantino', *Vanity Fair*, 14 October 2003

Prologue

Clarkson, Wensley, *Quentin Tarantino: The Man, The Myths and the Movies*, John Blake, 2007

Dawson, Jeff, *Tarantino: Inside Story*, Cassell, 1995, reprinted in *Quentin Tarantino: The Film Geek Files*, ed. Paul A. Woods, Plexus, 2005

Gross, Terry, 'Quentin Tarantino: Inglourious Child of Cinema', *Fresh Air*, NPR, 28 December 2009

Hollywood's Boy Wonder, BBC, 25 October 1994

Rose, Charlie, 'Quentin Tarantino', 14 October 1994

Secher, Benjamin, 'Quentin Tarantino: "All my movies are achingly personal"', *The Telegraph*, 8 February 2010

Tarantino, Quentin, and Roger Avary, The Video Archives podcast, 19 July 2022

The Moment with Brian Koppleman podcast, 28 July 2021

Waxman, Sharon, *Rebels on the Backlot: Six Directors and How They Conquered the Hollywood Studio System*, HarperEntertainment, 2005

Webb, Daisy, 'Film school rejects: Iconic directors who avoided the classroom', *Film Daily*, 26 December 2019

WTF with Marc Maron podcast, 28 June 2021

Chapter One

Biskind, Peter, *Down and Dirty Pictures*, Bloomsbury Publishing, 2004

'Blood, Sweat and Bullets – The Making of *Reservoir Dogs*', Death By Films

Child, Ben, 'Why Quentin Tarantino wants to be the next Howard Hawks', reporting on Tarantino's Alfred Dunhill BAFTA Life in Pictures Interview, *The Guardian*, 12 January 2010

De Semlyen, Nick, Chris Hewitt and Damon Wise, 'Once Upon A Crime', *Empire*, December 2017

Hollywood's Boy Wonder, BBC, 25 October 1994

Lawrence Bender interview, *Reservoir Dogs* UK Blu-ray

Pulp Fiction: The Facts, *Pulp Fiction* UK Blu-ray

Quentin Tarantino interview, *Reservoir Dogs* UK Blu-ray

Tate, James M, 'Michael Madsen Interview and Laurence Tierney's Nephew Tim', *Cult Film Freak*, 16 March 2019

Taylor, Ella, 'Mr Blood Red', *LA Weekly*, 16 October 1992

Woods, Paul A, 'Eastern Dogs', *Quentin Tarantino: The Film Geek Files*, Plexus, 2005

Chapter Two

Ayscough, Suzan, 'Stone giving berth to Tarantino "Killers"', *Variety*, 18 March 1993

Clarkson, Wensley, *Quentin Tarantino: The Man, The Myths and the Movies*, John Blake, 2007

Dawson, Jeff, 'Natural Born Killers', *Empire*, November 1993

Hollywood's Boy Wonder, BBC, 25 October 1994

Maslin, Janet, 'Young Lovers With a Flaw That Proves Fatal', *The New York Times*, 26 August 1994

'*Natural Born Killers* lawsuit finally thrown out', *The Guardian*, 13 March 2001

Salemme, Nadia, 'Quentin Tarantino's films are connected in "movie universe"', news.com.au, 19 January 2016

Smith, Kyle, 'Oliver Stone Q&A: *Natural Born Killers*', *New York Post*, 13 October 2009

Spitz, Marc, '*True Romance*: 15 Years Later', *Maxim*, 25 April 2008

The Moment with Brian Koppelman podcast, 28 July 2021

Zoller Seitz, Matt, *The Oliver Stone Experience*, Abrams, 2016

Chapter Three

Biskind, Peter, 'Four x Four', *Premiere*, March 1996

Dargis, Manohla, 'Quentin Tarantino on *Pulp Fiction*', *Sight and Sound*, November 1994

Hollywood's Boy Wonder, BBC, 25 October 1994

Lowry, Beverly, 'Criminals Rendered in 3 Parts, Poetically', *The New York Times*, 11 September 1994

Not the Usual Mindless Boring Getting To Know You Chit Chat, *Pulp Fiction* UK Blu-ray

O'Hagan, Sean, 'X Offender', *The Times Magazine*, 15 October 1994

Pulp Fiction: The Facts, *Pulp Fiction* UK Blu-ray

Quentin Tarantino interview, *Jackie Brown* UK DVD

Rose, Charlie, 'Quentin Tarantino', 14 October 1994

Webster, Emma, 'Pulp Action', *The Face*, October 1994

Chapter Four

Beeler, Michael, 'Humble Beginnings', *Cinefantastique*, January 1996

Biskind, Peter 'Four x Four', *Premiere*, March 1996

Gettell, Oliver, 'Quentin Tarantino, Robert Rodriguez look back on *From Dusk Till Dawn*', *Entertainment Weekly*, 3 November 2016

Hibberd, James, 'Robert Rodriguez Q&A: *From Dusk Till Dawn* and what's wrong with TV', *Entertainment Weekly*, 27 July 2017

Hollywood Goes to Hell, *From Dusk Till Dawn* UK Blu-ray

Hunter, David, '*From Dusk Till Dawn*: THR's 1996 Review' *The Hollywood Reporter*, 18 January 1996

McCarthy, Todd, '*From Dusk Till Dawn*', *Variety*, 21 January 1996

Tarantino, Quentin and Robert Rodriguez commentary, *From Dusk Till Dawn* UK Blu-ray

Udovitch, Mim, 'Tarantino and Juliette', *Details*, February 1996

Chapter Five

Archerd, Amy, 'Lee has choice words for Tarantino', *Variety*, 16 December 1997

Bauer, Erik, 'Method writing: Interview with Quentin Tarantino', *Creative Screenwriting*, 11 August 2013

Biskind, Peter, *Down and Dirty Pictures*, Bloomsbury, 2004

Bradshaw, Peter, '*Jackie Brown* review', *The Guardian*, 15 September 2022

Gravley, Garrett, 'We Counted Every Curse Word in Every Quentin Tarantino Movie', *Dallas Observer*, 30 July 2019

Hattenstone, Simon, 'I, Quentin', *The Guardian*, 27 February 1998

How it Went Down, *Jackie Brown* UK DVD

James, Nick, 'Tarantino Bites Back', *Sight & Sound*, February 2008

Maslin, Janet, 'Jackie Brown: Smarter Than She Is? Hah', *The New York Times*, 24 December 1997

Merida, Kevin, 'Spike Lee, Holding Court', *The Washington Post*, 30 April 1998

Quentin Tarantino interview, *Jackie Brown* UK DVD

Rose, Charlie, 'Quentin Tarantino', 14 October 1994

Rose, Charlie, 'Quentin Tarantino' 26 December 1997

Chapter Six

Biskind, Peter, 'The Return of Quentin Tarantino', *Vanity Fair*, 14 October 2003

Fleming Jr, Mike, 'Quentin Tarantino Explains Everything: Uma Thurman, The *Kill Bill* Crash & Harvey Weinstein', *Deadline*, 5 February 2018

Kotb, Hoda, 'From video clerk to box office icon', *NBC News*, 25 April 2004

Machiyama, Tomohiro, 'Quentin Tarantino reveals almost everything that inspired *Kill Bill*', Japanattack.com 2003, reprinted in Paul A. Woods, *The Film Geek Files*, Plexus, 2005

Rose, Charlie, 'Quentin Tarantino', 22 April 2004

Salemme, Nadia, 'Quentin Tarantino's films are connected in "movie universe"', news.com.au, 19 January 2016

The Making of Kill Bill Volume 1, *Kill Bill Volume 1* UK DVD

The Making of Kill Bill Volume 2, *Kill Bill Volume 2* UK DVD

Chapter Seven

De Semlyen, Nick, 'Quentin Tarantino Answers Your Questions', *Empire*, July 2019

Galloway, Stephen, and Matthew Belloni, 'Director Roundtable: 6 Auteurs on Tantrums, Crazy Actors and Quitting While They're Ahead', *The Hollywood Reporter*, 7 December 2012

James, Nick, 'Tarantino Bites Back', *Sight & Sound*, February 2008

Kurt Russell As Stuntman Mike, *Death Proof* UK DVD

Nashawaty, Chris, 'Bloodbath and Beyond', *Entertainment Weekly*, 27 March 2007

Rose, Charlie, '*Grindhouse*', 4 May 2007

Sharf, Zack, 'Quentin Tarantino Calls *Death Proof* Bombing a "Shock to My Confidence", Says His Films Lack Sex Because It Hasn't Been Necessary', *Variety*, 13 April 2023

Special Guest Director: Quentin Tarantino, *Sin City* UK Blu-ray

Stunts On Wheels, *Death Proof* UK DVD

Chapter Eight

Denby, David, 'Americans in Paris', *The New Yorker*, 17 August, 200

Fleming Jr, Michael, 'Tarantino reflects on *Basterds*', *Variety*, 17 May 2009

Goldberg, Jeffrey, 'Hollywood's Jewish Avenger', *The Atlantic*, September 2009

Happy Sad Confused podcast, 22 July 2019

Horn, Jordana, 'Glorious Bastard: Tarantino Talks About His Not-A-Holocaust-Movie', *The Jewish Daily Forward*, 21 August 2009

Lee, Chris, *Los Angeles Times*, 16 August 2009.

Rodriguez, Rene, 'Revisioning History: Quentin Tarantino on *Inglourious Basterds*', *Pop Matters*, 17 August 2009

Rose, Charlie, 'Quentin Tarantino', 21 August 2009

Sordeau, Henri, 'Quentin Tarantino talks *Inglourious Basterds*', *Rotten Tomatoes*, 11 August 2009

The Empire Podcast, 31 December 2021

The Moment with Brian Koppelman podcast, 28 July 2021

Chapter Nine

Appelo, Tim, '*Django* to the Extreme: How Panic Attacks and DiCaprio's Real Blood Made a Slavery Epic Better', *The Hollywood Reporter*, 10 January 2013

Child, Ben, '*Django Unchained* wins over Black audience despite Spike Lee criticism' *The Guardian*, 3 January 2013

Gates Jr, Henry Louis, 'Tarantino "Unchained" Part 1: *Django* Trilogy?', *The Root*, 23 December 2012

Gates Jr, Henry Louis, 'Tarantino "Unchained", Part 2: On the N Word', *The Root*, 24 December 2012

Gross, Terry, 'Quentin Tarantino, 'Unchained' and Unruly', *Fresh Air*, NPR, 2 January 2013

Guru-Murthy, Krishnan, Channel 4, 10 January 2013

Hiscock, John, 'Quentin Tarantino: I'm proud of my flop', *The Telegraph*, 27 April 2007

Hohenadel, Kristin, 'Bunch of Guys on a Mission Movie', *The New York Times*, 6 May 2009

Miller, Julie, 'Jamie Foxx on *Django Unchained*, Leonardo DiCaprio, and the Scene That Moved Quentin Tarantino to Tears', *Vanity Fair*, 16 July 2012

Rose, Charlie, 'Quentin Tarantino', 21 December 2012

Tarantino, Quentin, *Django Unchained* screenplay, 2012

Taylor, Ella, 'Mr Blood Red', *LA Weekly*, 16 October 1992

Williams, Kam, 'Quentin Tarantino The *Django Unchained* Interview', *African American Literature Book Club*, 2012

Wise, Damon 'Off the Chain', *Empire*, January 2013

Yamato, Jen, 'It's like *Cheers* for movie lovers: an inside look at Quentin Tarantino's New Beverly Cinema', *Los Angeles Times*, 2 June 2017

Chapter Ten

Baron, Zach, 'Quentin Tarantino Explains the Link Between His *Hateful Eight* and #BlackLivesMatter', *GQ*, 8 December 2015

Brown, Lane, 'In Conversation: Quentin Tarantino', *New York Magazine*, 24 August 2015

Fleming Jr, Mike, 'Quentin Tarantino on Retirement, Grand 70mm Intl Plans for *The Hateful Eight*', *Deadline*, 10 November 2014

Glorious 70mm, *The Hateful Eight* UK Blu-Ray

Happy Sad Confused podcast, 28 December 2015

Labrecque, Jeff, 'Quentin Tarantino: *The Hateful Eight* Interview', *Entertainment Weekly*, 31 December 2015

Lewis, Andy, 'Making of Hateful Eight: How Tarantino Braved Sub-Zero Weather and a Stolen Screener', *The Hollywood Reporter*, 7 January 2016

Lyman, Eric J, 'Italian Composer Ennio Morricone: I'll Never Work With Tarantino Again', *The Hollywood Reporter*, 15 March 2013

McMahon, Chris, '*The Hateful Eight* Hates on Six Strings: Film Includes Real Destruction of Antique Martin', *Reverb*, 2 February 2016

Scott, A O, 'Review: Quentin Tarantino's *The Hateful Eight* blends Verbiage and Violence', *The New York Times*, 24 December 2015

Tapley, Kristopher, 'Jennifer Jason Leigh on *Hateful Eight*, Anomalisa: "Two of the Best Roles of My Life"', *Variety*, 8 December 2015

Wise, Damon, 'All QT on the Western Front', *Empire*, January 2016

Chapter Eleven

Brody, Richard, 'Quentin Tarantino's Obscenely Regressive Vision of the Sixties in *Once Upon a Time. . .In Hollywood*', *The New Yorker*, 27 July 2019

de Semlyen, Nick, 'City of Stars', *Empire* July 2019

DGA Membership Screening Q&A with Paul Thomas Anderson, Los Angeles, 18 August 2019

Fleming Jr, Mike, 'Quentin Tarantino on 10 Oscar noms for *Once Upon A Time* and How Bumper Crop of 2019 Beat Back Notion That Superheroes and *Star Wars* Are Cinema's Future', *Deadline*, 13 January 2020

Fleming Jr, Mike, 'Quentin Tarantino on his *Once Upon A Time. . .In Hollywood* Novel, Retirement, Fatherhood and Other Great Tales', *Deadline*, 20 July 2021

Fleming Jr, Mike, 'Quentin Tarantino on *Once Upon A Time*, His Vision of *Star Trek* As *Pulp Fiction* in Space, and Hopes to Turn Leo DiCaprio 50s Western *Bounty Law* into Series', *Deadline*, 17 July 2019

Hainey, Michael, 'Quentin Tarantino, Brad Pitt, and Leonardo DiCaprio Take You Inside *Once Upon a Time. . .In Hollywood*', *Esquire*, 21 May 2019

Hart, David Bentley, 'Quentin Tarantino's Cosmic Justice', *The New York Times*, 6 August 2019

Lee, Shannon, 'Does Quentin Tarantino Hate Bruce Lee? Or Does It Just Help Sell Books? (Guest Column)', *The Hollywood Reporter*, 2 July 2021

Morgan, Kim, 'Tarantino on Hollywood', The New Beverly Cinema blog, 10 September 2019

Noble, Alex, 'Quentin Tarantino: *Once Upon a Time. . .In Hollywood* Novel Will Explore Backstory of Brad Pitt's Character', *TheWrap*, 2 June 2021

O'Connor, Roisin, 'Quentin Tarantino addresses backlash to Bruce Lee scene in *Once Upon a Time. . .In Hollywood*', *The Independent*, 1 July 2021

Restoring Hollywood: The Production Design of Once Upon a Time. . .In Hollywood, *Once Upon a Time. . .In Hollywood* UK Blu-ray

Travis, Ben, '*Once Upon a Time in Hollywood*: 10 Things Quentin Tarantino Told Us', empireonline.com, 22 August 2019

Zacharek, Stephanie, 'Nothing Lasts Forever. Quentin Tarantino on Sharon Tate, *Once Upon A Time. . .In Hollywood* and Retirement', *TIME*, 22 July 2019

Epilogue

Bamigboye, Baz, 'Breaking Baz @ Cannes: Quentin Tarantino Exclusive Part 1 – Surprise Directors' Fortnight Classic Revealed & Plenty More Detail on The Filmmaker's Next Project "The Movie Critic"', *Deadline*, 25 May 2023

Couch, Aaron, and Borys Kit, 'Quentin Tarantino no Longer Making *The Movie Critic* as Final Film', *The Hollywood Reporter*, 17 April 2024

Galloway, Stephen, 'Quentin Tarantino, Ridley Scott, Four More Directors on the Decline of "Middle-Class Films," Facing Retirement, *The Hollywood Reporter*, 10 December 2015

Kit, Borys, Pamela McClintock and James Hibberd, 'How Quentin Tarantino's *The Movie Critic* Fell Apart', *The Hollywood Reporter*, 24 April 2024

Secher, Benjamin, 'Quentin Tarantino interview: All my movies are achingly personal', 8 February 2010

The Empire Podcast, 31 December 2021

Wise, Damon, 'Off the Chain', *Empire*, January 2013

Zacharek, Stephanie, 'Nothing Lasts Forever. Quentin Tarantino on Sharon Tate, *Once Upon a Time. . .in Hollywood* and Retirement', *TIME*, 22 July 2019

Bibliography

Amazing Améziane, *Quentin By Tarantino*, Titan Comics, 2024

Biskind, Peter, *Down and Dirty Pictures: Miramax, Sundance & The Rise of Independent Film*, Bloomsbury, 2004

Clarkson, Wensley, *Quentin Tarantino: The Man, The Myths and the Movies*, John Blake, 2007

Rausch, Andrew J, *My Best Friend's Birthday: The Making of a Quentin Tarantino Film*, BearManor Media, 2019

Seitz, Matt Zoller, *The Oliver Stone Experience*, Abrams, 2016

Tarantino, Quentin, *Cinema Speculation*, Weidenfeld & Nicholson, 2022

Tarantino, Quentin, *Once Upon A Time in Hollywood: The First Novel From Quentin Tarantino*, Weidenfeld & Nicholson, 2021

Waxman, Sharon, *Rebels on the Backlot: Six Maverick Directors and How They Conquered the Hollywood Studio System*, HarperEntertainment, 2005

Woods, Paul A, ed., *Quentin Tarantino: The Film Geek Files – 2nd Edition*, Plexus, 2005

Picture credits

Acknowledgements

Thanks, firstly, to the editorial team at Quercus: Kerry Enzor, for selecting me as the launch writer for this cool new series and trusting in my career-long fascination with Tarantino; Anna Southgate, for gracefully enduring my overwriting and expertly making her edits; and Julia Shone at Greenfinch.

On a more personal level, I'm deeply grateful to Lucy Jolin for being my ever-valued first reader, and for picking up the slack on the domestic front while I scurried off down the QT rabbit hole for a few months.

I'd also like to thank Dorian Lynskey and Nick de Semlyen for their advice, support and friendship; my *Senet* magazine co-founder James Hunter for putting up with all my book-related talk in meetings; and all the commissioning editors I was unable to assist while working on this book. Namely: James Dyer, Alex Godfrey, Chris Hewitt, John Nugent and Beth Webb of *Empire* magazine; Charles Gant and Matt Mueller of *Screen International*; Phil de Semlyen of *Time Out* London; and Matt McAllister of *Dungeons & Dragons Adventurer*.